REVOLUTION BEFORE BREAKFAST

Revolution Before

Breakfast

ARGENTINA   1941-1946

BY *Ruth and Leonard Greenup*

Chapel Hill, 1947
THE UNIVERSITY OF NORTH CAROLINA PRESS

FOREWORD

THIS IS THE STORY of our years in Argentina. It is also the personalized history of a short period in the life of a nation. It was in Buenos Aires that we married in 1941, and there we lived and worked for four years. Those years were eventful ones for Argentina; they saw a succession of five presidents—Roberto M. Ortiz, Ramón S. Castillo, General Arturo Rawson, General Pedro Pablo Ramírez and General Edelmiro J. Farrell; they brought a revolution which to all appearances started out as a cut and dried military coup and turned into a major social upheaval; they witnessed the spectacular rise of an obscure army officer called Juan Domingo Perón to become the most powerful figure in all South America.

Argentina is insignificant, measured by all the traditional yardsticks of population, industry, wealth, armed power and position in the high councils of the world. Yet with her fourteen million souls she was large enough to be profoundly shaken by the late great turmoil in the outside world, even though she never became actively engaged in the war. There are two factors, however, which magnify the importance of Argentina far beyond that given her by the usual standards: One is her large trading capacity, making her one of the great importing and exporting countries; the other is her position as one of two leading contenders for dominance in South America, one of the few underdeveloped land masses remaining on the globe. In addition to all this is Argentina's own feeling that she is destined to a great future.

To us the four years we spent in Argentina was a time of significance in the life of a small nation during a period of great change in the world. And it was also a fascinating time, full of work, fun, of humor and enough excitement to keep it ever from getting stale.

Place the Argentine republic at the corresponding latitudes in the

v

northern hemisphere, and you find the province of Buenos Aires is Oklahoma in reverse. The federal capital falls almost on top of oil-rich Tulsa. And the cattle-dotted pampas of Argentina look so much like the prairies of Oklahoma and Kansas in the spring that it is difficult for a transplanted mid-western American to realize immediately that he is in a foreign country. Buenos Aires itself is like a Chamber of Commerce director's dream of a glorified Tulsa —the same evidences of enormous fortunes made in a generation or two and spent freely—palatial homes, exclusive shops, clean streets and well-kept modern apartment buildings.

Argentina has never been much of a place for a tourist. The River Plate is usually muddy, and Buenos Aires is flat, laid out mostly in modern squares and diagonals. The city can be "done" in a day, and even a slow plane can fly the broad pampas from Argentina's Atlantic shore and across the Andes to Chile on the Pacific in a few hours. But the country and its great shining capital grow on you, they need day-by-day discovery.

Buenos Aires to us was more interesting after four years than it was the first week. Even "foreigners" who have lived in Argentina twenty or thirty years say they still encounter things that surprise them in the country or its people. This is due to the fact that Argentina is a booming, growing country of changing moods, but it also derives in part from the unpredictability of the Argentines themselves.

In many respects Argentina bears a striking resemblance to the United States. Its extremes of climate range from the near tropical to the near Antarctic. Like the United States, it has vast areas of plains, a great mountain range and beautiful lake districts. It has high, arid regions, like Arizona and Nevada. Its cities are bright and modern, like the Pacific coast cities of the United States. The plumbing is as good and even more elegant in Buenos Aires than in New York. The constitution of Argentina is patterned after that of the United States.

But our version is that Argentina has something different. The people who migrated to Argentina from Europe never burned their bridges behind them as thoroughly as did the immigrants to the United States. Argentines sometimes refer in disparaging terms to the countries they left behind them, but there is less effort to steer away from everything European and much less emphasis on the "melting pot." An Argentine can be—and is—proud of his own country without slighting the others.

The Argentine has more liking and respect for European literature, art, music, architecture and thought development than has the American citizen. The American is more American than the Argentine is Argentine; both are transplanted, and both have flourished, but the Argentine basks in the rays of Europe's cultural sun, while the citizens of the United States want to make their own sun.

The result is that the Argentine nation is more of a hybrid than our own. It is fully as complex and difficult to understand. Argentina is a mass of complications and contradictions—economic, cultural and political—and the nation's changing moods contrive to make her the most unpredictable and exasperating country in this hemisphere, with the possible exception of our own.

It is difficult for a North American to understand the viewpoint of the Argentine man-in-the-street, for the average American in Buenos Aires lives on a higher economic level than the Argentine and consequently is not likely to associate with him a great deal or share his problems. We feel that we came to know the Argentines better than most Americans; not because we were gifted with any extraordinary insight, but simply because we had certain accidental advantages and opportunities not usually available to an American living in Buenos Aires.

For one thing, we had the "advantage" of a low income. When I, a sailor on the S.S. Argentina of the "Good Neighbor Fleet" of Moore-McCormack Lines, Inc., asked questions about living expenses in Buenos Aires, the Secretary of the American Chamber of Commerce advised me not to come to Argentina unless I had a salary of at least $250 a month. It seemed that was about as low as a self-respecting American could go and exist in the southern republic. Yet, when Ruth and I were married and went to work as reporters on the Buenos Aires Herald, our combined income, after deductions for a journalists' pension fund, was about $125 a month. The middle of each month inevitably found us—like our Argentine friends—down to counting our centavos carefully. We learned to make a peso go a long way, and uncovered some of the secrets of how the Argentines appear to live so well on such small salaries. The game of wits began when we moved into our first tiny furnished apartment. I handed Ruth our last forty pesos ($10 left over after paying the rent) and told her to buy our dishes, our silverware, our cooking utensils, our glasses and other household necessities.

With $10 Ruth bought all those things, plus a butcher knife and a real broom! It is only fair to report, however, that brisk stirring soon snapped the handles of at least three tablespoons from our best "silverware."

The little economies continued in the months that followed. We visited museums not in search of culture but because we couldn't always afford the American movies—even after an Argentine lad guided us to a shop where tickets could be had for half price. We often rode second class on the trains because it was cheaper—and found the people there friendlier. We learned which sidewalk cafes served the biggest free lunches, and the places to shun—the ones which gave us only peanuts and crackers with a ten-cent glass of beer. Our Argentine acquaintances—many of whose incomes were even more modest than ours—showed us many another way to save.

Ruth, meanwhile, was enjoying her dual role as housewife and full-time reporter for the *Buenos Aires Herald,* which provided blanket coverage of the doings of the 50,000 or more English persons and some 3,500 North Americans in and around Buenos Aires As she now tells the story:

"In the first place, reporters of the *Herald* and *The Standard,* the two English-language dailies, hadn't acquired the lazy Yankee habit of covering routine assignments by telephone. A meeting of fifteen or twenty English-speaking persons wasn't too small for personal coverage by a staff member from each paper. And most of the reporters consequently spent more time jumping on and off of trains, *colectivos,* and subways than they did at their typewriters.

"I soon learned that Buneos Aires covers an area almost as large as New York City and that the English have a special penchant for spreading out into distant suburbs and blind streets where the names and numbers have long since been dimmed by time and the weather. They also have a great number of schools, all of which like to stage plays and hold special prize givings, preferably in the dark of night. And the farther away a school is from the heart of Buenos Aires— such as St. George's College or even St. Hilda's—the greater its interest in getting the press out to see students cavort in front of the footlights.

"I tried to equip myself for these nightly excursions by purchasing a large map of the city and its environs. The map, measuring about five feet square, seldom failed to atract a crowd when I opened it at a dimly lit railway station and proceeded to study same. Chivalrous *caballeros* often offered to come to my rescue, for a woman alone in public after dark is still a novelty in Argentina. Invariably they approached with this question, 'Sola?' Then they began to murmur other things in Spanish, none of which were included in my little pocket book of helpful Spanish-English phrases."

At times during those first months in Buenos Aires Ruth complained she was a "livestock widow." The *Herald* discovered one day that I was born on a ranch in Montana, and therefore took for granted that I knew all about livestock. With the season of livestock shows almost at hand, the *Herald* desperately needed a livestock editor. One afternoon the pink-cheeked, grey-haired publisher, Mr. Junius Julius Rugeroni (whose double first name owes to the fact that it was never clearly established whether he was born the last minute in the month of June or the first thing in July) summoned me into his "inner sanctum" and appointed me to fill the post. He brushed aside my protest that I couldn't tell a Shorthorn from an Aberdeen Angus.

In the next few months it seemed I was travelling almost constantly. I covered more than a score of livestock shows scattered throughout the great cattle-raising districts. Before it was all over I had learned enough from Juan Ferrari of *The Standard* and his band of wine-loving, jesting colleagues of the Spanish-language newspapers—to fancy myself an expert on the dominant Shorthorn breed. We spent a good many hours talking—I mainly as an interested observer. It was on a train that I first heard the arguments for and against the industrialization of Argentina, with all the attendant problems of maintaining a stable economy and at least as much democracy as then existed in the country.

It was a rare opportunity for any man to learn something about the land and the people.

Among our Argentine acquaintances were men and women from many walks of life, from rich *estancieros* and their majordomos to white collar workers and copy boys. And if there is any political or social significance in what we learned from them, it is that there is a connection between the fullness of a man's stomach and his views on the importance of individual liberty.

The relationship between personal economics and political thinking was brought home to us sharply after the overthrow of President Castillo on June 4, 1943. One of the first things the revolutionary government did was to decree a substantial lowering of rents, and we gratefully accepted the reduction. We had known all along that rents were too high for people with modest incomes—including ourselves. We also approved when the government decreed a new work week of 36 hours for newspaper men, in contrast with the old 48-hour schedule which on some occasions had been stretched indefinitely without any payment for "overtime." These were some of the gains which affected us personally, and we would have been less than human not to be favorably impressed by them.

Argentina in 1943 was ripe for social and economic reforms. Much had been promised, but little had been done to raise the standard of living of hundreds of thousands of white collar workers and common laborers, including the thousands of peons who lived on the big estancias in conditions little better than vassalage. The peons and sharecroppers, except in the case of some enlightened estancieros, were fed well enough but were educated meagerly or not at all, ill-housed, ill-clothed and subject to the slightest whim of their rich employers. The miserable status of the peons and their lack of opportunity for a better life more than once was described by Argentine newspapers as a "national disgrace," a blot on a country which considered itself a progressive democracy.

That is why the revolution of June 4, 1943 gave new hope to a majority of Argentines. That is why they—and we too—watched lightheartedly while the army men took over the government house. A large percentage of the population expected there would be an improvement in their own lot, along with a closer hewing to the democratic line which would mean the end of the clumsy "neutrality" under which the old government provided a secure base for Axis activities in South America and forbade Argentines to debate in their forums and newspapers the issues involved in the Second World War.

The military men who seized power had a chance to correct the social and economic injustices which had beset Argentina for generations and which became more painfully evident as the country moved swiftly towards industrialization between the two world wars. With Argentine productivity increasing by leaps and bounds, it was a magnificent opportunity to effect some drastic changes which could greatly benefit the people as individuals and as a nation.

There was one man who grasped the opportunity. He used it skilfully. Juan Domingo Perón was elected to the presidency in a landslide on Feb. 24, 1946. He was in virtual control of the government for two years before that, and during that time some undesirable developments presented themselves. Argentina became a police state. Opposition to the government was not tolerated; politicians were locked in concentration camps. Talk of "national defense" reverberated throughout Argentina to justify vastly increased military expenditures. Student opposition was crushed ruthlessly, and schools were used as tools to indoctrinate young Argentines in the glories of the state. Independent trade unions virtually disappeared, their smashed organizations were brought under the government's wing. Organizations of manufacturers and businessmen were alternately cajoled and threatened by the government. Powerful opposition newspapers—and all of the influential ones *were* against the government—were closed or suspended so frequently that their suppression became commonplace.

It was thought by some that Perón's election might change all this, that the legalization of his status as head of the nation would leave Argentina free to pursue the goals of true economic and political liberties which the new president had proclaimed in his campaign speeches; and that Perón would confound his many critics at home and abroad by utilizing his mandate not for personal aggrandizement but for the benefit of the Argentine people.

Nearly a year after the inauguration, it is becoming clear that these hopes were ill-founded, even though Perón has relaxed some of the iron controls he maintained when he was the "strong man" of the Argentine government. Now that he is the "constitutional" president of Argentina the outbreaks of organized violence by his "descamisados" or "shirtless ones" have been less frequent; the prisons and concentration camps have been emptied; amnesty has been granted to his political enemies; the crude devices of closing or suspending newspapers which criticized his policies have for the time being been abandoned; some of the smaller labor unions are allowed to function independently; congress again meets.

But these apparent gains for democracy in Argentina have been offset, unfortunately, by the imposition of other controls having the unmistakeable stamp of totalitarian ways of thinking. The Perón government has demonstrated a dislike and disrespect for the free press, free schools, free enterprise, free courts and individual rights; all of which Argentina, in signing and ratifying inter-American agreements guaranteed to preserve as democratic institutions.

Perón has sought to consolidate and enlarge his powers to include not only the executive branch of the government, but the judicial and legislative branches as well; he has impeached the Supreme Court because it refused to sanction all his acts during the de facto government; he has condemned the capitalistic system and declared it was dying, and in so doing justified the extreme measures he took to gain control of the economic life of the country; he has persecuted liberal students and professors and driven them by the hundreds out of Argentine universities; he has almost succeeded in eliminating freedom of the press by surreptitious reprisals against opposition publishers, including manipulation of their newsprint supplies, tampering with their long-established distribution systems, and publicly urging readers and advertisers to boycott them.

With power firmly in his grasp, Perón has shown amply that he considers himself not the servant of the people, but the master. He has shown little understanding and even less faith in the checks and balances of the republican system of government. He has demonstrated that he is still the student of the German thinker Clausewitz and the Argentine tyrant Rosas, rather than the American Jefferson and the Argentine teacher-president Sarmiento; that he adheres firmly to the principle of the "leader" who knows what is best for his people and does everything *for* them rather than *with* them.

It would be a mistake, however, to think that all life in Perón's Argentina is grim and earnest.

Argentines have certain inalienable rights, and the man does not live who can curb the national love of horse-racing and lotteries, or destroy the impulse to lay another five pesos on red at the roulette table. And no government official has ever succeeded in getting traffic to stop and go exactly as he decreed. Nor has Argentina ever seen the man who could restrain the gallant *caballeros* on Calle Florida from tossing their compliments or gay quips at the beautiful girls who pass. Argentina has changed, but not that much!

LEONARD GREENUP

CONTENTS

ILLUSTRATIONS

*The photographs in this volume were taken by Ruth and
Leonard Greenup.*

REVOLUTION BEFORE BREAKFAST

THE REVOLUTION AND HOW IT GREW

W E HADN'T BEEN IN BUENOS AIRES FOR MANY WEEKS before we became painfully aware of a shortcoming in our equipment for attaining social success at such affairs as dinners and cocktail parties. Our conversation was seriously lacking in sparkle. It had none of the elements of drama, of blood and gore and desperate escape from certain death, the lively stuff that embellished the after-dinner conversation of our hosts and their other guests.

It seemed that all our new friends had been through at least one revolution, and they loved to tell about it! It was wonderful talk, but it made us feel woefully drab by comparison. We had only the one grim consolation that we had been popped into situations in which even the omniscient Dale Carnegie would have been properly stumped. You see, there is really nothing you can do to help yourself when the conversation swings 'round to revolutions, except to sit and listen and hope that someday you, too, will be caught in a revolution, and that you will live to tell the story of it happily ever after.

So we listened. And the things we heard were hair-raising. Most of our friends, of course, had had the rather ordinary experience of being trapped between snipers and having to run for their lives. Others, rated a notch higher in the social scale, had blood spattered on them from rebels who fell in the skirmishes of revolt. A privileged few had been caught in machine-gun fire, and one man detailed with justifiable pride how, when the guns commenced to rattle, he had thrown himself flat in the street to avoid being cut down, only to learn with disgust, after the shooting stopped, that his trousers were stained with evidence of the cavalry's recent passing.

Housewives, who had too much sense to venture out when the

horses and the bullets were whizzing by, also had their versions of revolutions in South America. Some told how they had been caught unprepared by uprisings and had nearly starved for days; others, real veterans of these periodic upheavals, cautioned me always to keep an emergency supply of canned foods on hand to tide us over the days when the stores might be closed.

Revolutions, we were informed, were bloody, gruesome affairs in which we might lose our lives. The garbage might not be picked up for weeks, and the stench of rotting food and rotting bodies would be overpowering.

So we settled back hopefully to wait for a revolution. And it came after two anxious years had passed.

As far as I am concerned, all these evil reports about the hardships, the horrors and the stench of armed revolt were put to rest by the Argentine military revolution of June 4, 1943, when General Arturo Rawson at the head of eight thousand troops marched on Buenos Aires.

That was a fine revolution. It delighted and intrigued me. But I, being at least one part housewife, feel compelled to report that it was probably the best smelling revolt in history. I believe that most correspondents neglected to mention this, they being far more concerned with the number of dead—which was about forty—and the necessity of predicting which way the political wind would blow henceforth in Casa Rosada.

Even before the troops had massed in front of the Government Palace, I could smell the approaching army and I sensed the revolution was going to be a success. So did nearly a hundred thousand curious *porteños* who had rushed out of their offices early that afternoon to see what all of this talk of a revolution was about anyway. They were assured when they saw their soldiers mounted on familiar metal conveyances out of which steam was puffing at an industrious rate. They recognized the smell and so did I. It was *puchero*, the national stew, the king of all stews where chicken, beef, hot red *chorizos*, potatoes, carrots and other vegetables blend into an ambrosia which in this case could be called quite appropriately "Surrender" or "Last Resistance."

A whole cloud of good smells enveloped the troops and wafted its way into the crowds. And I saw more than one *porteño* nudge his neighbor and exclaim, "*Puchero! Puchero!*" They smiled and looked as though that made everything right with the world and the revolution as well. The guns and the bloodshed were remarkably inconspicuous that day.

The troops, especially the ones manning the *puchero* kitchens, seemed to realize the responsibility of their positions and waved and smiled to the crowds. The field kitchens steamed ahead until they reached strategic, protective positions around Casa Rosada, the Government Palace which looks something like a layer cake in its pale pink frosting and elaborate baroque trimmings. Flowers were thrown from the crowds to the guardians of the *puchero*, and I saw some of the troops put blossoms behind their ears. The coziness was enhanced when a few girls jumped up on the kitchens to be near the unofficial conquerors of the day.

Peanut vendors from all over the city rushed into the plaza to do an unprecedented week-day business, selling the goobers from their portable stoves, built to look like locomotives.

It was almost an anti-climax in the festivities when the revolutionary leaders—General Arturo Rawson and General Pedro Pablo Ramírez, along with several Army officers—appeared on the balcony to receive the homage of the people. However, shouts of "*Viva democracia*" swelled through the plaza. And there were many "*vivas*" for Rawson and Ramírez. It was easy to see that most of the people thought the revolution meant a new democratic, pro-Allied government, and they seemed happy about it.

The country had been taken so easily and quickly that the new leaders hadn't had time to rig up an adequate loud speaker system in the plaza, but every word—whether it was heard or not—was greeted with enthusiastic applause. I was amazed to catch myself shouting a "*Viva Rawson*," now and then too, then nervously wondering whether I might be jeopardizing my American citizenship. I couldn't hear a word of what was being said, even though Leonard and I managed to elbow our way up to within twenty-five yards of Government House and could almost see the whites of the eyes on the balcony. Hence, it was quite a surprise to pick up the newspapers the next day and learn that I'd been among those indorsing the remarks against communism, graft and Godlessness.

Perhaps the *puchero* had conquered me too, for the field kitchens kept up full steam all through the shouting and speeches.

At any rate, when the officers finally left the balcony, most of the people seemed in a hurry to get home to their own kitchens and their own *puchero*. That is, all except groups of young men, the ones who had been the loudest to shout, "*Viva patria! Viva Rawson! Viva Ramírez!*" and "*Patria, patria, patria!*"

Suddenly, as if a signal had been given, they broke loose like so many hundred Katzenjammer kids! Until then, big buses and little ones called *colectivos*, all filled with passengers, had been speeding around the plaza ignoring the revolution as if it were some vulgar upstart unworthy of upsetting time schedules or causing traffic to be re-routed.

The young men, however, had other ideas. What revolution, worthy of the name, had been fought with so little loss of blood, so little destruction of property, so little fireworks and excitement?

True, a few unfortunate ones had lost their lives earlier this day when troops marching toward the city from Campo de Mayo forgot to warn the head of the Navy's Mechanical Training School, and he had ordered the school defended, resulting in some casualties among the conscripts and the passers-by. That had been a deplorable accident, the only hitch in this revolution before breakfast.

But the actual capture of the Government Palace had been accomplished with all of the smooth ease of a Boca Junior football victory, and with fewer bloody noses. Even the feeblest opponent of Boca had invariably put up more of a scrap than had President Ramón Castillo and his cabinet members, who had preferred instead to cruise the muddy waters of the River Plate in a gun boat.

So the young men set out to save the day for the newsreel photographers.

A *colectivo*—the smallest unit of public transportation—whizzed into the plaza. It was swarmed upon by a mob of whooping youths, who ordered the driver to stop and all of the passengers to get out. Then with an entire empty vehicle to play with, the Katzenjammer kids set to work. Windows were broken and seats ripped out. Then the wreck of a little bus was tipped over, while hoodlums gathered from all around to hammer at the sides of their fallen foe. Some stepped up just to kick it. Finally, when the tires had been shredded and the headlights smashed, the gasoline tank was uncapped to let the fuel spew out. A lighted match was flicked at it and the whole wreckage shot into flames.

This was so much fun that other *colectivos* were stormed, conquered and converted into flaming pyres. In a few moments, this had become a plaza-wide sport. When a big lumbering old gray bus limped into the scene filled with workers on their way home for the evening, a bigger gang of rowdies jumped on it and herded out the passengers. It was rocked back and forth by bands on the outside, while a demolition squad went to work within. The woven cane seats were hurled out of shattered windows and grabbed either as souvenirs or converted into torches. The bus made an impressive fire, and young men began dancing wildly about it and shouting for the *patria*.

The appearance of a street car provoked a sizable gang, who boarded it with lighted torches and methodically set each seat afire before derailing it. Its bulky hulk became a mass of flames.

Soon blazing street cars, buses and *colectivos* all around Plaza de Mayo and up the Avenida de Mayo itself cast a crimson glare over crowds which had grown excited by the sight of fire. Gangs of boys grabbed Argentine flags and began running madly up the Avenida, screaming and singing.

A few policemen were on hand to throw tear gas bombs when the crowds became excessively unruly but did not interfere with the destruction of vehicles, most of them owned by foreign companies anyway. However, it takes a good deal to make an Argentine miss a meal, and the revolution of 1943 was not one of those events. When the dinner hour came, it was time for the *porteños* to leave the ashes of the street cars and the buses to rest in peace. We deserted them, too, for some of Ann Stringer's Texas-style pork chops.

But not for long. The Stringers, Ann and Bill, would be on their way back to the States in a few weeks and weren't going to miss one gun shot of their first and only South American revolution if they could help it. Dinner ended, we hurried out to the street to find a city black and deserted. For the first time, we saw empty subway stations and sidewalks bare of people.

Avenida de Mayo, the scene of a milling crowd two hours earlier, was deathly still, with iron shutters down over every window and all of the bars and cafes locked for the first time that I could recall. Smoke still curled up from the skeletons of buses, and the fumes from the tear gas were still strong enough to make our eyes smart.

In strange contrast was the brilliant light that enveloped the Government Palace. We walked toward it, our heels clattering in the silence. But at the end of the Avenida we were halted by a bayonet-carrying young soldier who told us that we could go no further. His weapon glittered under the street light, and we moved on, but not before noticing that troops had surrounded the plaza.

Only the lights from newspaper offices on Rivadavia brightened the scene as we turned toward big and always noisy Calle Corrientes. Tonight it was just another empty street, dark and lonely. The four of us stopped at a street corner to decide where we would go next. The policeman near by blew his whistle and told us that not more than two people were allowed to walk together on the street that night.

Leonard and I then started toward home. We walked up Leandro Alem, where waterfront dance halls had for years welcomed visiting sailors with loud music and gaudy neon signs advertising the enticing attractions within. Tonight there was no welcome, no music, no neon lights. And the street was empty of men.

It wasn't until we got near our own front door that we saw any sign of life. The little park across from our apartment house was alive with people—all soldiers, and all busily setting up housekeeping as if for a long stay. They were pitching tents and patroling the little park with drawn bayonets. Their German-style helmets flashed as they passed the lighted corners of the grounds. The horses of the cavalry had been staked along a side street and we could hear them neighing through the night. The field kitchens were nearer, and still they were steaming. I gawked at a strange-looking weapon pointing skyward which was being installed in the center of the park, and Leonard said it was probably an anti-aircraft gun.

I was enormously impressed that our neighborhood had been so honored. And Leonard contributed a touch of the dramatic with the rumor that the Navy might oppose the revolution, and if so the harbor would be cannonaded. He didn't need to remind me that we lived only a block and a half from the river. Every time I heard a door slam in the apartment building during the rest of that night, I thought the bombardment had started. I wondered whether the kitchen floor would be a better place to dodge whizzing bullets than the bath tub.

Anyway, I took the precaution of sitting down Indian-fashion on the cold tile floor of the kitchen to write a letter to my parents, notifying them that I had survived the revolution with no greater hardship than a blistered heel. But it was no easy task to tell them anything about the men I had seen on the balcony of Casa Rosada that evening. I was ashamed to confess that I'd never even heard of General Rawson until that day. But all would surely be well from then on because he was a descendant of one of the few North American families to settle in Argentina.

I am astonished, when I think of it now, how little any of us knew about the men who had seized power that day.

Yet there was a sound, if unfortunate, reason for our ignorance of the Army and the men who led it. For one thing, Argentina has been at peace for so many decades that it is necessary to go back to the middle of the last century to find a military figure of any stature. There are no Pershings, or Fochs, or Eisenhowers or Marshalls who have won fame in modern battle. The only way a general could win real prominence in Argentina was for him to go into business or politics—whether by election or *coup*. In the second place, to Americans in Buenos Aires, the Army had always been a tight little circle with no ties binding it to Washington or West Point. The Argentine Army had always looked to Europe— and in particular to Germany—for its theory, its tactics and its equipment. Most of the small arms and infantry equipment were modelled after the German Army, much of it was actually of German or Swiss or French manufacture. The Argentine commanders read avidly of Clausewitz. They admired the old Prussian theories on the employment of infantry and accepted the German doctrines on the use of mechanized units as the last word in modern warfare. The new Wehrmacht, especially after its lightning conquest of the Low Countries and France, was their idea of professional perfection.

Many officers had studied in the war academy of Berlin or served with the German Army on maneuvers. And a large proportion of them returned to Buenos Aires voluble converts to German military efficiency as well as hospitality. Some of them wore high Wehrmacht decorations and told of lavish parties given in their honor by ranking Nazi officials.

Even before the rise of Hitler, the Germans had shrewdly capitalized on the Argentine Army's admiration of Prussian strategy and equipment. At one time, according to former Senator Eduardo Laurencena, three German generals formed part of the Argentine General Staff. A succession of others, top-notch men, taught in the Argentine War College. Argentine officers received a German military education, studying text books written by German officers; Argentine Army regulations were copied from those of the German Army; the organization, way of marching, the salute and uniform of the Argentine Army were of the same origin. The German influence was so strong that during part of the late World War, conscripts at the big Campo de Mayo army base outside Buenos Aires were discouraged from reading any newspapers other than the pro-Nazi *Cabildo* and *El Pampero*. They often found it difficult to secure copies of any of the pro-democratic newspapers. Even army officers and soldiers attending the classes offered by the United States air mission at Palomar air base studied carefully these two daily pro-Nazi and partially Nazi-financed publications. Naturally, they gave a very one-sided picture of the progress of the war, and it is no wonder that almost the entire Argentine officer class believed firmly in a German victory, many of them even after the Allies disproved the widely accepted theory that the invasion of Europe was impossible.

The German entree into elite Argentine Army circles also extended to civilian members of the large German colony in Buenos Aires, whose relation with the Argentine army officers was on a friendly social footing. Many of them belonged to the same clubs, and the Germans cultivated these contacts assiduously. Their social relations were smoothed by the fact that most of the Germans spoke Spanish fluently, had been in the country for many years and perhaps married Argentine women, and had learned to observe precisely the customs of the country. A substantial number of Argentine officers also spoke German and had visited that country during peace times with their families. Thus the Germans in

Argentina were in a position to exercise a potent influence on the Argentine army officers, especially at the time of the revolution in 1943, when the old-fashioned concept of democracy was achieving scant military success on the battlefields of the world against the dynamic new concept of totalitarianism.

The situation of the American community, and to a lesser extent the British community, vis-a-vis with the Argentine Army was in sharp contrast to the influential German position. The military attachés of the two Allied powers were, of course, in fairly frequent contact with Argentine officers, but I suspect that their relations were more formal than friendly and that not many confidences were whispered during any of those warm *abrazos* they exchanged at cocktail parties. And the average American in Buenos Aires was little better acquainted with the professional Argentine officer than he was with Timoshenko or the men from Mars.

In short, it seems doubtful that we knew enough of what was happening in the Argentine Army to assess its sentiments accurately on June 4, 1943; the confusion of Allied policy with respect to the revolutionary government tends to bear this out.

We had little time, during Rawson's administration, to learn what he stood for; on the evening of June 4 he proclaimed to the cheering crowds that he was the new president of Argentina, but on the morning of June 7, that same year, he was forced to announce his resignation. The only clue at that time to Rawson's political leanings was his decree No. 3 of June 5, 1943, dissolving Congress, and the naming of his cabinet, which included two well-known pro-fascists, General Domingo Martínez and José María Rosa, whose United States black-listed print shop published *El Pampero*. Rawson's resignation provided Argentina with the rare spectacle of three presidents within a week: Castillo, Rawson and then General Pedro Pablo Ramírez, none of them elected to office by the people.

General Ramírez was better known to the Argentines. He had been Castillo's Minister of War, and he had a long, distinguished record in the Army. However, the fact that he had served as a first lieutenant in the German Army prior to the First World War, and had been Military Attaché to Italy from 1931 to 1932, made the new president suspect.

Ramírez immediately launched a campaign to make himself popular. Thousands of pictures of the President were turned off the presses and distributed to business establishments all over the country. I saw his picture everywhere—in the windows of department stores, bakeries, bars, and beauty parlors; and one grocery store proprietor went so far as to place the color photograph in his window, where it was surrounded by an assortment of choice hams.

The months that followed were never dull, for the new government took itself very seriously indeed. No one in Argentina could escape being touched by the political upheaval, and Buenos Aires never seemed quite the same to me after that June evening when we looked across the street and discovered troops billeted in "our" park.

After hastily confirming the dissolution of Congress which had been ordered originally by Rawson, the Ramírez regime saw fit to call off the coming presidential elections and began to govern the country by decree. In other words, they not only enforced the laws, but also made them.

And so they launched an epoch where the pen was mightier than the sword, and a great deal busier. Probably for the first time in the country's colorful history, writer's cramp became an occupational disease of the government. Students of higher mathematics, rather than lawyers, were required to keep track of the host of decrees that marched out of the Government House. One report, which some sources discounted as being too conservative, had it that the military regime wrote and signed in the neighborhood of ten thousand decrees before handing the government over officially to President Perón three years to the day after the 1943 revolution. Some traditional democrats were wont to scoff at this phenomenal production of law and order, but even serious students calculated that the President would have required a day of forty-eight hours just to read the decrees he had signed.

Besides the official decrees, there was a multitude of other resolutions and orders issued by the various government agencies to plague further the bewildered citizens. No inhabitant of the republic, not even residents of the most remote corners of Argentina, remained unscathed; and not even the animals of the republic were left to roam their carefree way.

I was always sorry I didn't get to meet and personally congratulate Lieutenant Colonel Caccia, the Acting Mayor of Buenos Aires, who distinguished himself by one bit of legislation. It must have been one of those sunny but humid summer days when Caccia's heart went out to all of the residents of the municipality, whether they had two legs or four. So he ordered that all draft horses employed in the city must be supplied with straw hats or "hats of some similar light materials during the summer months."

The hats turned out to be picturesque, narrow-brimmed affairs, with the ears of the draft animals sticking out jauntily through the holes that had been tailored for them. I sincerely believe the horses were not only grateful for the shade, but also took real pride in their fashionable new appearance.

The Mayor of the city, General Pertiné, also extended his jurisdiction to the animal kingdom when he signed a decree modifying the zoo and appointing a colonel to run it. The action, he explained, was taken to carry out the "cultural purposes for which the zoo had been established."

The welfare of the human being was not neglected. The General Post Office authorities passed a resolution providing neck shades for all postmen to protect them from sunburn.

And the new federal government, concerning itself with various professional ailments, passed a decree including "telegraphist's cramp" among them.

The preamble to the decree stated that scientific investigation had established that the professional telegraphist's ailment arose on the opposite side from that on which he operated. It commenced by localizing itself in the left big toe and, rising through the thorax, produced a contraction which the operators qualified as "terrible," as it prevented them from breathing, causing them to require removal from their chairs, where they were fixed in a rigid position, resembling a mark of interrogation, curving toward the left hand side.

Affirming that it was the duty of the State to protect such a large section of workers, the decree ordered the incorporation of the ailment in article 149 of Law No. 9688.

One proprietress of a waterfront beer hall, however, indignantly declared one night that the State wasn't doing much to look after her welfare. Her establishment had been visited and the rest rooms inspected. The *oficial* warned her that some changes would have to be made. Instead of such plebeian designations as "*hombres*" and "*mujeres*" (men and women) on the two doors, the signs would have to be re-painted to read, "*caballeros*" and "*damas*," or "gentlemen" and "ladies."

The proprietress thought it was hardly worth the effort, so sharply had her business declined since the revolution. Indeed, an aura of piety seemed to exude from Casa Rosada and penetrate the entire city of Buenos Aires.

Leonard and I had always been impressed by how late the *porteños*, both adult and children, liked to stay out at night. We had been accustomed to finding the streets full when we went home from the *Herald* as late as 2:30 A.M. Sometimes we'd notice whole families out, including the grandmother and two- or three-year-old children.

But though General Ramírez rang out no curfews, most *porteños* began going home early for the simple reason that all places of entertainment began locking up before they had time to settle down and enjoy themselves. At the same time, some of the leaders broached the necessity of raising the birth rate. Drug stores were forbidden to sell contraceptives, and newspapers were notified that they must cease publishing advertising of divorce lawyers in Uruguay as "the State will not consent to propaganda tending to promote divorces and inciting the inhabitants of the country to violate the laws by submitting themselves to foreign jurisdiction." Publication of news concerning persons getting divorces in other countries also was frowned upon.

At the same time, song writers, music publishing houses and theaters were advised to clean up the lyrics of the tango—to cut out all reference to immorality, of unfaithful wives and erring husbands.

The purity campaign even extended to the nation's speech, and radio stations were warned about broadcasting slang or otherwise corrupting the language.

Movie houses and theaters which had been operating up until 1 A.M. or later were ordered—because of the fuel crisis—to close

Andean hut against a background of
snow-capped mountains

Banks of clouds hover about the
summits of the Andes

Monument on Cerro de Gloria, Mendoza, marks the site where San Martín gathered his liberating armies for the plunge into Chile

Clock of flowers and shrubs, San Isidro

their doors at 11:30 every night and at midnight on holidays. *Confiterías*, or music halls, long the favorite haunts of after-theater crowds, were decreed shut before 12 P.M. too.

Some *porteños* began to grumble and talk of the good old days when they could listen to unexpurgated tangos and drink *vino* until 4 or 5 A.M., or as long as their pesos lasted. They began to blame the dreary city on a Catholic priest and contended that he was responsible for the new program of piety, not General Ramírez. They were referring, of course, to Father Wilkinson Dirube, army chaplain and presidential adviser, who was an important behind-the-scenes figure in the early days of the military government. Father Wilkinson soon found so much attention by the public unwelcome and quietly retired from the spotlight of Casa Rosada. One of his personal friends told me that he had been a much maligned man.

With or without Father Wilkinson, however, Casa Rosada never let the decree production line lag.

One day the government decided that it wasn't doing enough to conserve fuel, so it passed this unusual decree: "Shops situated on the even side of the street must close at 18:30 o'clock on the even days of the month, and at 19:30 on the odd days. The reverse applying to shops on the odd sides of the streets."

The newspapers, at least, profited from this, for most stores found it necessary to publish advertisements informing their customers whether they were on the odd or even side of the street.

It used to be an amusing sight to wander around the streets in the early evening, for they would be brilliantly lighted on one side and in obscurity on the other. Big theater signs would be flashing on the odd side, while their neighbors on the even side would be blacked-out as if enemy planes were approaching.

This proved to be good practice for them, however. For soon big posters made their appearance all over the city showing Buenos Aires in flames and planes circling overhead, and subsequently certain sections of the city were blacked-out at different times.

All of this was a mere step to the big occasion when all of Buenos Aires would go black, hiding her splendor from any jealous power. The night came, and all was dark, except for special blue lights placed at street corners and on street cars, and occasional squares of light to be seen in the tall apartment buildings. Anti-aircraft guns were scheduled to go into action to give *porteños* a sample of what a real raid was like. But no guns sounded in the night skies. The thunder and the rain came instead. Lights began to flash on in apartment buildings, and soon the street lamps followed suit. Citizens hurried toward the nearest movie, for the radio had just announced that the black-out had been called off because of rain. In a headline the next day, *The Standard* pronounced, "Black-out a Wash-out." The fear-inspiring posters and the blue lights were gone in a few days, and that was the last time we ever heard of hiding Buenos Aires under a blue light.

The musical comedy touches were many in those days, but few Argentines saw anything remotely humorous in the ruthless eradication of some of the country's most vital democratic institutions.

The Junta de la Victoria, a nationwide women's club of some fifty thousand members, was one of the first casualties of the new regime. Headed by Mrs. Ana Rosa de Martínez Guerrero, a member of one of the country's most distinguished families, the club had devoted most of its activities since its founding in 1941 to preparing clothing and other aid for the Allied nations. But just three weeks after the revolution succeeded, the club was ordered closed by government officials. At the same time, about $75,000 worth of garments, ready to be sent to the Allied nations, disappeared, never to be seen again by any of the club members. The excuse for the closure was that Communists had infiltrated into it, the charge apparently being based largely on the fact that a good share of the clothing was being sent to Russia.

Other organizations suffered a like fate, and before the purge had subsided, some 345 had been closed as a result of alleged Communist or subversive influences within.

Leonard and I watched the throttling of one of these. It was the big pro-Allied Acción Argentina, which had a membership of over seventy thousand persons and great influence in the country. Known as a middle-of-the-road group, its directors were some of the nation's most able leaders. We arrived at the Acción Argentina headquarters just a short time after it had been raided. We saw firemen drive up in a truck and proceed to remove the big sign bearing the name of the organization and then scrape off the group's posters. A crowd gathered to watch, but no *"vivas"* were being shouted that day.

The other principal casualties were Comisión Sanitaria para la Ayuda de los Pueblos Libres and the Confederación Democrática Argentina de Solidaridad y Ayuda a los Países Libres. But dozens of obscure little clubs were also either closed or had policemen on hand to attend their meetings. This finally reached the point where a woman felt positively subversive to be caught with a pair of knitting needles in her hands.

As societies providing garments for the various Allied nations appeared to be singularly vulnerable, some Scottish and British matrons began to consider themselves daring souls to venture out to their own sewing circles. I knew of one woman who made it a practice to telephone her husband at least once during a meeting to let him know that she was still outside the clutches of the law.

The least desirable accomplishments of the Ramírez government, from the democratic point of view, were the closure or suspension of many newspapers, the suspension of eight federal judges who normally hold office for life, the closure of some Jewish newspapers, the establishment of Catholic religious instruction in public schools which had for many decades been non-sectarian, the dissolution of all political parties, and the imprisonment of thousands of persons on flimsy or nonexistent charges.

Violations of civil liberties were many and spectacular, but the military authorities developed a highly effective technique of keeping the public quiet. They gave as they took away.

Seldom had the "common man" basked in so much solicitude for his pocketbook. At times, I too developed a kindly feeling for the military dictatorship, especially when the landlord came around one day and said that from then on our rent would be 15 per cent less each month.

I am sure he and his colleagues were the only men in Argentina not jubilant over decree No. 1,580 which ordered rentals on apartments and houses reduced from 20 per cent to 5 per cent monthly. The most popular feature of the decree was that persons paying $12.50 or less for their homes got the 20 per cent cut, while those over the $100 bracket benefitted least.

Those were the honeymoon days of the Ramírez administration—

his first month in office—when the price of butter was set at twenty cents a pound in markets, milk at five cents a liter (approximately a quart), and other basic foodstuffs lowered as much as 20 per cent in some cases.

Not content to win fame and popularity by means of such handsome gestures, the Ramírez regime sought to dramatize itself to the people in the Argentine newsreels, which blossomed suddenly as they became required screening in every theater of the land. The newsreels were dedicated not so much to "news," as to glorifying the generals and the colonels in power. We saw by way of the screen the whole impressive ceremony at which the Virgin of Mercedes was made an honorary general of the Argentine Army. We saw His Excellency, President Ramírez—in the presence of high government and army officials—read a decree naming the Virgin a general, then solemnly pin a general's sash on the image. The Virgin was then removed to a room behind the altar, the key to which was presented to Ramírez. I wondered who got that key when he fell from power.

I never heard of any man being laughed out of public office, but one story helped prepare the people for General Ramírez' abrupt return to private life.

The President, it was related by anecdote tellers in the cafes around Buenos Aires, one day entered a subway station on a tour of inspection. Seeking to test the qualifications of the attendant, Ramírez inquired where he would be able to ride on the subways of Buenos Aires. The attendant thought quickly of the Retiro and Constitución railway stations at opposite ends of his line and another subway nearby which ended at the big middle class cemetery of Chacarita. Then he replied respectfully to Ramírez: "*Señor Presidente*, for you the subway has three destinations: Retiro (retirement), Constitución (restoration of legal government) and Chacarita (burial in the cemetery)."

As far as the quick-witted Argentines were concerned, the humble attendant had shown the president three ways to step out.

Ramírez chose the first, or rather fellow army officers chose it for him soon after he signed a decree breaking relations with the Axis. His picture soon disappeared from store windows, not to be replaced by that of his successor, General Edelmiro J. Farrell.

The "Old Andine Condor," as Colonel Perón liked to call the new president, soon became the target of the sharpest wits in the nation.

His kindly, homely face was the subject of many a jest, and the stooge rôle he played for Perón provided the favorite anecdotes of the pampas.

One joke became so popular that it will probably find itself in the pages of Argentine folklore some day. Farrell lost his handkerchief while attending a big parade, and an officer tried to give him another. Farrell, however, insisted that he wanted his own, remarking wistfully, "After all, that's the only thing Perón will let me stick my nose into any more."

Even Farrell's education was scrutinized and found wanting. The *porteño* wags insisted that he had been presented with a beautifully bound copy of *Hamlet* while on a visit to one of the provinces. "Who wrote it?" Farrell courteously asked the donors.

"Shakespeare," he was informed.

"Then please send him a card of congratulations," he told the amazed group.

"But Shakespeare is dead," a man whispered in his ear.

"Then send the card to his family," Farrell suggested.

"But the family is dead, too," he was told.

Farrell wiped a tear from his eye, the jokesters claimed, and sighed sorrowfully, "Ah, what a tragedy that San Juan earthquake was, to wipe out the entire Shakespeare family!"

I believe that even the bitterest enemies of the military regime found it just a little difficult not to like—or at least sympathize with—General Farrell. He always seemed much more *simpático* to me than the dapper Ramírez, who never ceased to look cold, austere and plagued with liver trouble. Farrell, on the other hand, reminded me of nothing so much as a big, friendly St. Bernard dog. He was about as glamorous as an old shoe.

There were quite a few differences between the Ramírez and Farrell regimes. The outstanding development under Farrell was the swift but carefully engineered rise of Perón's star. True, he had been one of several powers behind the throne in the days of Ramírez. But with Farrell in the president's chair, Perón didn't even bother to conceal that he was running the show.

The barbs grew sharper when Perón swaggered into the anecdote picture with Farrell. The President and the Vice-President, according to one story, left on a river vessel together for the nothern city of Corrientes. A crowd gathered to see them off, and one man, undoubtedly inclined to morbid speculation, asked a friend, "Supposing the ship is sunk, who do you think would be saved?"

"The nation," his friend replied without hesitation.

The era of piety became history. I suppose even the men in power sensed how ridiculous they would appear to keep up the fiction of reforming the people. The scandalous stories that spread about the private lives of the men in Casa Rosada were suggestive of those that filtered out of Germany about Goering and Goebbels and Hitler.

More momentous, however, was the introduction of a new weapon into Argentine life; the instrument of fear to squelch opposition. This was achieved by means of enlarging, strengthening and centralizing the police into the most powerful and brutal arm of the government. To say that Argentina became a police state under Farrell and Perón is certainly no exaggeration, as any of the thousands arrested can testify. True, there had been great numbers of arrests during the days of Ramírez, but instead of cells being emptied with his departure, they became only more crowded.

At the same time, military expenditures reached the highest peak in the history of the country. They rose from 535,000,000 pesos in 1943, at that time the greatest on record, to 973,000,000 pesos in 1944, and further advanced to 1,428,000,000 pesos in 1945. Perón further startled the people by announcing the reorganization of the Army, providing for pre- and post-conscription training to include male citizens from twelve to fifty. The establishment of a women's auxiliary also was provided for under the decree.

It was interesting to watch the steps employed by Perón to smash independent labor unions or turn them into tools to help him become president. The whole road show campaign of "Perón for President," which began two years before his election, was one of the more spectacular domestic features of the Farrell government. It included the wooing of all phases of labor by a whole series of wage increases and benefits, and the mushroom growth of a gigantic government propaganda machine dedicated largely to seeing that Perón became the next legal president. The government-sponsored demonstration came into full flower in this period, and the sound truck became the Paul Revere of this revolution.

Whereas Ramírez had been cautious enough to have only the smaller newspapers suspended, his successors rushed in where no angel would think of treading. Mighty *La Prensa* was closed for several days, and the United Press for nearly a month. Few newspapers in the republic were left untouched by the iron hand in Casa Rosada.

The arrest or exile of thousands of the government's opponents, the fascist-like utterances and theories of the leaders, coupled with their totalitarian methods of oppression, left the Farrell-Perón regime wide open to accusations that theirs was a Nazi-type government; and the almost unhindered operation of Nazi spies in Buenos Aires, which was the center of German espionage in the Americas, strengthened that impression.

I have never believed that the Germans financed or even took an important part in the military revolution of 1943; that was entirely unnecessary. However, in their long years of intimate social and professional association with the Argentine Army the Germans successfully had laid the foundation for the Army's seizure of power and subsequent imposition of totalitarian rule. From the German point of view, the situation in early 1943 was something like this: the Argentine Government might do something "foolish," such as breaking off diplomatic relations or even declaring war on the Axis, thereby jeopardizing Argentina's proper position in the totalitarian world that would follow a German victory. But an army revolt would prevent this and would also assure the Germans of a continuing safe base of espionage and propaganda operations in the Western Hemisphere; similarly, there was a chance the army government could create a bloc in southern South America which would disrupt inter-American unity and prove a real thorn in the side of the Allies. The Germans had everything to gain and nothing to lose by talking up an army revolt in Argentina; and the Army perhaps required no great amount of persuasion to attempt the *coup*.

Any suggestion that a foreign power had any part in the revolution of June 4 was vigorously refuted by the military men who had seized power, including the parade of officers who thereafter inhabited the Government Palace in the frequent and confusing changing of the guard. In fact, they said so many times, and with such emphasis, that this was strictly a home-made revolution designed to clean out graft and inefficiency in the government and that it had no relation with international affairs, that few observers were willing to accept the Army's statements at face value. They protested too much. The military men beat the drums too loudly for the *soberanía* of the *patria* and announced too often that the new regime wanted nothing of foreign ideologies.

To maintain their pretense of indifference to world affairs brought forth in the new military rulers a dexterity of the tongue which would make the average *yanqui* congressman look like a stuttering school boy. The Spanish language naturally lends itself to the flowery and ambiguous phrase, and the army men soon learned the full artistry of its use. Their speeches—with the exception of a few blunderers who did not last long in responsible positions—became such masterpieces of the double meaning that often two persons could listen side by side and come away with entirely opposite ideas of how the general or the colonel stood on any given issue, including the current conflict between the Allied and Axis powers.

The standard reasoning became, "Well, he said this, so he must mean this...." The foreign observer became a political detective, seeking for the real thought underlying the gilded subtleties of official words.

How deeply Argentina was involved in the struggle for power in the outer world was amply shown, however, not only by the Allied nations which blew alternately warm and cold toward the succession of governments in Casa Rosada, but also by the high mortality rate of the foreign ministers under the Army regimes.

General Rawson shocked the public by choosing as his foreign minister, General Martínez, the ruthless federal capital police chief. But Martínez was out before he ever got in—with the fall of Rawson. The new government of General Ramírez then named Rear Admiral Segundo Storni to the post. Storni retired in crushed humiliation after his naive request for Lend-Lease aid from the

United States met with such a stern rebuff from Cordell Hull, then Secretary of State. On leaving office, Storni gallantly said, "I accept full responsibility for the note to Mr. Hull," but his friends were of a different opinion, saying the whole thing had been devised by Ramírez and his friends. General Alberto Gilbert followed him, and despite pronounced Axis leanings, was the man who delivered the Notes to the representatives of Germany and Japan officially rupturing relations. After that, his tenure in the Foreign Office was brief, and his place was filled temporarily by Rear Admiral Benito S. Sueyro. Sueyro resigned as Acting Minister in the turmoil which followed General Ramírez' delegation of his powers. The Minister of Agriculture, General Diego I. Mason, agreed to fill the job temporarily, and when Farrell became President, it was Mason who reassured the world that there would be no change in the country's foreign policy. He kept his job for several months, giving no indication of overwork, for at that time Argentina's relations outside her own boundaries were at a bare minimum. General Orlando L. Peluffo was appointed the Minister of Foreign Affairs in May, 1944, when the revolution was less than eleven months old, and it was during his term that the United States, Great Britain and most of the United Nations recalled their ambassadors from Buenos Aires. On more than one occasion, Peluffo denied charges made by Cordell Hull that the country was the headquarters of a Fascist movement which was spreading throughout the continent.

Leonard and I began to take a keen interest in General Peluffo when we went to call on an American couple one night who lived in the same neighborhood as the minister. They passed on a piece of gossip they had heard from their maid, who was distinguished for her curiosity as well as her cooking. The servant had learned from a servant in the Peluffo building of strange happenings in the block. Each night plain-clothes men were posted at the entrance of the apartment and still other police at the corners. The servant had been a good reporter and obtained the address. Leonard and I were so eager to see these mysterious things for ourselves that we hardly bothered to bid our host and hostess good night. We headed in the direction of General Peluffo's residence and were gratified to find a policeman at the corner, sitting on a motorcycle and with a gun in his holster. Another policeman was near by, and when we reached the apartment entrance, there were two men standing there, wearing double-breasted suits. They inspected us carefully and then tried to look nonchalant when we stared back at them. We strolled ahead to the other corner, only to find another armed officer mounted on a motorcycle. There was something afoot, no doubt of that. Of course, I jumped to the romantic conclusion that an attempt had been made on the general's life. Not until he had resigned a few days later because of "differences with the President on internal policy," did I learn that the men weren't placed there to protect the minister, but to watch him for his rivals in the cabinet.

His successor, Dr. Cesar Ameghino, the Minister of Finance, fared somewhat better, for it was during his days as Foreign Minister that Argentina re-established diplomatic relations with the other American nations, declared war on the Axis and was admitted to the United Nations.

His resignation came, however, in one of the periodic upheavals of the cabinet, and when the curtain went up again, Dr. Juan Isaac Cooke was the new Foreign Minister. He had hitched his wagon to the rising star of Perón but soon found the road ahead a rough one. Before he left the stage to make way for a whole new cast of characters which came on after Perón's election as President, he had had the job of trying to refute the charges in the U.S. State Department Blue Book that the Argentine military governments had given aid and comfort to the Axis.

In many ways the Argentine show resembled a Cecil B. De Mille production, so many and varied were the actors that wandered on and off of the stage. Some of the men who were in and out of office were able and even brilliant. Others were eccentrics, clowns that provoked laughter when tears would have been more appropriate.

This kaleidoscopic shifting of the men in Government House led to some exceedingly curious paradoxes, among them being the fact that several high officials, who were blanketed in obscurity immediately after their fall from favor, later attained some stature as champions of democracy. Their sins apparently were wiped out by the greater sins of the succeeding administrations.

There was, for instance, the case of General Rawson. His speech proclaiming the victory of the revolutionary cause had been notable for what it had not said about the new government's stand in regard to the Axis. Yet a few months after his "retirement," many a pro-democratic Argentine looked to him as the white hope of the pro-Allied forces within the country, and it was bruited about that the real reason he had fallen from power was that he had wanted to break relations with the Axis without delay, that he had even desired to declare war on Germany in 1943. And, conveniently forgetting that it was Rawson who had taken the initial move against Congress, many Argentines looked to him as the logical man to overthrow the military government and restore democratic liberties. That Rawson was willing to serve in this rôle is indicated by his arrest in September, 1945, as the leader of an unsuccessful plot to overthrow the Farrell-Perón government. He was always waiting in the wings for the new actors to muff their lines.

Another Johnny-come-lately democrat was Ramírez. He went temporarily into oblivion after he signed the decree rupturing Argentina's relations with the Axis, and numerous of his satellites were vaporized along with him, some never to be heard of again by the public.

Then came the liberation of Paris, which brought a great surge of joy and hope to democratic forces all over Argentina. Huge spontaneous demonstrations were staged, and all of Buenos Aires went crazy with thanksgiving. And with it came the resurrection of the politically dead—including Rawson and Ramírez.

Groups began to march through the streets waving flags and shouting. When one group of several hundred passed the home of Ramírez, it paused to yell, "*Viva democracia*," and with some incongruity, "We want you back, we want you back!" Ramírez popped out on his balcony in a curtain call which was cut short when police appeared on the scene and dispersed his enthusiastic audience with tear gas bombs.

After that, the men in power made sure that Ramírez would take no more curtain calls. Plain-clothes men were kept in the neighborhood, some posing as eskimo pie peddlers, others as street cleaners and still others as peanut vendors. In fact, the neighbors began to comment on the excellent service they were getting from the tradesmen of the street. This attention so annoyed the former president, however, that he is reported to have warned the police chief that the next plain-clothes man he saw lurking in front of his home would be shot. After that, Ramírez discovered that the climate was more healthful in the town of Rosario, where it was said his interest in selling real estate dwarfed his political ambitions.

What we saw in Argentina was not a single revolution, nor was it a series of uprisings; in the long range view, it consisted of only two—but very distinct—revolutions.

In the first revolution, which was an army affair, the characters on the stage changed interminably, but the lines they read were virtually always the same. The first revolution was a farce, and most of the dialogue and the elaborate posturing were screamingly funny. The Argentines rolled in the aisles, watching the army men on the stage trying to run the government; they chuckled to see the military men take themselves so seriously.

I believe that, for better or for worse, the Argentine people gossiped and laughed themselves into the second revolution. They had grown so accustomed to lampooning the latest array of funny men on the stage, they had been so lulled with the pantomime of government, that they realized too late that the play had been rewritten. The Argentines were slow to discover that before them was a new and serious document, written by a vastly different playwright, run by a new director and enacted by a new leading man who stuck carefully to the new revolutionary script; all these functions performed by one man whose sense of humor did not extend to comedy on a national scale, a man with ambition and magnetism and intellect.

The new man was Juan Domingo Perón, the army officer who substituted grim drama for comedy in Argentina and reminded the Argentines that they are the people of the tango—sad and ambitious. Subsequently, Perón was elected president—the first constitutional ruler of the land since June 4, 1943. And now playing on the Argentine stage is Perón's revolution—which is an entirely new chapter in the life of a nation.

LAND OF THE STRETCHED BELT

I N ARGENTINA THE CAT, ALLEY VARIETY, HAS A MARKED AIR OF independence and indifference to human beings. He never need worry about where his next meal is coming from, for he obviously thrives on the leftovers in this land of overwhelming plenty. And eventually he grows into a super-cat, a glistening, aristocratic and full-bellied giant of the alley. As a matter of fact, he probably eats too much.

For humans, Argentina is likewise the land of the stretched belt.

The Argentine nation is probably the best nourished in the world. The people are plump, look well-fed. Theirs is not a land of the "three square a day" but of four or five meals, at least two of them huge repasts sufficient to founder the newcomer to Buenos Aires. All this the Argentines take for granted, yet with a feeling of some pride in the overflowing cornucopia and their ample sharing in it. For instance, each little storekeeper arranges his good things—his fruit, his vegetables or meat with all the care of an artist preparing a masterpiece.

The great Mercado del Plata, in the heart of Buenos Aires, is one of the sights of the hemisphere. I visited it again and again, not so much to buy food as to convince myself that I wasn't dreaming. I had never thought of cabbages and carrots and egg plants as objects of beauty until I saw this giant food emporium, where they are polished and sprayed and arranged so each vegetable harmonizes in color with its neighbor. It would be wonderful in technicolor.

Evidence of the abundance of food is everywhere. Standard window equipment for the city's hundreds of restaurants is a large barbecue spit, on which great sides of meat, a dozen or so chickens and quantities of fat sausages turn round and round to a sizzling golden brown.

Pasta shops are filled with big bundles of spaghetti, and workers can be seen making neat rows of raviolis. Heads of cheese are stacked ceiling high in neighboring stores. Plump, baked turkeys lie in regal elegance in the windows of delicatessens. And there is so much good, fresh meat for sale, that Buenos Aires looks unpleasantly like a giant slaughter house during the morning food-buying hours. Besides *almacenes, ferias, mercados, fruterías* and *verdurerías* to keep the *porteño* from ever knowing the pangs of hunger, countless carts filled with fruit and vegetables stop from apartment house to house each morning all through the year.

Learning to cook in food-abundant Argentina was a pleasant experience, made more interesting by such novelties as the fact that tuna fish was more of a luxury than chicken, because a small can of tuna then cost more than a large chicken.

Lack of prepared foods such as mayonnaise keeps cropping up from time to time to annoy the American housewife, and we had been keeping house for at least two months before I was able to find a potato. Finally a friend told me that potatoes in Argentina are sold in coal stores—why I'll never know, except possibly because both coal and potatoes come out of the ground. I have yet to find a potato in an *almacén*, the Argentine equivalent of our grocery store.

It was a surprise to find neighborhood *almacenes* and bars frequently combined, with the bars complete with rails, sawdust on the floors, and a table or two where the customers were welcome to shoot dice or play *truco*, the most popular Argentine card game.

The *almacén* sells all sorts of canned goods, sugar, flour, cheese, sometimes eggs, wine, beer and crackers.

There are no big general grocery stores in Argentina where fresh meat, vegetables and canned goods are sold as in our Safeway and Piggly Wiggly stores. But Argentina has one institution—the *feria* (street market)—that puts our most modern super-markets to shame. I'd love to take you to a *feria* right now—for with $12 or $15 you could buy enough fresh vegetables, fruit, meats and fish to keep a family of four well supplied for a week.

There was a big open air market near us on Calle Córdoba. This *feria* filled an entire street for about three blocks. It was a whole series of open air stalls selling nearly every kind of food and drink imaginable. We even bought champagne there one Christmas holiday.

The *feria* people wear white uniforms and are very friendly. The prices of their products are all marked as required by law, and you stand much less chance of being over-charged there than in any other place.

Our favorite Córdoba *feria* always put its best foot forward to the general public. The part of the *feria* facing upper-class Avenida Callao was devoted to flowers. Here it was possible to buy as many as a dozen red roses for an American dime. There were flowers the year round. Daisies, huge dahlias, poppies, gladioli. If we spent as much as a quarter for a bouquet of flowers we considered ourselves extravagant.

After the flowers, came stalls of all kinds of fruit. Some stalls sold only oranges. Others had strawberries, cherries and bananas. Curiously, lemons were extremely difficult to buy in stalls, but were hawked among the crowds by small boys.

Vegetable stalls then followed. Some men sold only asparagus, which in Argentina is noted for its quality and size. I've seen tender "spears" nearly a foot long and about an inch in diameter. Leonard and I used to buy huge bunches for 20 cents, pour melted butter over them after simmering, then sprinkle them with Parmesan cheese. When asparagus is served, people don't bother with knives and forks, they just grasp the big end in their fingers and chew quickly before the butter runs off.

The *feria's* meat stalls extend for at least a block and simply bulge with all cuts of the kinds of meat eaten by civilized people anywhere in the world. Most of it is freshly butchered and hangs in rows in the open air. In the early 1940's a pound of filet mignon was about 20 cents, and ground beef about seven cents a pound.

Another section of the *feria* is devoted to poultry. Dressed chickens hang fat and naked from the top of each stall. Then come booths with mountains of fresh eggs, others with thick, sweet cream and cheese of every variety, some with spaghetti, and last of all the fish. This is placed at the lower end of the *feria* and the smell keeps maids from loitering to exchange gossip.

During the New Year and Christmas season, bottles of champagne and *pan dulce*, a sweet raisin and nut bread, are sold at low prices in the open air market.

Late 1946 still finds Argentina a paradise for the stomach, but not at the bargain basement prices which prevailed up until the end of 1944. Prices of food have spiralled there along with the other necessities of life, but store shelves are nearly as groaning as ever and the only adjustment being made to belts is the customary one of letting them out that extra notch.

Filet mignon has skyrocketed to the unheard of price of 34 cents a pound, and a large baking chicken to as much as $1.75. The Argentine *señora*, not yet educated to substituting cottage cheese for butter, is beginning to grumble because she has to pay 25 cents a pound for her *manteca*.

Tenderized ham has climbed to 50 cents a pound, while Canadian bacon is more than double its 1944 price. During the war years eggs were 20 cents a dozen, but had risen to 37 cents a few months after V-J day. Milk, which once cost five cents a quart, now is up to six cents. Prices of staples likewise have risen, a pound of bread to five and a half cents, potatoes to three cents, sugar to six cents and flour to three cents.

Canned goods are out of the reach of the average white collar worker, with a small can of tomato juice selling for 21 cents, and a quart of cooking oil at 55 cents.

Fruit prices reached such unheard of figures in 1945 and 1946 that the newspapers began to write editorials about the orange, and housewives seldom passed a fruit stall selling oranges at 75 cents a dozen and grapefruit at 12 cents each without exclaiming, *"Qué caro!"* The situation gave rise to a joke which became popular in Buenos Aires: A man is seen buying fruit in a market. A friend asks another, "What is he, a vegetarian?" "No," his friend replies, "He's a millionaire."

As for eating places, there are hundreds of them in Buenos Aires alone, including dozens of excellent restaurants. The Argentine eating out doesn't have to confine himself to the regular restaurant, however. He may have his coffee and French rolls in the morning at a bar or sidewalk cafe. He can have lunch in a modern quick lunch establishment about like one of Child's restaurants. He can

Street scene in Córdoba

Ancient cathedral, in Córdoba

Lujan cathedral attracts candleman

Country boys in old Lujan

drink tea in any one of dozens of *salones de te* in the heart of
Buenos Aires, where he may take his choice of four kinds of
sandwiches brought to him on a heaping platter and a dozen small,
valentine-like cakes. He can eat to the tune of a tango, American
jazz, a Strauss waltz or a rumba. If he likes, he can stay on for
the cocktail hour at any of the tea houses, and with his San Martín
will be brought free an assortment of cheese, crackers, hot sausages,
potato chips, potato salad and peanuts. If he orders a second cocktail, he gets a "repeat" on the free lunch.

Dinner in Buenos Aires is anywhere between 8 and 10 o'clock.
Since the Ramírez regime ordered midnight closing for the movies
to conserve fuel, there has been a tendency for earlier dinners.
When Leonard and I were working on the *Buenos Aires Herald*, a
morning paper, we were allowed and took two hours for dinner.
It is almost impossible to get dinner in less than an hour anywhere
in Argentina.

One of our early discoveries of restaurant life in Buenos Aires
was a little place not over a block and a half from the office. Here
the waiter brought a huge four-wheeled cart of hors d'oeuvres for
us to choose from—fish, salads, cold meats, pickles and *mayonesas*.
After stuffing ourselves on these, we were then expected to proceed
to the main course.

La Cabaña, where Leonard took me to dine after our wedding,
is the most famous restaurant in South America. The entrance very
much resembles a de luxe butcher shop, with sides and cuts of
young chilled beef displayed under glass. Two dark red Shorthorn
yearlings—stuffed—stand guard, one on each side of the door. Huge
demijohns of wine are lined along the floor going into the restaurant. The whole place is done in typical *criollo* style, and wine
bottles hang all around the walls. But the chief attraction is food.
There isn't any music here—with such food there doesn't have
to be. My first dish in La Cabaña was its famous "Virginia" tenderized ham, and I'm still wondering if Virginia can equal it. The
baby *bifes*, which fill a plate and are at least two inches thick, are
brought to the table on individual charcoal stoves. These big pieces
of beef are washed down with red wine.

Estancia, on the same street, was another one of our favorite
places for eating out on pay day or when guests were in town.

We had many other favorites for regular week-day eating.

Some of the best restaurants at low prices were on or near the waterfront. One was the Napoli, always crowded and with the inevitable decoration of rows of wine bottles in shelves around the wall. We used to go there for *panqueques de manzana* (apple pancakes). Most restaurants in the center of town had good *panqueques*, but none quite like the Napoli. They were brought to the table on big platters, with the rum sauce covering them aflame. I always wanted to go into the kitchen and ask the chef for the secret of his thin, crunchy *panqueques* that covered the whole plate with fire and rich flavor of rum. I've lived to regret that I lacked the nerve.

In Buenos Aires there is a restaurant for every kind of food. There is French, Spanish, Argentine, American, Russian and Italian cooking.

The best chicken à la Maryland I ever ate was in a little Hungarian restaurant on Calle Reconquista in Buenos Aires—it's La Corneta del Cazador. The chicken is fried in meal after the bones have been removed. With it is served creamed corn in patty shells, banana fritters which have been dipped in orange juice, and fresh peas.

We used to eat Canelones à la Rossini every Sunday night at the Mogador, an Italian dish in a French restaurant in a South American city. Sometimes we ate steak and kidney pie at the same place.

It is a fact that in Buenos Aires it is difficult to find a restaurant which has really "bad" food.

The sad thing about it all is that the food is too good and too plentiful in Argentina. That is, it is "sad" for the stomach and the figure. Most tables are equipped with siphons of soda water to aid the overworked Argentine digestion. Drug stores do a thriving business in Carter's Little Liver Pills, but still people go on joyfully eating all they can. So did we.

A curious thing about food in Buenos Aires is the scarcity of typical Argentine dishes. You could list them all on your ten fingers. There is the *bife;* the *asado* or barbecue; a special *criollo* steak sauce, *puchero* and a few others. But there is one dish—the *empanada—* which is just as much Argentine as the hamburger or ham 'n eggs is American.

The *empanada* is a fried meat pie, and it has high standing with the nation's palate. It is eaten at quick lunch stands before an evening at the movies. It sometimes serves as a first course in fine restaurants and homes. It is a favorite at cocktail parties. There are all kinds of *empanadas*—chicken, ground beef, corn, cheese and fruit. But the most popular is ground meat, with chopped olives, hard-boiled eggs and raisins blended together. Each province produces its own particular kind. A *correntino* swears by the *empanadas* of his province and will insist that he can't get any fit to eat in Buenos Aires. A *cordobés* will drive for blocks when he gets to Buenos Aires just to find a shop selling *empanadas de Córdoba*.

Our Austrian maid, Anastacia, favored other Argentine dishes, such as corn, rice and *chorizos* cooked in a big earthen-ware casserole. She also introduced us to *puchero*—a real boiled dinner of potatoes, carrots, onions, beef, chicken and red *chorizos*. This was our regular Friday meal.

We had never tasted melon and ham combined until we got to Argentina, but it is so good I am convinced it ought to become universal. In the French *pensión* where we lived for a few months before returning to the United States, the *cocinera* used to put some fancy touches on this dish when we had guests. For the first course, she would send us a huge platter of ice-cold delicate golden melon, ham sliced and fashioned into rolls and fresh figs nestling in a bed of lettuce. What meals we had in that boarding house! We would have a five-course lunch—which usually started with soup, and some such thing as an omelette stuffed with tomatoes and cheese, then a filet mignon with lettuce salad, dessert (usually a bowl of fruit) and coffee.

Dinner was a meal such as this: a plate of half a dozen artichokes with hollandaise sauce for two persons; then spaghetti with sauce, and a baked meat with sherry-flavored gravy; then a cake and coffee. When we had guests, the *cocinera* would outdo herself. She might start with a shrimp salad, then have a special French toast sandwich with melted cheese and ham between the slices, and for the main course, baked chicken with a fresh vegetable salad, and a French cake for dessert. For this we paid $100 a month for board and room for both of us.

Buenos Aires has no monopoly on good food in Argentina. Mendoza, in the foothills of the Andes, delighted us as much in a culinary way as in a scenic one. On our arrival in Mendoza, one of our first excursions was to the Bola de Nieve (Snowball) to sample *empanadas mendocinas* with an ice cold white wine in tall, dark bottles called Suter Semillón. We stayed there for hours sampling more *empanadas* and drinking more of Mendoza's favorite wine. In Mendoza were also black grapes the size of plums served in big bowls with fresh figs, apricots, pears and peaches, over which chunks of ice glistened.

Beautiful Córdoba, noted for its multitude of lovely churches, was another place where we found eating all it should be. We still dream of a *bife* smothered in mushrooms that we had in one Córdoba restaurant for 25 cents. Here we ate our first *humita con choclo*, praised by Argentines as a typical dish of their native land, but seldom listed on restaurant menus. It looks like an oversized tamale, but is not hot. Hot dishes such as found in Mexico are unheard of in Argentina.

Argentines shudder at the Yankee habit of putting mayonnaise on fruit salad. They seldom have any salad other than mixed vegetable or plain lettuce. Fruit salad is a dessert and a little wine is mixed with the juice of the fruit. Ice cream grows more popular every year.

The big fluffy American-style cake is unknown. Argentine cakes are usually very flat and heavy, but beautifully decorated. Leonard and I stopped many an evening on our way home for dinner to admire the elaborate decorations in Dos Bulevares, the excellent bakery at the corner of Santa Fe and Callao. I remember one window displayed frogs molded in sugar on each cake. Some were ready to hop. One extra large cake even had a classroom of small frogs sitting at desks with a big frog, complete with eye glasses, supervising the class. The shop was very stylish inside too, with huge crystal chandeliers.

The cake baker is truly a sculptor. Some icings are adorned with such things as life-sized baby chicks of sugar, others with school-houses, castles and even the likeness of the current president. I was impressed with one cake in the New China tea shop window designed especially to appeal to the nation's gamblers. It was decorated with a sugar dice cup and five dice all ready for the popular game of *generala*.

This great abundance of food and the tendency of the Argentines to luxuriate in it—particularly in Buenos Aires—in part explains the ease with which military men at various times have been able to seize and hold power in spite of the predominantly democratic sentiments of the Argentines; and most politicians know instinctively that they are safe to raid the nation's treasury and infringe on civil liberties. For who ever heard of a people rising up in bloody revolution on over-loaded stomachs? What man ever assassinated a tyrant after consuming a pound of filet mignon washed down by a quart of sparkling red wine?

An Argentine doctor friend of ours had a novel theory: "We're all suffering from chronic constipation," he diagnosed. "We eat too much. We'll never have any real democracy or make any nation-wide progress until more of us get discontented, and that's hard to do on a full stomach. Life is just too easy for us."

It is true there are large areas in Argentina where the masses lack some of the elements of a balanced, health-giving diet, but the problem of "filling the stomach" simply does not exist.

Despite rising prices, 1946 sees the Argentine stuffing down just as many calories and carbohydrates as ever, most of them coming from the tenderest, most delicious beef found anywhere in the world.

For even though Argentina exports more beef than any other country, this outgoing amount is only 30 per cent of her total production. Per capita, the Argentine nation eats more meat than any other on the globe. During six months in 1944, the 2,501,812 inhabitants of Buenos Aires ate 440,000,000 pounds of meat, or some 176 pounds per person. In other words each man, woman and child in the city ate about a pound of meat a day. For the entire country the per capita average is 300 pounds of meat a year, of which 88 per cent is beef. Beef consumption in Buenos Aires even increased in 1945, when the figure for cattle slaughtered in the municipal yards rose to 1,350,000 head, against 1,320,000 head in 1944. This is for Buenos Aires alone, and consumption in some parts of the interior is much larger. In the same period, slaughter of cattle for export fell from 2,490,000 to 1,630,000 head, a reduction of 34.5 per cent. Slaughtering of sheep for export decreased 10.1 per cent in 1945, while home consumption was gaining 12.6 per cent.

The people of the United States, long envied by the rest of the world as a country of enormous meat consumption, must fold up their napkins and leave the table when an Argentine enters the dining room. *Norteamericanos* have long been regarded as something akin to vegetarians by their neighbors of the River Plate.

Besides the meat, enough poultry is available to make "two chickens in every pot" more than a campaign slogan to the middle-class Argentine. And if he is still hungry, there is always fish. In the 1937-1942 period, Argentina consumed 76,446,000 pounds annually, or about 5.7 pounds per capita.

These gargantuan meals have been responsible for the growth of one of the country's most flourishing industries—the production of *yerba mate*. This "Paraguayan tea," first used by the Guarani Indians of Paraguay before the arrival of the Spanish *conquistadores*, is said to aid the digestion and prevent rheumatism, believed to be aggravated by heavy meat consumption.

The Reuter office in Buenos Aires wouldn't have seemed natural without a little kettle bubbling away near the copy desk where the Argentine desk men and translators worked and drank *yerba mate*. So popular is this pleasant yet beneficial drink that Argentina's internal consumption of *mate* in 1941 amounted to 235,731,000 pounds. Colonel Perón, well aware of the importance of *mate* in the life and digestion of Argentina, distributed thousands of *mate* gourds with his picture on them during his presidential campaign.

Even with this digestive aid, Argentines are unable to eat all of the food on their plates. Visiting journalists often write of the overflowing garbage pails, some claiming that Buenos Aires throws enough away in one night to feed a small European country for a day.

It is extremely difficult for the people of Argentina, who have never known real hunger, to realize why visitors are so amazed at their food consumption. When they read statistics of the number of grams of food consumed in Czechoslovakia and Poland, they comment "*qué triste*," but they have less firsthand knowledge of privation than the people of the United States. It isn't that the Argentines are selfish, either. I've noticed the way they almost invariably drop a coin or two in the cup of the infrequent beggar they pass, and they are kind and generous to their friends. But to ask an Argentine to understand starvation, is something like expecting a New Yorker to know how the people of Hiroshima felt when the atom bomb hit. We had one Argentine friend who described himself as a man of simple tastes because he could get along on a couple of baby *bifes* a day, one for lunch and one for dinner, plus *papas fritas* and red wine.

A little *criolla* maid who worked for us for a year liked to consider herself among the downtrodden of the earth. Piously, she refused to eat the food from our table and said she was used to living on a little, so she broiled herself a T-bone steak each noon and evening after she had served us. A devout follower of Colonel Perón, she often complained to us of the hardships of the working class. She told us that some of her friends were so poor that many a night they had only platters of spaghetti with meat sauce, cheese and wine for their dinners.

One day, however, she came in all smiles. She had with her a page from *El Pampero*, the Nazi-financed newspaper. "Just look how fortunate we are," she said, pointing to an article with pictures which the newspaper had lifted from an issue of *Life* magazine that had just reached the country. The series was entitled "All the Meat You Can Eat" and showed pictures of food in Argentina, among them a Chateaubriand steak at the equivalent of 40 cents, and tea with sandwiches and cakes for 25 cents. The pictures showed how the super-abundance of "good red meat" in Argentina was "ironically, the wages of neutrality." *El Pampero*, of course, had seized on the story to show Argentines how much better off they were than the rest of the world, how the country's refusal to side against the Axis was the reason they could eat better and cheaper than their rich neighbors to the north. The same story was also picked up by *Cabildo*, the morning Axisphile sheet, and soon nationalist papers and politicians were all congratulating themselves to the tune of, "See how fortunate we are." Even some of our pro-democratic friends began to tell us of acquaintances wavering in their enthusiasm for siding actively with the Allies because, "See how fortunate we are now."

As a matter of fact, Argentina's bulging storehouse in the early days of the war caused her more uneasiness than any fear of hunger. When shipping to the River Plate was curtailed, the granaries began to overflow with huge quantities of wheat and corn that couldn't begin to be consumed at home. In a few months, reports began to trickle into the federal capital of the swarms of rats that were multiplying and growing fat in the seas of golden grain stored without adequate protection in various parts of the country. Some alarmists went so far as to predict that such a great army of rats might cause an outbreak of bubonic plague. The plague never materialized but Leonard and I did see rats running through the streets of downtown Buenos Aires on more than one occasion— they looked well-fed too. We were strolling along Calle Florida, the Fifth Avenue of South America, one evening, when a commotion was caused by a big, bewildered rat racing through the crowds.

As one of the four great wheat exporting countries of the world, Argentina's production has averaged about 240,000,000 bushels a year for the past decade, with nearly 60 per cent of it being exported. This export volume fell off drastically during the war while production remained virtually the same. At the same time her imports of coal and oil dwindled, so Argentina began to burn her enormous wheat and corn surplus as fuel.

In the fall of 1944, Argentina promised wheat to the U.N.R.R.A. And when Paris was liberated, government officials with a great fanfare of publicity announced they would give 100,000 tons of wheat to suffering France. Before that, when the Allied march into Rome was in the headlines, the Argentine government announced a gift of 50,000 tons of wheat to Italy. All of these gifts were hailed with editorial approval by the Argentine press, and government leaders frequently referred to them as tangible proof that Argentina really had made a substantial contribution to the Allied cause.

But after the war ended, the Argentines found they had more generosity than surplus food. Considerable drouth and locusts had cut production, and the government announced that Argentina's exportable wheat surplus was far too small to meet the demands being made. One sobering announcement was that the 1946 surplus totalled only 1,800,000 tons, of which 1,100,000 had already been promised, mostly to other Latin American buyers.

On top of other difficulties, there developed a shortage of rail and motor transport. Rail facilities had been weakened by six years of neglect enforced by shortages of steel and rolling stock during the war. Grain exporters also complained that at one time ten foreign ships in the great southern grain port of Bahia Blanca were unable to load wheat because freight cars formerly used to haul grain from the interior were now filled with cement and other materials for a new airport and army barracks.

In the months following, European governments learned to their dismay that the government in Buenos Aires talked of generosity but was determined to get the highest possible price for its wheat and corn. The French government, for example, purchased a large quantity of corn and sent ships to carry it from Buenos Aires; but by the time the ships arrived, the price had gone up and Argentina refused to issue export permits for the contracted corn until the French agreed to pay 25 per cent more.

The U. S. Commodity Credit Corporation, which was buying flaxseed for the Allied governments, struck a similar snag. The Argentine government refused to issue export permits at the contracted price, and the European governments to which the flaxseed finally went, found they had to pay more than double.

In late 1946 the U. S. Department of Commerce issued figures showing that Argentina was getting a higher price than either Canada or the United States—the world's two other main exporters of wheat. In August, Argentina had exported 4,600,000 bushels of wheat at approximately $2.80 a bushel, the United States shipped 16,000,000 bushels at about $2.25, while Canada got under $1.55 a bushel for the 8,400,000 bushels she exported.

The government, realizing there was gold in those grain bins, also extracted all the traffic would bear from her South American neighbors. Uruguay, Peru, Brazil and Bolivia were unable to get wheat for which they had contracted in Buenos Aires, until they agreed to higher prices. Even then the export permits were slow in coming.

Charges were made that the Argentine government was using

food as a political weapon. Shipments were suspended to Montevideo and the position of the Uruguayan government thereby weakened, until the United States stepped in and promised to make up the deficit that had suddenly developed because of Argentina's withholding. Then Argentina resumed small-scale shipments. Bolivia, following the revolt that overthrew Perón's friend, President Gualberto Villarroel, in July, 1946, also complained she was being pinched on wheat and other food for political reasons. Angry cries went up in Chile when Argentina, which had plenty of sunflower and other oil seeds, stalled for months on previous commitments to her western neighbor. President Perón later explained that his government, which controlled grain exports, found it necessary to get high prices for Argentine food abroad in order to finance farm subsidies that would ensure low prices at home. That was his answer to critics who accused Perón of creating a reservoir of ill will abroad that might in more abundant years deprive Argentina of part of her traditionally great share of the world's agricultural markets.

As a matter of fact, the lead rôle Argentina might have played as the great breadbasket for the hungry victims of the war had already been whittled down to a secondary part. Her lack of permanent storage facilities to handle surpluses she might have accumulated, the abandon with which her railways, factories and power plants burned wheat, flaxseed and corn as fuel during the war, plus her own unstinting consumption of food throughout the war and since, left her with disappointingly small reserves for the hard years now at hand.

Yet it would be ungrateful of me to condemn the inadequacy of Argentina's food policies. I would literally be biting the land that fed me, fed me better than I had ever eaten before or ever expect to eat again. And that would be too big a bite for anyone, even for me who learned how to eat in the land of the stretched belt.

PICARDIA CRIOLLA

SOME NORTH AMERICANS HAVE TOLD ME THAT THE REASON
they like the Argentines is that these South Americans are
so much like themselves. "Why, they're just like we are,"
they often say admiringly after a few days in Buenos Aires.

And it is a fact that the inhabitants of Buenos Aires have much in
common with the people who live in New York. They have the
same respect for the shining gadget, their love for the peso at least
equals the Yankee love of the dollar. Both peoples consider themselves the last word in modernity. Both like automobiles and good
clothes and air travel. The city-dwelling *porteño* promotes a good
sun tan at Mar del Plata with the same enthusiasm as the New
Yorker does at Miami Beach. Both think the depth of their tan
is an index of prosperity. The atmosphere of bustle and getting
things done is almost as pronounced on the shores of the River
Plate as it is on the shores of the Hudson.

Another similarity exists between the North American "city
slicker" and the Argentine *"tipo de pocas pulgas"*—meaning a "guy
with very few fleas." However, there is a difference in the attitude
of the American toward the city sharper and the Argentine view of
the man who thinks and operates with such speed that the fleas can
never catch up with him. What the American believes he should
deplore, the Argentine frankly admires. The dissimilarity in the
psychology of human relations is the result of education, practical
training and history.

While young North Americans learn in primary school about
George Washington and the unfortunate cherry tree, little Argentines get this advice at their father's knee: *"No seas zonzo,
aprovecha todas las circunstancias, que la vida es corta."* Don't be
a dope; life is short, and you have got to take advantage of all the

circumstances. Or: *"Este mundo es para los vivos, los zonzos que se embromen."* In other words, this world is for the smart guy, and the fool is just out of luck.

It usually takes the American longer to arrive at the same conclusion; and before he does, his conscience has pricked him along the way. Sometimes he never arrives. But even those who do, find that the Argentine has a running start, for he has been weaned on the *picardía criolla.*

This phrase means native trickery, but it would be more inclusive and accurate to call it the full-time application of Argentine wit power, the development of intelligence. It extends almost from the cradle to the grave. It shows itself, in its petty and most obvious forms, in the scissor-minded little Argentine maids-of-all-work, who through years of practice have developed fool-proof ways of snipping from household expense accounts into their own poorly-paid pockets. It extends, in subtle ways, to international dealings, in such a fashion that it is often discovered that Argentina has left herself a loophole through which to escape doing something which other nations had generally supposed she had agreed to do. It gives Argentine diplomatic representatives a head start on some of their Anglo-Saxon colleagues.

Among other things, the *picardía* keeps Argentines on the alert. They are always looking for the "catch." They are not a naive and trusting people. When they listen to a man's speech, or read about it in the newspaper, they are not apt to take his words at face value. They look between the lines for what he really meant. They have skeptical minds, and their suspicions extend to every phase of life.

Leonard came home chuckling one day between livestock shows, and reported that the judges were lifting the tails of bulls. They did so, not so much to inspect the bone formation thereabouts, as to insure against sprucing up the bulls with paraffin injections. If the tail dropped limber and naturally back into place, the judge knew that the bull had not been waxed; but if it fell stiff like a board, the bull was scratched off the list. Warm paraffin, Leonard said, was sometimes injected to fill out the small hollows next to the backbone and give the impression that not only would the animal provide his offspring with fine rump steaks, but also was capable of carrying a great weight of meat himself without sagging or becoming flabby.

Another discovery was that some enterprising *estancieros* burned the spots off noses of bulls they expected to show in the lesser exhibitions. A black spot on the muzzle automatically disqualified a Shorthorn because it indicated the bull might not be purebred. To avoid this reflection on the animal's ancestry, the unscrupulous owner would sear off the spot and put vaseline on the bull's snout. This apparently was a fine art. If the burning was done too early, the spot might grow back before the show; but if the owner used the irons too late, the blisters on the nose would tip off the keen-eyed judges.

We immediately pigeon-holed these bits along with what we considered other interesting but useless information.

The *portero* in our apartment building taught us our next elementary lesson on the facts of life in Argentina. This happened when we ordered groceries from a store outside his sphere of influence. Of course, they were never delivered to us, and we were eventually reduced to doing business with the *almacén* where he received a "cut." That was the only way he had of making a decent living—obtaining tips from grocery stores, milk men, dry cleaners and other establishments patronized by his tenants. In return, he discouraged outside buying by halting deliveries at the entrance hall.

We learned a more painful lesson when we went off to Mendoza for our first vacation.

One day we climbed to the top of Cerro de Gloria to photograph the imposing and beautiful bronze statue of General San Martín, placed on the site where more than a hundred years ago he stood to review the *gaucho* troops he had assembled for the march across the Andes, which liberated Chile from Spanish rule. It was a hot afternoon and on the long trip down we paused for *laponias*, Argentina's best known brand of eskimo pie. Later, on the bus going back to Mendoza, Leonard made the unnerving discovery that he had lost his billfold with our vacation money, and he began to retrace his steps. As the ice cream man saw Leonard returning, a broad smile came to his face and he waved the billfold happily.

Leonard beamed back at the honest man, looking into the billfold for an appropriate bill to present as a reward. Then his face fell, for 200 pesos was missing. He carefully recounted, and then pointed out his shortage to the ice cream vendor, who began to clamor so loudly for his reward that a policeman came sauntering up. After hearing both sides of the case, the policeman turned to Leonard and with a stern face lectured him roundly on his ingratitude and told him he was lucky to get his billfold back at all. I wasn't there to see it, but Leonard in a weak moment later admitted that he had been so bewildered by the swift zig-zagging of events that he had suddenly thrust a ten-peso note into the man's hand, muttered *"gracias,"* and beat a red-faced retreat before he was talked into more expenditure than the 210 pesos his forgetfulness had already cost him.

The incident had a dampening effect on us, for 210 pesos is the equivalent of what most reporters then earned in Buenos Aires in a month. Feeling the need of sympathy, we recounted the story to an Argentine army officer friend, who congratulated us instead on our good fortune in getting most of the money back. With a twinkle in his eye, he also murmured something about a *"picardía criolla."*

Back in Buenos Aires, we began asking our friends if they knew of a *"picardía criolla."* They did, of course.

Ethel Clapp, wife of the *Herald* night editor, obliged with a story of how she had fallen hard, even after she had been many years in Argentina. One day a man came to her door with assorted cages of canaries, and she and the children had picked a brilliant yellow bird which the owner guaranteed was as fine a singer as it was beautiful. They waited for days for their bird to sing, but in vain. It must be too young, they decided. Then its plumage began to dim, and all their loving attention and frequent baths failed to revive the little bird. It grew drabber by the day. They were afraid it had taken sick and would die. But one morning the sun shone brightly into the kitchen, and it was plain for all to see that their lovely canary had become a common sparrow. All the bright yellow paint had come off. But of course by that time the family had become so attached to the bird that they didn't care what color its feathers were.

On one of those bitter and windy nights when after-dinner con-

versation in Buenos Aires drifted easily to the subject of fuel—
which is so scarce and expensive that it is sold in small quantities
by weight rather than by cord—the weather brought a humiliating
memory to Mrs. Ward. She was the only third-generation *norteamericana* we ever met in Argentina, and she admitted she should
have known better, but when a couple of men drove up to her
house and offered her a bargain in firewood, she couldn't resist
them. They appeared to be honest, conscientious men, for they
not only carefully weighed the wood but insisted that she be there
to watch them. When Mr. Ward came home that night after his
day in the Bank of London, he looked at the wood and commented
favorably upon the price per kilo, but unfavorably on the small
size of the pile. Then he borrowed scales from a neighboring store
and braved the chill night air to weigh his wife's purchase. When
the entire amount had been weighed, it was something less than
half that recorded by the woodcutters' scales.

The morning paper brought the Ward's their answer. It carried
a warning to beware of certain woodcutters—sharpers who had
imported a scale in pounds, probably from the United States. A
pound, the paper pointed out, weighs less than half a kilo, and
people who picked up this particular "bargain" might freeze
before spring!

Once you are aware of the *picardía*, there is no need to dig up
the landscape in search of examples.

When our faithful old Austrian servant had to give up her job
because of ill health, we soon acquired another of those "jewels"
that people we knew were always praying for. This one came
pedaling up to our door on a shiny new bicycle one afternoon and
proudly informed us she was a wonderful *cocinera*, having been
second in command of the kitchen of the Hotel Mar del Plata
back in her home town of Tandil. We hired Lita on the spot when
she promised to cook dinner for us that night.

What a dinner it was! There was a crisp *mayonesa de legumbres*
to start, and Lita had even transformed the radishes into rosettes.
Then came *arroz con pollo* in a big earthenware pot, topped off
by *flan* custard. After that we relaxed and began congratulating
ourselves on the good life, deciding it was well worth paying Lita

$20 a month, even if that was a little higher than the unofficial ceiling wage.

Our household began to bloom and flourish. So did our waistlines, and so did Lita! The first week she bought a new pair of shoes, gloves and hose the second week, and a blouse the third. She began getting her hair waved and her nails manicured every week. When she bought a new radio, I congratulated her on her fine management. I began to tell our friends of our wonderful find, and of Lita's thrifty habits which enabled her to put on silk stockings every evening when she served the table.

When a charming Argentine *señora* and her daughter came to tea one afternoon, I again recited the virtues of our Lita. They merely smiled and asked politely how much I had been paying for a dozen eggs or a kilo of meat. Then they told me how Lita had been able to buy a radio on her salary.

Here is how it was being done: The servant went to the butcher and the dairyman and promised to bring them the business of the household in return for a ten per cent "cut." The amount was either received in a lump sum at the end of the month or daily, depending on how the bills were paid.

Their amused revelations started a never-ending battle of wits between Lita and me. It was a simple matter of pride not to be duped. But on the other hand, being a laborer myself as well as a housewife, my sympathies were divided. I didn't want exploitation on my conscience, and I didn't want to leave Lita any excuse to resort to the *picardía*. So I gave her a raise, and at the same time asked her to make out itemized lists of each day's food bill. This she did conscientiously. When I complained about the price of eggs and told her they were twenty centavos a dozen cheaper at a store where I had asked the price, she remarked that the ones she had bought were *"más frescos."* And when I informed her she had "paid" too much for fruit or vegetables, she reminded me that only *"ricos"* lived in our suburb of Olivos, and naturally they had to pay more.

Unless I were to fire Lita and take a chance on her successor, there was only one sensible thing left to do. Thereafter each day after work, I went to the *lechería*, then the *quesería*, stopped to buy meat at the *carnicería*, vegetables in the *verdurería*, sugar in the *almacén,* fruit at the *frutería,* and bread at the *panadería.* Most nights it took me about two hours to go to all the places necessary to gather a well-balanced meal, while Lita just stayed in the kitchen and sulked.

My revolt against the household *picardía* was working fine, until the night I tabulated our food budget and found it was just about the same as when Lita wheeled out on her bicycle after provisions. I couldn't check prices because shopkeepers had an unfortunate habit of not marking their wares, in addition to which my decided Yankee accent left me an easy mark. In two weeks Lita was back in control.

Some housemaids, however, have come to regret their mastery of the *picardía criolla.* A smart cook in a wealthy household can by careful managing amass a small fortune of 6,000 or 7,000 pesos over a period of a few years. And the fatter her bank account, the more vulnerable she herself becomes to the *picardía criolla.* It usually gets whispered about that she is a lady of fortune. If she is single—no matter whether she is 25 or 45—suitors begin to make their appearance. Many a servant girl has succumbed to the matrimonial lures offered by a smooth-talking *caballero.* If she is trustful, she may get no nearer the altar than an engagement, especially if she makes the mistake of giving her life savings in advance to her *novio* to buy furniture or pay on a house. It may be the last she will ever see of him. Sometimes the *caballero* finds it necessary to actually marry the girl before getting her cash. His disappearing act becomes more difficult then, but it has been done. He can count on his bride's reluctance to admit she has been a sucker—a confession that never gets much sympathy in Argentina.

It was about this time that Leonard became convinced that the men of Argentina must come from a race of bank examiners. In restaurants, he noticed how they got out their pencils when the waiter brought their bill, then very deliberately added and re-added to check the waiter's total. He tried this himself one night, much to the embarrassment of an American friend, and was surprised when he was able to deduct four pesos from a sixteen-peso check. After that, he kept a well-sharpened pencil next to his billfold and was not too much of a *zonzo* to count his change on subways and buses.

No one is better aware than the Argentines themselves of the need of constant vigilance in their dealings with their fellow men.

Even the drinking habits of this wine-loving people are not exempt from trickery. Some liquor stores feature bottles of wine covered with what appears to be a very heavy and slightly caked coating of ancient dust. The contents are said to be rare, old wines, and they bring higher prices than the stuff in the clean, new bottles. Only after he has reached home and taken a few sips of the expensive vintage does the purchaser discover the recipe of its production, which is: Take a bottle of ordinary table wine, roll it twice in the rich mud of the River Plate, let it dry and then sprinkle it liberally with dust. That gives you the sort of good old stuff the clerk solemnly declares can't be bought these days.

And, in spite of the great vineyards of Argentina, porteños have found that not all the wine they drink is of the grape. Quebracho extract, legitimately used for tanning shoes, also has been known to play a considerable part in the production of lower-priced wines. At one time this practice became so general that an ancient vintner, who wished to preserve the honorable traditions of his profession, called his son to his death bed and instructed him how to manage his estate and the bodega. His last words are said to have been, "And, my dear son, don't forget that wine is also made from grapes."

In Argentina I always admired the beautiful machines installed by the National Cash Register Company. They were everywhere, perhaps more widely used than any other expensive gadget sent out with the U.S.A. label. They were the key to any purchase, the unquestioned center of an elaborate sales mechanism in which the customer first selected his article, then went to another counter to get the bill checked, to still another counter to pay, and finally to the wrapping counter with a duplicate of the bill to pick up the purchase.

The check and double-check system can be found even in little hole-in-the-wall hot dog stands. One man takes the money and gives the check, while another takes the check and hands out the hot dog.

The Argentine takes great pride in getting a bargain. A friend told me of a little group of painters who jumped at the chance to get five kilos of coffee for the amazingly low price of three and a half pesos (or more than ten pounds for about eighty cents). They went home chuckling about the great bargain they had driven, but came to work the next morning much-chastened men. Their wives had opened the cans and found an inch of coffee at the top. The rest was sawdust.

From one classic *picardía* we were mercifully exempt, mainly, I suspect, because we too obviously never possessed the kind of money it requires to buy street cars. The slick urbanite who "sells" them preys on country folk who have money. The slicker engages one of these well-heeled characters in conversation, long enough to confide that he is the owner of the street car approaching and invite the provincial to take a ride as his guest. Once on the car, the city man casually points out the driver and the ticket man as his employees and shows how much money is being taken in. The conversation grows more and more personal until the city man confesses that he has a great weakness for playing the races and has lost so much money that he is forced to sell one or two of his street cars in order to meet some bills. The story seems plausible enough and the thrifty country boy can see that the vehicle is a rolling gold mine. With visions of making a fortune and showing the folks in his home town that a really smart fellow can get ahead in the big city, he turns over his life savings of three or four thousand pesos—and takes possession as the former "owner" steps off with a last word of instruction on how to make the business pay. When the new owner demands the collections from one of the attendants, he suffers a rude shock; once recovered, he usually tells his story to the police and then either heads back to his province a broken man, or uses his bitter experience as the foundation of some get-rich-quick scheme of his own.

Casual reading of a daily newspaper is enough to demonstrate the necessity of watchfulness. Here are a few typical headlines:

"EASY MONEY" IN SANTIAGO DEL ESTERO, Extraordinary Case Brought to Light

A BANK CASHIER'S LUCRATIVE "SYSTEM"

GETTING RICH QUICKLY, A Police Investigation

NEW VERSION OF OLD TRICK

WILES OF THE TIRE DEALER

LAWYER WHO WAS TOO TRUSTFUL

ROBBED HIS FRIENDS SO HE COULD GET MARRIED

TURNING A DISHONEST PENNY

MUNICIPAL OFFICIALS CHARGED WITH FRAUD, DISHONEST CITY FATHERS "SHOWN UP," A Tale of Graft and Corruption

THE MEN WHO MADE THE MONEY, More Increased Banking Accounts

EL PALOMAR LAND SWINDLE, Guilty Sentenced to Six Years' Imprisonment

GIPSY TRICKS AGAIN

One of the most audacious examples of piling up a fortune through wholesale trickery, humbug and misrepresentation cost the patients and the employees of a so-called "sanatorium" over half a million pesos. Two men, both of whom the newspapers described as possessing "extreme sagacity and savoir faire" obtained a lease on a building, bought hospital equipment on a grand scale on credit, and then secured working capital for their institution by the novel means of requiring all applicants for jobs to deposit a large sum as a "guarantee" of their honesty while working in the institution. One man deposited $750 for a job as porter! The total amount of "guarantees" thus secured from poor but thrifty people looking for work was more than $20,000. After working for 12 to 15 days, the employee was dismissed and his deposit was kept by the operators, who then lured other unemployed persons to their economic downfall.

The operators even used Argentina's great disaster, the San Juan earthquake of 1944, to facilitate the perpetration of their fraud. Purporting to be deeply grieved by the loss of thousands of lives and the large number of injured persons, the partners offered 40 beds to the government and these were accepted in an appreciative letter signed by the President's secretary. Shortly afterwards, on the beds being requested, the tricksters explained that their offer could no longer be complied with as they only had 20 beds vacant. Later, they reduced their offer to eight, four and two beds, and finally stated that they could not give any; for their confidence game, however, they made good use of the original letter of thanks from the high government official. It helped them get more material on credit for their promotion scheme.

Looking back on such illegal activities, I must admit that for a time I became smug about the prevalence of law and order in my own country. "Well, thank goodness, we don't have anything like that going on in the United States," I became accustomed to say. I once admitted under pressure that we had sold the Brooklyn Bridge to a few suckers, but I argued that the bridge was so big and expensive that really not very many people could afford to buy it.

Being some 6,000 miles from home, I placed a shining halo around the brow of my fellow citizens, and I became convinced that we were more honest and virtuous than the Argentines.

Yet I can remember reading about only one bank hold-up in all the time we were in Argentina. It caused a tremendous sensation. Such things simply were not done there. Why, one Argentine objected, "Someone might have been killed! Was it necessary to be so violent?"

You see, the Argentines would much rather watch the practiced maneuvers of the untarnished wit, than the nervous quivering of the polished .32 automatic.

One friend explained the evolution of the *picardía* to its position of an almost patriotic factor in the national life. Many years ago the inhabitants of what is now the Argentine republic found the need of trickery. The Spanish Crown planned to stifle import and export trade through Buenos Aires by sea and thus maintain Lima and Panama as the political and commercial centers for South American relations with the mother country. But Spain's project wilted under the answering strategy of the men of Buenos Aires, who sneaked thousands of tons of tallow and hides onto English and Dutch ships lying hidden at anchor in the Río de La Plata. Through several decades of smuggling and bribing, the transplanted Spaniards quietly but effectively thumbed their patrician noses at the Crown and proceeded to build up Buenos Aires.

Then the *criollos*, offspring of Spanish *conquistadores* and the Indians they gradually subdued, stamped their own trade-mark on the *picardía* in more than a century of violent blood-stained commerce between the exporting city of Buenos Aires and its hinterland, with the inland inhabitants never quite able to get their fair share of the trade profits or the political spoils.

Today, the *picardía* is still a factor to be taken into account by everyone in the land. This was recognized by the brash young military government, which in 1943 began to issue long and frequent statements of how it had cleaned up corruption in the country. From time to time, it issued sizeable lists of former government officials, detailing how little money these persons had on taking office and how large their fortunes were when they left. A general indifference always greeted these "exposés," a lackadaisicalness which either indicated disapproval of the new regime altogether, or a sympathetic feeling towards the unfortunates who had been caught.

One of the government investigation stories which attracted comments of "how clever!" was one concerning Modesto González, a respected merchant in the province of Santiago del Estero. Modesto not only admitted that he had been refunded about 650,000 pesos in back taxes which he had never paid but told how he had accomplished this miracle.

First he had filed a suit for the collection of 21,000 pesos in sales taxes, and after making sure the province lawyers would put up token resistance only, took it to the Supreme Court where it was ruled in his favor, as he had expected. This, he said, was only the spade work for bigger things. Thus encouraged, he brought a second suit—this time for the return of 827,275 pesos in taxes. A man of great foresight and obvious ingenuity, he had been neither surprised nor disappointed when certain records "conveniently" disappeared from the tax office. His own tax payment documents, of course, were among them, making it impossible to prove that he had only paid 192,000 pesos in the first place.

But Modesto confessed his was not a 100 per cent success story— that he had not harvested the full crop. Only a modest 400,000 pesos remained to him, he said, after giving the governor 100,000 pesos to convince the provincial legislature to settle the matter out of court. The legislature was convinced, but not before the governor's term had ended and his successor had demanded another 50,000 pesos to put the deal across. Before he got through, González complained that officials had eaten a full 250,000 pesos of his gravy.

Just a few days after the army authorities disclosed that tale of graft, we heard an English businessman match the story of the Santiago del Estero merchant. His story began when the firm with which he was connected had difficulty in collecting a debt from a client with a small fruit box factory up in the Tigre river section. "I would willingly pay you," the client explained, "but no one wants to buy my boxes. Do you suppose you could find a buyer for them?"

The businessman replied that he would try and went to call on a friend, a captain in a certain artillery division. The captain was very cordial but said that he could do nothing to oblige. However, he introduced the businessman to his major. The major told the businessman that he would help all he could, but it was a matter for the colonel to decide.

In due course, the businessman was ushered in to the colonel, who gave him a warm welcome. After the traditional exchange of pleasantries the businessman got around to the point. "Do you think the —— artillery could use some fruit boxes?" The colonel believed they could and asked the price.

The businessman knew that the box factory owner quoted the boxes at 20 centavos each, but having in mind the little courtesies already extended to him by the army officials, he quoted the price of a box at 50 centavos, allowing 15 centavos each to the captain and the major as tokens of his appreciation. When the businessman mentioned 50 centavos, the colonel hesitated, cleared his throat and said, "No, I believe that 90 centavos would be a more reasonable figure."

With the price and sale agreed, the businessman sent trucks out a few days later to the factory to obtain the boxes from his client. The trucks were loaded and driven to the artillery's supply warehouse. When they arrived and the drivers began to unload, the superintendent came up and asked, "What do you have there?"

"Fruit boxes," was the reply.

"What in the world do you think we want with fruit boxes here?" he asked. As the superintendent couldn't be convinced, the trucks were turned around with their loads and sent back.

The businessman then hurried to the colonel and notified him that the boxes had not been accepted. "They'll have to be dismantled," the colonel explained. "We can always use wood. Let me see, how many sides does a box have?"

"Six," he was told.

"Well, I think we ought to pay you one peso a side, since they're going to be dismantled," the colonel said.

The businessman vows that the boxes were dismantled and sold at six pesos each, with the factory owner getting his usual price of 20 centavos, thus enabling him to clean up his debt.

Even lawyers, generally the canniest of people, must watch their step in Argentina. *La Razón* one afternoon told the story of an extremely worried-looking man who was ushered into the office of a lawyer at Calle Venezuela 1501 and blurted out this question:

"Tell me, doctor, what sentence would a father of a family, who stole through necessity, receive?"

The lawyer, evidently a good-hearted man, listened to the tale of woe and then murmured that he had to look up the matter in his library and left the room. His idea was, he later recalled, to return with a ten-peso note which he would give to the father in distress to restore his faith in humanity.

However, the lawyer's own faith in human nature was rudely shaken when he discovered, on his return, that not only was his "client" missing, but also the lawyer's 800 peso watch, which he had carelessly left on his desk. The "father" had been a polished actor.

The most exciting night of the year for the police and fire department is not New Year's, Christmas or Independence Day, but the "Night of the Three Kings," when the Wise Men brought gifts to the infant Jesus. Instead of exchanging gifts on Christmas Day, the Argentines save both their gifts and merrymaking until the *"Reyes"* night, when so much Latin whoopee is made that the little businessman with the deficit can count on the police being fully occupied elsewhere. It is the ideal time to burn down the old shop; and the evening has come to be known as the "Night of the Fires."

If the fire goes well, the man collects his insurance and later moves to a new establishment. There was one thrifty soul, however, who wanted his cake and insurance too. When the "Night of the Fires" came along, his combination store and home went up in flames. He moaned that everything he owned in the world—from furniture to pots and pans—had been destroyed. The building had been enveloped in flames so rapidly that the man hadn't even been able to save a wine glass. But after an appropriate interval, the luckless man moved into a new and finer establishment. This was as his old friends had expected. They congratulated him on his changed circumstances. But when they were invited inside their friend's new living quarters, there was a surprise awaiting them. Before their eyes were the very chairs they had "watched" shoot up in fire. Even the old curtains were hanging without a sign of smoke on them. The friends were too polite to question the phenomenon. It was easy to see that their frugal friend had taken the wise precaution of having his household goods stored first before facing the hazards of the "Night of the Fires."

Others have not fared so well.

One elderly man was desperate. He had become involved with a young girl and spent all his profits on her, now he needed some capital to keep up the courtship. His store must be burned. But in recent years the companies had become very suspicious of any losses on the "Night of the Fires." His fire would have to be different. He rigged up a bomb and inserted it between the plate glass window and the iron shutters, which had been designed to protect him from revolutions and thieves.

In good time the bomb exploded, but it merely smashed the window and tore a big hole in the shutter. There was a dismal lack of fire, and a large part of the bomb remained for the police to discover when they arrived. The storekeeper was arrested, and while he was being hauled away for questioning by the overworked police force, loiterers took the gaping store window as an invitation and cleaned out the remaining stocks.

It seems like a terrific jump from that to Argentina's dealings with the great outside world, but the *picardía* easily bridges the gap. Until the appearance of the Argentine delegation at the meeting of the General Assembly of the United Nations in New York in late 1946, Mr. Gromyko had a virtual monopoly on using the veto power in the United Nations. This was very disturbing to the small nations who felt they had been shrugged aside in the game of power politics. But there was nothing they could do about it; that is, until the Argentine delegate, Dr. José Arce, found the loophole. Dr. Arce proposed that, since a quorum was required to transact the business of the United Nations, the so-called small members could all walk out and bring the United Nations to a standstill by depriving it of the number of votes required. This, he proclaimed, would in effect give the small nations their own "veto." I doubt very much that the practice will be used, and only wish to point out, that it was an Argentine who was clever enough to think of something everyone else apparently had overlooked.

GAMBLING AND DRINKING AND SIN

D
OCTOR MERENGUE WAS THE MOST AMUSING ARGENTINE we ever met. The good doctor was a split personality, the pen product of the talented cartoonist, Divito. He was, as nearly as any one watching his daily life could see, the perfect professional man, a very upright soul who always did the proper thing, who treated his wife well and had an apparently successful practice which enabled him to own a Cadillac—the supreme luxury in Argentina—and go to the best places with the best people. He dressed impeccably and maintained a superb, unblinking poise come what might.

But the other self of this Dr. Jekyll and Mr. Hyde was a racy, impish, irresponsible, vain, gaudy and entirely lovable character who went leering shadowlike into the faces of pretty girls and looking down their dress fronts with bulging, eager eyes. He also gambled heavily, ordered champagne in a loud voice to show people how prosperous he was, and was a completely uninhibited show-off.

While all these things were going on in his other self, Dr. Merengue presented a smart, barrel-chested, unruffled exterior. He was to all outward appearances bored by losing a thousand pesos at the casino in Mar del Plata, but his other self was racing into the luxurious establishment with the look of a devil on his face and a bomb smoking in his hand. He showed up stiff and unflinching for his duel with the retired colonel he had unwittingly insulted; he proudly sneered "never" when his seconds asked him if he wanted to call off the duel, but his other self was grovelling in front of the colonel and crying, "Mercy, mercy!"

Dr. Merengue's social behavior and his views on the other sex were unimpeachably correct. He never stared at beautiful girls, he picked up their handkerchiefs and politely restored them without even giving them the once-over; he followed a beautiful pair of legs up a stairway and never saw the under-pinnings because his aloof gentleman's gaze was always far over their heads; he treated his gorgeous secretary with the most dignified courtesy and kept his distance. But all the while his other self was calling him a sucker. The other self was a lady-killer, he held the luscious secretary on his lap, he never missed a chance to inspect a bosom or a pair of calves—higher on a windy day—and he recorded, with a lascivious leer, the telephone number he had overheard a sweet young thing give to her girl friend.

I suppose the reason we became so fond of the balloon-chested Dr. Merengue and his balloon-pricking other self, was that the less admirable half presented to us in rib-tickling fashion the most human qualities of the Argentine people—their gambling and drinking and sin.

When I first arrived in Argentina I was always somewhat nervous around a casino, a lottery shop or even in a bar where dice games were being played; I kept looking over my shoulder, expecting the county sheriff and a couple of his deputies to come in thumbing their badges, announcing the place was being raided. It was shocking, the way the people went about their gambling. There was nothing furtive about them, they were quite as calm shooting dice at a sidewalk cafe as Americans are playing bridge in a fashionable hotel.

There is a peculiar, dry rattling sound in the air of Buenos Aires. It is a characteristic sound unlike anything I had ever heard in New York, San Francisco or Missoula, Montana. It is the sound of Buenos Aires; it is equally intense in the middle of the day and late at night; it is always loudest in front of coffee shops and bars, yet it is a mellow, hollow clicking, rather than the harsh clatter of breaking dishes. We discovered what it was when we went into a bar to celebrate the first pay check we earned on the *Buenos Aires Herald*. The sound is the chatter of a million rolling dice.

In the bar were men shaking dice in big leather cups and throwing them out on the small tables. Some groups were shooting with five dice, while at other tables the men were playing with only

three. Old staff members of the *Herald* told us they were playing
generala and *bidú*, the two most popular dice games.

Bidú, the real favorite, is played with three dice. The first player
rolling a pair of ones and a deuce wins that round of the game and
therefore doesn't have to pay for his own drink. *Generala* is longer
and complicated and requires score-keeping. The dice games are
played for cocktails, for lunches and even for 15 centavo coffees.
There is good sound sense in this practice, we were told, for the
Argentine male is never willing to "go Dutch" for a drink or anything else; by gambling over it, he saves a lot of time and breath—
and face.

When Ruth expressed a willingness to learn these fascinating
games without any further delay, she was told that ladies do not
play *bidú* or *generala* in public bars or coffee houses, although they
may be wizards with the dice at their own firesides. Later we
learned that this is the only form of strictly masculine gambling in
the country. Women are eager addicts to other games of chance.

Every Friday afternoon I used to notice both men and women
rushing to grab either *Crítica* or *Razón*. At first I attributed this
to their interest in the Russian war, but closer observation revealed
that they were rushing past the front page to an inside page where
they kept their eyes glued for five or ten minutes. A ride on a
subway or a bus any Friday afternoon found most of the passengers
studying that same inside page—the one with the week's lottery
results published in full. But in spite of our kibitzing, Ruth and I
didn't succumb to the national gambling fever until we had been in
the country nearly six months.

In early December a strange, feverish excitement settled like a
fog over Buenos Aires. The lottery shops became filled with crisp
new tickets bearing an engraving of the Virgin Mary holding the
infant Jesus—and the magic figure 6,000,000 pesos, or about
$1,500,000. Shops which had sold winning tickets in previous years
posted signs in their windows giving the winning number and the
amount received by the lucky holders. Less fortunate shops resorted
to other methods of enticing customers. They posted a list of the
ending numbers over the years, so that confirmed gamblers could
decide mathematically whether this year's *grande* was more likely
to end in seven or nine. If the winning ticket ended in eight last

year, and three the year before, would the chances be better for it to end in two or four this year? Little groups often gathered in front of lottery shops to debate these fine points, and tickets ending in the number the experts thought most likely to win, according to the law of averages, were in brisk demand.

I began to hear the most conservative Englishmen planning how they would spend their riches come Christmas Eve, when at last the winning *grande* ticket would be in their hands.

Our laundry woman asked for her wages early so she could get a ticket, and in all seriousness informed Ruth that even though she would be a millionaire next week, she would continue working for the Señora "Root," which was as near as she could ever come to pronouncing my wife's name. She then inquired if the Señora Root had bought a *boleta* yet. Ruth told her that she had not, and that if Anastacia won the lottery, Ruth would have to go to work for her. But Anastacia viewed that with disfavor; she thought Ruth ought to have an equal chance at great riches.

That evening returning from work, Ruth and I saw a beautiful lottery ticket hanging in the window of a shop on Callao near our apartment. It ended in seven, and seven was due to come up this Christmas because it hadn't been the winning termination in many years. However, the shop was already closed, and we didn't have the necessary 17 pesos anyway. We had to pass it up.

While broiling a *bife* that night, Ruth began to sing, "You Are My Lucky Star," and it just happened I was humming it simultaneously in the next room. We were sure that it was a good omen, so we rushed down to the *Herald* early the next morning and got a slight "advance" on our January salary, then hurried back and bought the ticket ending in seven.

I'm afraid neither of us did much work the next day. Mere reporting seemed pretty prosaic when we were going to be millionaires in a matter of hours. Other members of the *Herald* staff also wore an air of suppressed excitement. They too had bought *vigésimo's* (twentieths of a ticket) and were dreaming their money away. Nearly everyone we talked to had come within at least two numbers of holding the *grande* ticket at one time or another. One friend told us of dreaming the number of the *grande*, waking up and writing the figures of the ticket down, then starting a search for that particular ticket. He walked from shop to shop, and even called his office to say that he was "ill" so that he could continue the search. He never found it, but he swore that the number of his dream did win the *grande* that year.

Archie Clapp, the night editor, had his own system. Every year he went into a lottery shop, asked the owner for a ticket, then put it in his pocket without looking at it. He would never look at it until after the drawing. So far, his system had never worked. Some old timers tried to prepare us for disappointment by recalling the evil fate that had befallen the persons they knew who had won the *grande*. On us, however, that sort of talk was wasted.

That night, Ruth and I were still too busy spending money to bother about sleep. We bought the *South Pacific Mail* from Mr. Peddar in Valparaíso, Chile, and turned it into a daily. We toured the world and invested our money in Oregon real estate and even decided we would not let our forthcoming prosperity go to our heads. We debated at length whether we would keep on working at the *Herald* and finally agreed that it would be the sensible thing to do, as otherwise we might be plagued by fortune hunters.

But no fortune hunters hounded us that Christmas.

We hurried out to grab an extra edition of one of the newspapers the next day, but our number wasn't the one printed in big black type across the front page. Ruth thought this was probably a typographical error, which the newspaper later would be forced to correct. Eventually, however, we decided we had better look down the list for the smaller prizes of 50,000 pesos, etc. Our number wasn't there, either. We bought extras of other newspapers, but our number was as inconspicuous as ever. By that evening, Christmas Eve, Ruth said she was feeling like the victim of a Wall Street crash, and no stock plunger in '29 ever brooded more about his bad luck than we did Christmas Day—especially since the money we had squandered on the lottery ticket should have gone to buy a turkey.

To rub salt into our wounds, all of the newspapers that Christmas Day carried long stories and pictures of the persons who had won the *grande*. Some pictures showed the winners feasting and drinking champagne. There was no champagne for us that year, only a bottle of cider with the misleading label, Cidra Champagne.

We never learned, though. We kept on being millionaires once a year all the time we were in Argentina.

The nearest we ever came to joining the nouveau riche was a 100-peso prize, my share of the 20,000-peso winning ticket purchased by a pool of United Press employees one Christmas. It was wonderful what happened in that office when the news spread. Every man expanded into a millionaire. Half of the staff walked out to celebrate. Copy boys refused to work while they decided what they were going to do with their sudden fortunes and debated the relative merits of Buicks and Cadillacs. Cables from New York and London piled up neglected in the All America chute. Hot incoming war copy was left unattended in the radio room. If it hadn't been for a wet blanket performance by big, genial Bill Mooney, I suppose the paralysis would have lasted for hours. Bill got out pencil and paper and figured the copy boys would get about $10 each, since they had purchased only small shares of the ticket. In spite of this it was a marvelous feeling for all of us, the fact that we shared in a 20,000-peso prize. I took my winnings and went to buy Ruth a pair of soft leather *gaucho* boots. I mentioned to the salesman that I was doing my shopping with my lottery winnings, and the news spread. The salesman called the manager, and soon an admiring group had gathered around to congratulate me on winning the twenty thousand. I lacked the nerve to admit that my "fortune" was an infinitesimal fraction consisting of a mere $25.

More than a hundred million pesos—about $25,000,000—is gambled annually on lottery tickets in Argentina, and we didn't know a person who had never succumbed to the fever of the big Christmas and New Year's drawings. So great is the demand for tickets that a few days before the Christmas lottery it is impossible to find a ticket except in a "black market" at much higher prices. We've walked miles trying to find tickets when we neglected to do our shopping early.

Since this is big business, the drawing for the *grande* is watched with hawk-like vigilance, and woe to the government or individual who allows fraud to creep in anywhere. Take the case of Cirilo Maidana in 1944.

Maidana worked as a mechanic in the City Transport Corpora-

Small church in Córdoba

Courtyard in Lujan after rain

tion. One night he dreamed the winning number—11,880—and the next day he told his fellow employees about it. They wrote it down, and nine of his friends chipped in with him to buy three-twentieths of the ticket bearing that number. Maidana was sent out to buy it during his lunch hour. When the day of the great drawing came, Maidana's number won, and the humble transport men went crazy with joy over their good fortune. Inasmuch as the lottery offices were closed that evening and the lucky mechanics were unable to collect their 300,000 pesos, the winners borrowed a thousand pesos from a businessman to help them celebrate in the required style. Champagne flowed freely, and the borrowed pesos vanished swiftly—but what did it matter, when there would be plenty tomorrow to last them for the rest of their lives? In the early morning hours, Maidana was escorted home to his boarding-house by his friends, whose parting admonishment was that he keep the tickets safe until they came round in the morning to accompany him to the lottery office to cash in on their good luck.

However, shortly before seven o'clock that morning, the entire neighborhood was alarmed by the shouts and screams coming from Maidana's room, to the effect that thieves had broken in and stolen the winning tickets. The police were summoned immediately, and the first examination of the room seemed to offer some support of Maidana's story, as the window of the room showed signs of having been forced. Maidana tearfully told the details of his horrible misfortune. He said he had originally placed the tickets in a small cash box and hid this under his pillow, but during the night he had found it uncomfortable and had moved the box to the night table, from which it apparently had been stolen. But the excited Maidana talked so much, and gave so many contradictory stories, that he was taken under suspicion to police headquarters.

Once behind bars, he told another story. He had tried to buy the ticket with his number on it but had been unable to find it, so he had purchased another ticket with a very similar number. He hadn't informed his friends of the change, thinking that the number of his dream wouldn't come up anyway. On the other hand, his second number might be the winner, in which case he could quietly collect and keep the entire amount, without his friends ever being any the wiser. Maidana told other stories as time wore on, and in the end nearly everyone was convinced he had never bought any ticket at all. His fellow workers, however, continued to insist that he still had the winning ticket and was merely welching on dividing the proceeds. The controversy raged for weeks, with newspapers printing editorials, along with pictures and whole pages of news matter. Maidana received as much unfavorable publicity in Argentina as Al Capone did in Chicago. According to last accounts, the garage mechanics were back at their old jobs, finding it harder to pay back the thousand than it had been to spend. And if Maidana did have the fortune, he was keeping very quiet about it; if he has the money, he will never be able to spend it in Buenos Aires, at least not around his former friends.

Of all the forms of gambling, horse racing is probably the most satisfying to the Argentine, who loves horses and is willing to back his judgment with pesos. Over a million dollars has been bet in a single day at one track alone. Friends who have followed the races on both continents contend that Argentine horses are the finest, most beautiful animals in the Western Hemisphere.

Rich and poor alike play and enjoy the horses. I've seen hundreds of workers crowd into Constitución Station and line up for second class tickets to La Plata when a big race was being run in the provincial capital. They make the hour's trip standing or sitting on the floors of the swaying train, all the while studying their racing sheets. At the race track they don't get the choice seats, but they are even more enthusiastic than the members of the swank Jockey Club.

Mixed pleasures are enjoyed by well-to-do racing devotees. Each race track has an elaborate paddocks restaurant, all boasting superb menus. Prosperous Argentines have developed the custom of watching the races between courses, and their gargantuan luncheons may drag out through the afternoon. If there are more races than courses—which sometimes happens—the patrons can always repair to the bar.

One of the most beautiful race courses in the country is San Isidro. The track is surrounded with climbing red geraniums. Masses of climbing pink roses surround the Palomar track just north of Buenos Aires. Owners of race horses are wealthy, as a rule, but a moderately successful businessman can own one. Some grocery store owners have turned their profits in sugar and beans to horse flesh, paying from $2,500 to $10,000 for a good animal.

Sometimes jockeys have a more impressive following than the horses, and some jockeys have become national figures, better known than senators or provincial governors. Leguisamo, for example, has become an almost legendary character, and we know some persons who invariably placed their bets on the mounts Leguisamo was riding that day. This didn't always pay, they admitted, because occasionally the kind-hearted Leguisamo would agree to ride the horse of an old friend, even though it wasn't conceded a chance to win. Such turf figures as Leguisamo are often in their fifties and have held their reputations intact for many years. When a nationally famous jockey dies, the newspapers give as much space to his obituary as they do to that of a distinguished statesman.

The Argentines take their horse racing seriously, whether they have gambled two pesos or two thousand on the race. Any obvious irregularity is acted upon promptly by the fans, who show their anger by showering bottles and other missiles on the track. Workers especially hate being made to feel like suckers, and in flagrant cases they surge out onto the track, shouting their disgust. Sometimes the police have to resort to tear gas to disperse these ardent fans who want a fair run for their money.

A poor man may play the races and buy a lottery ticket every week, but there is one form of gambling that is pretty well confined to the upper income bracket. Roulette and baccarat, the plush-lined ways to lose your money, are limited to palatial casinos open only during the resort seasons. Mar del Plata, on the sea, boasts the biggest casino in the world, while a smaller casino is operated in a hotel at Mendoza, the city in a jewel-type setting in the foothills of the Andes. When summer comes and ladies of fashion begin collecting beach clothes and *alpargatas* in matching colors, the men of the family debate weightily over "systems"—fool-proof ways of winning at roulette.

Ruth and I were equipped with a "system" before we started on our first vacation. Ruth got it from Dolly Tow, who had acquired it from a friend who claimed that for years he had not lost at roulette.

It is easy for me to laugh now about how dense I must have seemed to Ruth when I questioned Dolly's claim that with this system you could play both the opposing red and black colors (in roulette there are only two colors) at the same time and win on both over a series of perhaps twenty or thirty plays. I can see now that it was the fault of my education—too much algebra and trig and economics. But anyway, I was perfectly prepared to demonstrate it couldn't be done. So Ruth with a little smile got out a 20-centavo piece and a box of matches and demonstrated the system. I took heads for black and she played tails for red, and we flipped the coin about fifty times, keeping score according to the system. And of course I was a red-faced idiot when we both won. Believe it or not, we both won! And I was persuaded after another hundred flips of the coin that we had been introduced to a fool-proof way of licking the house. We were so elated over the discovery that Ruth insisted on calling all her friends and telling them how they too could get rich. These telephone calls, following the usual preliminaries, usually found Ruth issuing an invitation like this: "Now you come over right away, and we'll show you our system. It's wonderful. You play the red and the black, and you win on both. What? Well, Leonard says it works, and you know how sensible *he* is. . . ."

This evangelism bore fruit. Some of our friends became firm believers, and one couple planned to borrow a few thousand pesos and make a special trip to Mar del Plata to put it to the test.

Before our friends could report on their findings, however, Ruth and I had already started in the opposite direction to test the system at Mendoza, where we were allowed to play the colors for as little as five pesos. With sharpened pencils and pads of paper we set out for the casino in the Plaza Hotel, accompanied by our partners, John Hoopingarner and Ricardo Bunzl. We had convinced them that there was money to be made with each spin of the wheel.

The croupiers lifted amused eyebrows when the four of us came in and methodically began to play against each other, jotting figures down in the little notebooks we had brought along for the purpose. Ruth, now that we were putting the system to the acid test for the first time, said nervously she wished now that she had worked her own problems back in grade school arithmetic. She was book-keeper for the black, and the little ball insisted every time on stopping at red. Every time red won, the figures she was adding became larger.

The arithmetic on my side—the red—was simple. All John and I had to do was to cross off figures and add up winnings. But—and it may be that this is the basic weakness of the system—Ruth and Bunzl were losing on black at a tremendous rate that dwarfed our winnings on red. After red came up twice more, John had to hand our entire winnings and most of our red capital across the table so that Ruth and Bunzl could stay with the system on the black.

It was at that instant that the Goddess of Fortune proved that she was Argentine and not *yanqui* when the ball stopped at zero, a calamity that the "system" had not foreseen. For when "zero" comes up, the house takes everything on the table, including every peso being bet on the other 36 numbers and the colors. Only a few cautious souls had bet on zero itself, and we were not among them.

We crept out of that casino, bereft of our capital, and our faith in the "system" a little shaken. However, we still maintain that the system is really fool-proof. All you need to win is a little luck and a bankroll of 10,000 pesos to handle your losses if red and zero come up fifteen times in a row while you are playing black.

It would be a pleasure to report that the casino was swallowed up by an earthquake and that we never went back there again. But of course the earthquake didn't and we did. On a subsequent visit we forgot about the system and won back enough pesos so that we could again look the croupiers in the eye and enjoy ourselves. And we learned that a casino is not a den of iniquity, but an attractive and fashionable place. We were impressed by the large number of women, most of them elderly, bejewelled and respectable, playing for high stakes. It is one of the few places a lady can visit unescorted in the evening. It is considered a harmless pastime for a couple of wealthy matrons to dress up in their finest gowns and most expensive jewels and stroll over to the casino for a few rounds of roulette.

Just to keep this from getting to be a habit, however, casinos are located only in vacation centers, and Buenos Aires is as free of legal roulette as Kansas City. In areas where the church is the most strongly entrenched, such as Córdoba, casinos have not been established, despite the pleas of resort owners who claim it will bring a vast flow of new pesos into the province.

The most prosperous industry in Mendoza is not the roulette wheel, however, but the vast underground *bodegas* where a large portion of the wine consumed annually by the nation's drinkers is processed and aged.

There is a great deal of drinking in Argentina, but there is little drunkenness. In four years there I can remember any number of American and British friends who drank more than they could hold, but I can remember only one drunken Argentine.

Argentines are extremely moderate tipplers, in spite of the fact that they consume an enormous annual quota of white and red wines, vermouth, imported Peruvian *pisco*, Paraguayan *caña*, French champagnes and cognac—in short, just about all the intoxicating beverages that man's ingenuity has devised anywhere in the world. Most of them prefer wine to whisky, except when they want to create an impression of affluence in public. I never understood why, but it is thought to be a mark of social distinction for a man to step up to a bar and order a *whisky con soda*.

The great middle class drink, however, is the San Martín cocktail. This combination of vermouth and gin, similar to North American martinis, enjoys universal popularity at bars, in homes and as a drink before dinner in a restaurant. Rivaling the San Martín in popularity—at least during the summer time—is the gin tonic, which is said to fortify one against the heat.

Champagne isn't the luxury in Argentina that it is in the United States. Up until the war, the finest French champagne was on sale at comparatively low prices. Today, Argentina is turning out some fine champagne of her own in the *bodegas* at Mendoza, and this is priced within reach of the average white-collar worker who wants to celebrate Christmas, the New Year, his birthday, or some feast day in elegance. *Cidra*, which is really nothing more than carbonated cider, is bottled to look like champagne and tastes a little like it; it is substituted for champagne on occasions which do not quite demand the real article. It is popular with big corporations giving a Christmas or New Year's party to gain the good will of their employees.

But for ordinary drinking, the Argentine sticks to *vino*. In most families, lunch or dinner wouldn't be complete without a bottle of red or white wine, and boys and girls of all ages dutifully drink the small glass of wine, usually diluted, that is set before them. Workers who stop to cook their *bifes* at a building under construction or in a street they are repairing, wash down their bread and meat with good-sized bottles of wine, which is so cheap that almost no one is forced to do without it, no matter how poor he is. We used to buy regularly a good dry white wine, called Vino Toro, for 22 cents. Rarely did we pay more than 50 cents for a liter— an over-sized quart—of wine, which also can be purchased more economically in glass, wicker-encased bottles of five- and ten-liter sizes. The low price of wine, combined with the national love for it, accounts for the amazing consumption by the Argentines, which averages about sixty-five quarts a year for each man, woman and child in the country.

The Argentines thus have every right to consider themselves real connoisseurs of wine and champagne and other intoxicating beverages. And they do. Yet the fact that their drinking seldom leads to total inebriation tends to block any prolonged discussion of the subject. The Argentine male is far more apt to confide in you about the progress he made with the blonde last night than how plastered he got after he switched from scotch to rum and cokes.

The devilish, goat-eyed other self of Dr. Merengue who leers down the inviting dress fronts of the Argentine beauties he passes on the streets is, if anything, a sizable understatement of the average Argentine's attitude toward the other sex. Our friend, even when he is being a rakish Mr. Hyde, never quite dares exercise one of the most ancient and cherished prerogatives of the Argentine male: To reach out and gingerly pinch the *nalga* of any lady who happens to strike his fancy.

The fates, and a succession of hostile, pious governments, have conspired against those gallant *caballeros* who once made Buenos Aires the only place in the civilized world where a *mujer bonita* could measure her popularity by the number and blackness of the bruises on her dainty behind. Today, most of the bruises have faded, but the legend lingers on.

It was as recent as the early forties, that one fatherly American ship captain felt it his duty to brief his female passengers, before entering port, on the feeling perils they might endure at the hands of the *porteños*—and he did mean feeling. He had been giving these warnings, he confessed, ever since he had had to comfort a tearful tourist who had set out from the ship years back for a joyful day of shopping and sight-seeing in the Argentine capital. Even before she had had time to load up on souvenirs, she noticed a handsome, dark-eyed man move towards her, his eyes full of obvious admiration.

While she was still wondering what beautiful romance was in store for her, he had without warning reached down and with his fingers expertly nipped her neat posterior.

Her shocked screams soon brought a policeman rushing to her side, but not to her aid. To the lady tourist's surprise, she was hurried off to a police station with the young man. Her impetuous admirer was soon turned loose, but she wasn't. And she spent several hours there before she was freed to return to the ship, an outraged woman if there ever was one.

It was meagre consolation for her to learn from the captain that she had been merely an unfortunate victim of one of the government's intensive efforts to eliminate the pinching practice. One law made it possible for a woman to go to a police station and bring charges against any man molesting her. This had a sobering effect and the practice abated somewhat. However, the situation was confused when a few unscrupulous women developed the racket of preying upon young men belonging to some of the best families. One of these women would sight a young scion approaching, would sidle close to the young man and then would shriek that she had been pinched, whirling and pointing to the wealthy young man as the author of the foul deed. Before the police arrived, of course, she would accept a bribe not to make trouble.

Learning of such practices, the police understandably kept the female complainants in the station for two or three hours while they looked into their records to determine if they were honest women. Under such unfavorable circumstances, most women preferred to keep silent when pinched or to retaliate by jabbing the pincher savagely with their hat pins.

Yet, almost inevitably, the decline and fall of the pinch came in the late thirties and was all but conquered by the military government which came to power in 1943. The ultra-pious Ramírez regime changed the regulations so that a woman had only to report the slightest incident to 'the nearest policeman, pointing out the man, and justice would take its course. The fact that guilt was all but presumed instilled caution in male hearts and forced the pinch to a height of refinement which experts conceded it might not have attained in generations of normal evolution. Under pressure of the new political and social theories, the pinch was tailored into a quick, flattering little pat which could give offense to no one, a new and artful reconnoitering of the posterior which was, to some women, reassuring proof of the enduring charms of their best curves.

Thus the pinch became little more than a gentle caress, a hand slithering gracefully across a silk-clad passing hip. If the practitioner happened to be passing his quarry in the opposite direction, his swinging hand might collide unobtrusively with a thigh, all so gracefully that the lady could never swear it was anything but an accident.

With the decline of the pinch, another traditional element in the street relations of the sexes came fully into its own. This was the *piropo*—the quip ranging from the picturesque and extravagantly flattering phrase to the rude though humorous remark addressed to the passing woman.

A pretty girl passing a man may hear such phrases as, "What beautiful eyes you have, angel," and if she shows the slightest sign of being pleased by the compliment, she may be accompanied by poetry, either extemporaneous or plagiarized, for the next few minutes of her walk. Such outcroppings of masculine culture more than once drew down the wrath of the editorial writers of *El Pueblo*, the Catholic daily newspaper, who described the perpetrators in the following words:

"The pest is the precocious youth of the whipper-snapper persuasion who passes much of his time in smirking fatuously upon the school girls and young women who have the misfortune to cross his path, and, growing bolder as he smirks, whispers inanities into their ears until violently rebuffed."

The editorialist goes on to describe the youths who wait near the schools to plague the pretty girls as they come by in their smocks: "Sporting his first full length trousers, with a cigarette between his fingers and a shock of well-plastered hair upon his head—a veritable mane of hair—this budding Don Juan awaits his prey. At the first sign of a white smock, he adjusts his tie, passes his right hand affectionately over his well-oiled locks, and clears his throat. His 'Good afternoon, *simpática*,' meeting with no response, he ventures to ask, 'Are you always so silent and demure?'

"The young lady replies, 'Go away, young man, you are compromising me,' while breathing an inward prayer that he may continue his unbelievable inanities.

"With a little luck," the editorial concludes almost hopefully, "he may exhaust his vocabulary of sweet nothings before the charmer declares that she must wend her way."

With this training, the young men venture in later years into the fashionable streets to joust gaily with any attractive young woman who will listen to their polished phrases. Other men, developing along different lines, exhibit a rough and ready wit calculated to deflate the recipient and amuse passers-by. One American girl discovered this type of *piropo* because she had a weakness for chewing gum. She was walking along the street, chewing contentedly, when a man with a polite voice quipped, *"Buen provecho,"* which means "good appetite" and is usually reserved for a friend seated at a table with plenty of food in front of him. The quotation was embarrassingly apt in this case also, however. Yet the girl was glad she was chewing gum; otherwise the commentator might have found something else about her appearance or conduct deserving of a *piropo*.

One Englishwoman who dresses elegantly was nearing her office one day when two men began discussing her in loud tones obviously for her benefit.

"Che, Ramón, she's not bad," said the first.

"Not bad for forty!" Ramón bawled in an even louder voice. The woman, who was only 34, was understandably indignant.

A Dutch girl who usually stands out in an Argentine crowd

because she is both blonde and tall, had on a new and fairly bright green suit one afternoon. Seeing her, one Argentine *caballero* of the street remarked to the world in general: "Look at the long, green she-grasshopper!"

Another friend, an American far along in her pregnancy, ventured out on the street one afternoon to buy some clothes for the expected child. A strange man looked her over carefully as she approached, then said courteously, "I hope it will be a boy."

With rare poise and good humor, our friend inclined her head and murmured, *"Gracias, señor."*

In spite of the stranger's good wishes, the child proved to be a girl.

On the whole, the façade of courtesy is preserved by the men directing remarks at passers-by, because they can never be sure when their fishing is going to get a nibble from some one of the passing stream of womanhood.

The girl to whom a *piropo* is addressed may be flattered to the point of expressing her thanks, in which case the man will follow her to elaborate on his thesis that she is the most beautiful thing he has ever seen. And after ten or twelve blocks of this, she may finally stop and engage him frankly in conversation or allow him to take her to tea or cocktails. In either case, the Argentine male being the virile Don Juan he thinks he is, the road to conquest may be neither long nor full of detours.

This route seldom leads a girl to the altar, but oh, what a beautiful primrose path it can be! Instead of thorns, if the girl is young and lovely and shrewd, she finds her way freshened with pink champagne and strewn with fur coats and luxurious apartments. That is, if she has been fortunate enough to become the mistress of a *niño "bien."*

These perfumed and lacquered lovelies haunt no sordid back streets but boast addresses as fashionable as any to be found in the republic. The lady's prestige and the fun she has are determined by the prominence and prosperity of her lover and are heightened by the luxuries he showers upon her.

We knew of one middle-aged mistress who was the envy of all the women in the fashionable apartment building in which she lived, not because of her beauty, which was considerable, but because she slept in chartreuse chiffon nightgowns between peach silk sheets. This intriguing information was relayed to us by a bedazzled young American matron who paid a neighborly call one day on her fascinating neighbor in the apartment above.

Our friend's entree into such exotic circles soon made her one of the most sought-after tea table guests in the English-speaking community, and many a party was enlivened by her tales of sin in high places. Ruth delighted in hearing these scandalous bits and in passing them along to me. One day, she succeeded in getting her popular friend over to our tiny apartment. It was an enlightening visit. Her friend looked around our apartment with an amused eye and then headed for the kitchen—which wasn't any bigger than a clothes closet.

"Say," she shrieked, "don't you know you're living in an *amueblado?*"

Ruth replied that of course we knew our apartment was "furnished."

"That's not what I mean," our worldly visitor giggled. "Come look at this kitchen. Can't you see it was designed for a kept woman and not for a wife? Nobody was ever supposed to really cook in this, it's just to mix drinks and fix up a midnight snack."

Then our friend proceeded to instruct us on the facts of life in Argentina. "A woman's respectability is in direct ratio to the size of her kitchen," she observed. Inspecting the bathroom, which was large and elegantly equipped, our friend said that that was all she needed to convince her that our building was dedicated to bliss— but not the wedded kind.

Recovering somewhat from the pleasing shock of learning that we were living in an apartment equipped for sin, we recalled noticing more activity about the place in the middle of the night than at noon, and it had seemed unusual that all of the "wives" in our building looked young enough to be the daughters of their "husbands." They were always so bright and cheerful, too, with never a cross word for each other, and never any baby carriages.

"But we looked for apartments all over this town," Ruth apologized, "and they all had little kitchens."

Our guest beamed like the cat that has just licked off the canary feathers. "Now isn't that just what I've been telling you?" she asked, with a wicked toss of the head.

There have been many changes in social customs in the last decade or two, our friend pointed out, but the institution of the mistress flourishes just the same today as it did in grandfather's time. And a man's success in life can still be gauged, not only by the pretentiousness of the home where he keeps his wife and children, but also by the number of his mistresses and the style in which he maintains them.

Many a good woman complains that the mistress has more fun and often enjoys a more lavish style of living than the wife, yet the outward appearances of the irresponsible delights of the mistresses can be deceptive.

The rules for living in sin properly, our visitor emphasized, are just about as iron-clad as diplomatic protocol. A man may take his mistress to a night club, to dinner and even the theater, but he must not escort her to an official function or a big party where wives are present. If he has taken his mistress to a dinner and dance place, and there encounters a married couple he knows, he refrains from speaking to them, and they also ignore him. Yet the mistress is not cut off from society. She may act as the man's unofficial hostess when he entertains a group of men friends; if other women are there, none of them is likely to be the wife of any man present.

The kept woman, notwithstanding, need not wait in lonely elegance for the sound of her lover's key turning in the lock. Very often, she is clever enough to persuade him to finance her in a little lingerie or specialty shop, or even to underwrite her career on the stage. Many an actress has been helped to fame by discreet whispers that she is the mistress of a general or some socially prominent gentleman.

Some of these clandestine alliances last for years, strengthened by bonds of deep affection. There was the intelligent mistress who was the devoted friend of her lover's two children. She was even chosen to chaperone the daughter on a long sea voyage, and the son was a frequent visitor at her apartment.

To educated Argentines, prevalence of the double standard does not mean moral decadence. Americans are apt to be informed that it is no worse for an Argentine man to live with his wife and keep another woman in an apartment elsewhere over a period of twenty years than it is for an American man to live legally—by means of divorces—with three or five women during the same period. In fact, it may be argued that the Argentine home and the children in it are far more sacred than their northern counterparts.

It is protected both by law and social custom. It is legally impossible to get a divorce in the country. But if an Argentine woman should be divorced in Uruguay or Mexico and then re-marry, she would find herself hardly more socially acceptable than a mistress in the conservative circles of both Buenos Aires and the interior.

By long custom, the wife is meant for child-bearing and family management rather than for companionship with her husband. In her entire lifetime, she has little opportunity to develop friendships with the other sex as in the Anglo-Saxon sense. If a young man calls upon her more than three times, always in the presence of the family, he is made to feel painfully aware that it is time for him to declare his intentions. If they do become engaged, the young man and woman have few chances to be alone together. Some member of the family usually accompanies them even when they go to the movies.

However, the rigid standards of the *dueña* tradition are crumbling somewhat. Old Spanish customs at home must now compete with a whole new sugar-coated way of life portrayed nightly by Hollywood in the packed movie houses of Argentina.

Many young Argentines are beginning to compare their lives with those they see on the screen. And one of them once asked me hopefully, "Is it true that a man in the States can trade in his old wife for a new one any time he feels like it?"

BACKWASH OF THE WAR

NEWSPAPER DISPLAY WINDOWS IN BUENOS AIRES SERVE A variety of purposes.

Some forty or fifty years ago, according to newspaper legend, an irate Spaniard who felt his name had been soiled by a story appearing in a fairly important daily challenged the editor to a duel. Now in those days it was customary for the editor to be held personally responsible for everything that went into the paper; so he saw that it was his duty to fight. He named his seconds and the duel was fought at dawn, with pistols. The editor, a big, fat man, was killed. Then the publisher, full of gratitude to the man who had defended the honor of his paper, had the body brought in and put on display in the office window. There it lay in state for three days. To all who passed on the street, it served spectacular, if gruesome, notice that the journalists of that paper were men of principle. The story does not say if the publisher found a successor to his heroic editor, but presumably he did, for the paper continued publishing for many years after.

Newspaper display windows have another use—the release of pent-up emotions. When a man disagrees with the policy of a newspaper, he smolders in silence for a time. Finally, when he can stomach its politics no longer, he heaves half a brick or a good-sized stone through its plate glass front. This is supposed to ease his feelings, and probably his satisfaction is increased by the thought of the hundreds of pesos the publisher will have to spend replacing the glass.

Destruction of the fourth estate windows became almost a ritual during the war, when feeling for the active participants in the conflict ran high in the breasts of the officially neutral Argentines. The pro-Allied papers were older and more prosperous than the Johnny-come-lately Axis press, and their big, fat windows made inviting targets for the Hitler men. There was many a spectacular crash as the democratic plate glass tumbled. However, the smaller panes belonging to the pro-Axis press were also shattered in forays by enthusiastic young Argentines, most of them university students.

But there is plenty of glass manufactured in Argentina, and nothing in the world could induce the publishers to shutter their windows permanently. The newspapers went right on exposing a tempting footage of window pane.

To do otherwise would have been to deprive the *porteño* of one of his favorite customs and inalienable rights—that of reading the news before it gets into print. The newspapers display bulletin boards in their windows, and it was on these that the average Argentine read his daily preview of the historic events of the Second World War.

The habit has become so ingrained that news agencies supply special summaries of the world's big happenings for use only on the bulletin boards. These short dispatches are either lettered out neatly in type much like small-scale theater signs or are carefully written in white chalk on a blackboard. A newspaper may have anywhere from five to thirty of these messages in its window at the end of the day, depending on the importance of developments.

I was particularly impressed with the emphasis the newspapers laid on war news, which was played up to the almost total exclusion of local events. The few times I recall having seen Argentine news on the bulletin boards came during the first days of the 1943 revolution. Also the winning numbers of the Christmas and New Year's lotteries, and occasionally the Sunday football scores, would be scrawled on the boards. But by and large, the newspaper bulletins indicated the average Argentine was most deeply concerned in the conflict taking place on the other half of the globe.

During the war years, *La Nación* distinguished itself for its fine bulletin board service. It used both the block letter sign and the blackboard. The smart letter display in the front entrance on Calle Florida invariably had a crowd around it, and Leonard and I on our way to work nearly always visited the blackboards on the less pretentious Calle San Martín entrance to learn what was happening.

Blue mosaic church tower glistens in the heart of Córdoba

A glimpse into a patio, San Isidro

There were half a dozen blackboards at the back, and the news usually was carefully classified. For example, news of bombing attacks was on one board, and the activities of the western ground front on another. The Russian front occupied still another and sometimes two, if the news was big enough. The Pacific theater was given much less space, mainly because of the sporadic nature of the sea warfare and the fact that the Argentines had little interest in Asia and the islands of the Pacific, which very few of them had ever visited.

These bulletin boards were apparently reliable guides to the reading interests of the Argentines. No matter what the weather was, or the hour of the day, there was invariably some *porteño* curious enough to stop and read the war bulletins. Frequently, when big stories were breaking, the sidewalks were so crowded around the newspaper offices that it was difficult to pass.

The printed newspapers themselves appeared designed to satisfy a voracious appetite for war news. There was little else but war on the front pages.

This may seem remarkable, considering that Argentina was several thousand miles from the nearest land front and had little or no chance of getting into the war. Yet the fact was the Argentines had traditionally been closely bound to Europe—their motherland and their market—and had a definite stake in the outcome of the war. There was also the Battle of the Atlantic, which literally rippled along the shores of Argentina and rolled into the River Plate.

Porteños could almost smell the smoke of big guns when the German pocket battleship, *Graf Spee,* was ignominiously hounded into the Río de la Plata by British warships in the early days of the war. There, almost under the very noses of the Argentines, the *Graf Spee* was scuttled, and hundreds of the crew were interned on Argentine soil. The excitement of the chase into the river mouth was kept alive by the antics of the German officers and sailors, who tried again and again to escape from Argentina to Germany; many of the attempts failed, but a third of the German sailors did sneak back across the Atlantic, and some of them rejoined the Nazi navy. This was a titillating international scandal, with the Argentine authorities belatedly tracking the young Nazis through mountains and forests and doing it so half-heartedly that the Germans were seldom restrained for long. Many Argentines were incensed about this, not only because their authorities had been derelict in duty, but also because they felt that the German sailors had misunderstood and abused Argentina's traditional and liberal hospitality.

When the escapes could no longer be officially ignored and the government cracked down on the interned Germans, *La Crítica* heaved a pious editorial sigh and welcomed the new get-tough-with-sailors policy.

The newspaper commented, "It is already almost four years since the celebrated naval combat of Punta del Este took place. The crew of the German battleship came to Buenos Aires after the defeat. The condition of the beaten sailors, the tragic death (suicide) of their captain and the youth of them all combined to arouse sympathy among us, which was all the more notable considering that the cause for which they had fought unsuccessfully did not merit any support from a country, like ours, of strong democratic tradition. It was sufficient for us to see them deprived of their ship and of their arms as a consequence of the defeat, and to understand the sorrow produced by their forced exile ... (but) neither the officers nor the majority of the sailors knew how to reciprocate the treatment received. They did not use the freedom which was so generously given to them—they preferred to abuse it. Some of the officers, in complicity with persons who later became known as perpetrators of subversive maneuvers and espionage, escaped from the country. Others went even farther: They replaced the law of the country in which they were, and employed violence and even sanctions against those crew men who wanted to found in this land a new home and repudiate in this way their earlier conduct ... and it must be noted that they never vacillated in attempting a political propaganda that could not possibly bear fruit among us. ... From now on, the sailors of the scuttled German warship must be concentrated in groups, under the vigilance and responsibility of Argentine Army and Navy authorities."

As a matter of fact, a number of the German sailors did marry Argentine women and became the fathers of Argentine children. The close of the war found them clinging to their hospitable new homes as tenaciously as any native *ombú* tree, apparently far happier to be living in the land of plenty than in their devastated fatherland.

The *Graf Spee* had settled deep into the mud of the River Plate when I came to Argentina in 1941, but bookstores still did a brisk business in post cards portraying the dismal end of the ship. It was a dramatic experience that few Argentines were willing to forget. And, at that time, it represented to most Argentines just about the only major positive achievement of Allied arms against Hitler in almost two years of the European conflict. The Germans then dominated western Europe, from northern Norway to southern France, and were grooming themselves for a big push in North Africa. A German invasion of England was an almost constant threat.

Some Argentines were convinced they were witnessing the prelude to the destruction of the British Empire. But the majority of pro-democratc Argentines, who might have been inclined to resign themselves to an Axis victory after the fall of France, were never allowed for one minute to forget "there'll always be an England" by some fifty thousand Britons in the River Plate area. There were benefit shows, giant fêtes combining the attractions of a night club with a carnival, beauty contests and auctions all designed for the express purpose of raising money for the British war effort. There was probably no busier person in the entire republic than Lady Ovey, the lovely wife of the British ambassador, who not only encouraged Britons to further efforts, but was instrumental in winning many Argentine friends to the Allied cause.

In this land of abundance, the English and Anglo-Argentines began to tighten their belts to buy Spitfires—and there was hardly a member of the community who was not having a regular amount deducted from his pay check to help Britain fight the war. This differed from the American system of buying savings bonds, for the British contributions did not draw interest and could not be cashed in. Nor was the sacrifice entirely financial.

Seldom did a British ship leave an Argentine port without English and Anglo-Argentine volunteers aboard. Some of these had never seen England, and others were the great-grandchildren of settlers from the United Kingdom. By the end of 1944, the British community was almost decimated of young men, so great had been the response for volunteers. Many women "joined up," and I knew of one middle-aged couple, both of whom had seen service in the last war, who quit their jobs and sold their furniture to return to England and enter the services.

Some of these Argentine-born volunteers lost their lives in the submarine-infested South Atlantic, others in the sands of North Africa and many in Europe.

I arrived in Buenos Aires about a week before Germany invaded Russia, and for the next two years I saw hardly a banner headline which did not contain the name of a Russian town or river. The dramatic sweep of the Wehrmacht into Russia was relayed to the excited *porteño* reader with maps to guide him through the mysteries of Russian geography. Almost no person I met during the first month of the Russo-German war thought that the Soviet could last more than a few weeks at the most. The situation of the Allied powers therefore seemed just as grim as ever. Then came the epic battle of Stalingrad, which the Argentine public followed literally inch by inch and foot by foot. The Russian communiques were printed in full, and editors used their blackest type to detail the desperate struggle of the wounded Soviet. The turning-point victory of Stalingrad, when it finally came, was something of a twentieth-century miracle to the Argentine, who had been deeply shocked when the vaunted French army crumbled under the Nazi machine and the invincible British were forced to evacuate Dunkirk.

Thus the Argentines came to feel a considerable admiration and even a liking for the giant-killing Russians. Many good and devout Catholics momentarily forgot that the Russians were also Communists; ideological differences were overlooked, and bars patronized by upper and middle class conservatives began to offer Timoshenko cocktails. For the first time since the fall of the Czar it became respectable to be discreetly pro-Russian; and some Argentines, growing enthusiastic about the whole thing, named their pet dogs for the Soviet generals. The general atmosphere became so friendly to the Russian cause that even some White Russians felt encouraged to venture out and take bows for the Red Army feats. In the carnival that year, hundreds of Argentines dressed up in colorful "Cossack" costumes and tripped along the avenues, throwing confetti at friends more conservatively attired.

In the meantime, the Japanese had struck their staggering blow at Pearl Harbor. The Argentines were impressed with the damage the U. S. fleet had sustained, but this was far overshadowed by their knowledge that at last the United States was in the war, which had truly become a world conflict. Their main interest still lay in Europe, and the United States declaration of war on Germany and Italy meant that the Allied powers might finally swing the balance against Hitler. The Argentines, who had little use for American "culture" and were wont to sneer at U.S. preoccupation with the assembly line, nevertheless had a profound respect for the material things the assembly line could produce.

More than that, Pearl Harbor for the first time posed a real problem for Argentine policy with respect to the war. Should Argentina consider that the attack on Pearl Harbor and the Philippines was an attack on the hemisphere and hence on Argentina? Or should she remain neutral? There was a real division of opinion on the issue, but the Argentines never had a chance to air their clashing views thoroughly, for Acting President Castillo clamped down a "state of siege" to avoid public discussion which he feared—rightly or wrongly—might lead to a deep national rift and even violence.

Thereafter, the rôle of the other Latin American nations—especially Brazil—in the world conflict was watched with keen interest by the Argentines. And the American newsreels kept the *porteños* well informed of the growth in military strength of their big neighbor to the north. A jeep was something of a curiosity in Buenos Aires when a member of the U.S. Air Mission drove one through the streets, but when a *porteño* went to the movies he saw great numbers of these miniature vehicles rolling through the streets of Rio de Janeiro with Brazilians at the wheel. A great fuss was made over the manufacture of the first tank in Argentina and thousands of Argentines lined up to inspect it. But when they attended the movies, there were the Brazilians already manipulating scores of bigger ones through the avenues of their beautiful capital. Nor were the tanks and jeeps all they saw in the hands of the

Brazilians. There were big guns and other arms, most of which had been obtained through Lend-Lease from the United States.

Such spectacles were galling to the proud Argentine Army, which talked of the upset in the balance of power on the South American continent. To the man on the street, long nurtured on the theory of Argentina's superiority to Brazil, the pictures were bewildering. Then the Axis press hit on the happy slogan, "Argentina can't be bought with a check book," and before long many Argentines were referring with some pride to their country's invulnerability to Uncle Sam's bank account.

Meanwhile, rumors began to circulate in Argentina of the outcome of permitting United States troops on Brazilian soil. One Argentine officer told me quite indignantly that Brazilian officers were unwelcome in American officers' clubs, and the *yanquis*, based on the soil of Brazil, wouldn't even allow members of the Brazilian Army to patronize the same bars and restaurants that they frequented. Such a situation was held out as one of the possible evils of siding actively with the Allies; it might mean having American service personnel quartered in Argentina.

Despite Brazil's shining new guns, however, the pro-Axis press continued to depict Brazil as a Negro in bare feet, an attitude not altogether repugnant to the Argentine. Even our pro-democratic friends took great pride in the fact that their own nation was pure white and had been ever since Rosas employed the Negroes in the country as first line troops to kill the Indians, a maneuver that had resulted in the near extermination of both the black and red races. Brazil, they explained, was under the handicap of having Negro blood.

Brazil's contribution to the Allied war effort could not be ignored, however. The Argentines eventually learned that Allied troops and arms funneled through Brazil had played an important part in the North African campaigns.

The Montgomery-Rommel feud caught the imagination of the Argentine readers, and as Monty's Eighth Army checkmated the German at El Alamein and pushed him back on Tunis, Timoshenko had his first Anglo-Saxon rival. Montgomery berets soon went on sale at Harrod's.

War events moved faster. The Allied landing in North Africa

made a big splash in the headlines and hardly had time to die down before the Argentines were heatedly debating the ethics of the "deal" with Darlan. The discussion was so fervent that someone unacquainted with the news would have supposed it was an Argentine rather than an Allied general who had been involved with the "suspect" Frenchman.

After that, Allied victories—Tunis, Pantellaria, Sicily and the surrender of Italy—came so fast that well-informed Argentines were sure Hitler was going to be beaten. They were less excited by the war. There was thanksgiving, rather than fervent rejoicing, when Rome fell into Allied hands and first reports showed the Holy City almost unscarred.

The lull between the downfall of Mussolini and the invasion of western Europe was punctuated with hundreds of mass raids which the Argentines observed with mixed feelings. The *porteños*, a thrifty race with a respect for beautiful towns, were sad to see some of the cities they knew or had read about disappear in ruins. But this regret was tempered by their knowledge of what the Luftwaffe had done to Coventry and London in 1940. With their high regard for the family, the Argentines were horrified by the terrific losses to women and children who had played no part in the war for either side. Yet most Argentines also believed in the simple justice of an eye for an eye and a tooth for a tooth, and I think they did not judge the Anglo-American powers too harshly for their concentration on the air blitz in reverse.

Arm chair strategists were also engaged fully in a parlor battle speculating about when and where the Allies would open their long-awaited second front.

Would General Eisenhower strike the "soft under-belly" of southeastern Europe or the rocky shores of France or Norway? Pro-Axis die-hards, including at least one high officer of the Argentine Army, wrote learned articles doubting the feasibility of amphibious forces penetrating Hitler's west wall. These doubts were confined mostly to the pro-Axis press and its readers, who were in a distinct minority.

We ourselves were living on pins and needles waiting for the newspaper sirens to announce the great day. The big dailies were equipped with sirens on their roofs and their enormous racket was reserved to herald catastrophes or bring tidings of great, good events. World-shaking flashes from the news agencies always started a race of hired hands to the roofs to set off the sirens. Each newspaper wanted to be the first to blow. One Sunday morning we were awakened by their terrific shrilling and—assuming that Eisenhower had finally landed—we dressed like fury and scurried to our respective offices. It was quite a letdown to learn that the "invasion" we expected had been only the return to Argentina of Vito Dumas from a globe-circling tour in his tiny yacht.

Nerves were tense in those days and twice in the next few months *La Nación* set off its siren to announce the invasion of Europe. Both times the newspaper learned it had been given an erroneous alarm by the Associated Press, and when the invasion finally did come *La Nación* ventured to blow its siren only after the other newspapers had been bellowing for several minutes. *La Nación's* "honor" was rescued only towards the end of the world conflict, when *La Prensa* blew its siren to announce the surrender of Japan based on a premature United Press flash.

When the Allied troops landed in France the Argentines promptly relegated the Russian front to a secondary place. Many Argentines had travelled or lived and studied in France, and they knew and loved the country second only to their own. The cultural and social ties were many, and the Argentines watched the progress of the liberating armies with joyful interest, which reached its climax in the liberation of Paris.

It was like a great dyke breaking loose. For three whole days the Argentine people, their democratic sentiments pent up ever since the imposition of the state of siege, marched, and yelled and sang through the streets of Buenos Aires. I saw old men, tears in their eyes, cry, *"Viva libertad! Viva Francia!"* and little children solemnly place tiny clusters of flowers on the white marble statue in Plaza Francia.

Even before Paris was officially liberated the rejoicing began. It was the morning of August 23, 1944. Men who paused to read the newspaper bulletin boards, stayed there. The Allies were entering Paris! Huge crowds began to collect around the newspaper offices, and before any paper had time to reach the street, there was already a festive atmosphere about Buenos Aires. Flags began to pop out. Businessmen either forgot or ignored the fact that the government's state of siege regulation forbade the display of any foreign flag without official permission. The French tricolor—and I've always wondered where so many came from on such short notice—was unfurled on store after store. By noon, the shopping center was a riot of red, white and blue. There was bunting, and flags, and rosettes and flowers; Argentine flags were beside French ones, and in a few places the red, white and blue Union Jack and the Stars and Stripes shared in the tribute. Merchants hastily began to redecorate their shop windows. Some cleared out all of the merchandise to put in elaborate and beautiful floral arrangements— Crosses of Lorraine, big V's for Victory, and the French tricolor, all done in blossoms.

In one window, I noticed a display of red, white and blue bedroom slippers. Another had red, white and blue dressing gowns. A knitted goods store covered its windows with white and red and blue sweaters.

Stores which didn't have products in those colors, put in flags or flowers and often both. Jewelry and perfume shops along Calle Florida outdid themselves in the lavishness of their tributes in roses and carnations and cornflowers. And the strains of the "Marseillaise" could be heard from phonograph and radio shops and from hundreds of lips.

Street corner flower dealers hurried to prepare masses of red, white and blue corsages then quickly sold them all. Yellow and pink flowers wilted in neglect that day. Vendors did a land office business in little red, white and blue ribbons to be pinned in men's coat lapels. Miniature French and Argentine flags sold by the basketful. Women lucky enough to own red hats or blue suits put them on and joined the parade of *porteños*, who poured out of offices and factories to participate in the biggest spontaneous mass celebration in Argentine history.

The tide swept towards Plaza San Martín, the lovely tree-filled park which faces the Foreign Office and the Cavanagh building, the tallest in the country. Gigantic flags—French and Argentine— were suspended from the highest windows of the skyscraper, and the banners of the two nations fluttered from the roof. In contrast was the Foreign Office, totally bare of any decoration or tribute to Paris. The procession to the plaza and the statue of General San Martín became something of a pilgrimage that evening, a symbol of Argentina's gratitude and love for France. For the great national hero, whose bronze statue stood in the center of that plaza and many others throughout Argentina, had spent a quarter of a century in exile in France and there died lonely and poverty-stricken.

By 6 P.M. that day, the statue was literally smothered in flowers. There were the great wreaths from the American and British embassies, the French society, from student and other organizations. It was easy to identify each, for wide streamers stretched across the flowers and were lettered in gold with the name of the donors. Besides the big sprays, there were dozens of small bouquets with no identification marks. *Porteño* after *porteño*, who stopped at the foot of the statue to pay homage to San Martín and to France, looked up and gasped. Amid all the wreaths, one stood out. It read, "From the Political Prisoners of Villa Devoto."

No high official of the military government appeared before the statue of San Martín that afternoon—although it was reported that Colonel Perón really wanted to but had been over-ruled by his colleagues in Casa Rosada. But when any of the nation's former democratic leaders were recognized amid the throng, the crowd broke into cheers. Former Senator Palacios was spotted easily, and at the urging of the people, made a brief but eloquent speech, ending it with "Long live Free Argentina!"

The Argentine people took up the cry and added some of their own as they dispersed into small groups. I was walking along Calle Florida, intent on the beautiful window displays, when a group of young people, about a hundred of them, headed my way. They were carrying Argentine and French flags and chanting, "We are the people! Long live liberty! We are the people! We are the people!" Spectators along the sidewalk cheered them, and some joined them, shouting, "*Viva libertad! Viva democracia!*" The first thing I knew, the shouts for liberty were interrupted by a loud clatter. People started scurrying for cover, and I don't think I ever saw a densely packed street crowd thin out so fast. They were wiser than I, for I had to stop to look back.

Too late, I saw that the *cosacos* were coming. That's the way nearly every pedestrian in Buenos Aires refers to the dread mounted police, the fierce, saber-wielding men on horseback. In the next few seconds, I found myself trapped, backed into a small recess on a side street. There were five or six persons caught with me, and the wild men in blue were bearing down on us. Then two *cosacos* skidded their mounts. They were over us, their horses' front hoofs in the air. Sabers slashed at some of our little group, but missed me. The police yelled for us to move on but unobligingly kept their horses where they were.

I was so frightened that I froze in my tracks and might be there yet if a thoughtful *porteño* gentleman hadn't grabbed me by the arm and steered me to shelter in the nearest doorway.

My first close contact with the *cosacos* was comparatively pleasant, however, for hundreds of persons were cut with the slashing sabers or bruised by the police clubs.

That night, Leonard and I ran into a friend who worked in the American Embassy and who spoke such fluent Spanish that he was often mistaken for an Argentine. He had a friendly habit of chatting with the police near the Embassy building. After the day's hectic activities, our friend stopped at the Embassy corner when he saw a young policeman rubbing his arm, his face screwed up with pain. "What's the matter? Can I help you any?" he asked.

The young policeman continued to rub his arm and explained, "Oh it's nothing, I've just clubbed so many people today that I've strained my arm."

This police brutality, instead of intimidating the Argentine people, only seemed to exhilarate them. The restaurants looked that night as if every housewife in the city limits had liberated herself from the kitchen. And a table without an ice bucket and champagne on it was actually conspicuous. Leonard and I felt almost like traitors because it was before instead of after pay day, and we could only afford a modest white wine. We felt under further suspicion because we didn't know the words of the "Marseillaise," in either French, or Spanish or English and therefore were unable to join in any group singing. Every bar and restaurant and *confitería* was playing the French national anthem time after time that night. Even our favorite orchestra, which felt more at home with the "Blue Danube," had memorized the "Marseillaise" before the Paris celebration ended.

It was enough to possess a French flag to become the leader of a singing, enthusiastic group. And for the first time in many a month, demonstrators who paused in front of *La Nación* and *La Prensa* stopped there to cheer the two democratic papers instead of to stone or boo them.

The steps of the dark and bolted Congress building—which stood like an ornate but ghostly reminder of the days of constitutional government—became the lively scene of another pro-democratic gathering. French and Argentine flags were waved as the crowds cried for democracy, the constitution and France. When one man sounded the off-key note, *"Viva Perón,"* he was cracked over the head with an Argentine flag. The police kept busy that night, and the arrests were many. There was no discrimination, and the victims came from all walks of life, lawyers, school teachers, laborers and the rich unemployed. Many a good and highly respectable matron saw the inside of a jail cell for the first time in her carefully sheltered life.

It was nearly midnight when Leonard and I started for home. Police were thick, on horseback and on foot. We walked through Plaza San Martín, but when we stopped at the flower-bedecked statue a uniformed man told us to move on. Nearby was a group of some 50 other police in a circle, looking for all the world like an over-sized football team in a huddle.

The day's activity, however, was only a mild introduction of what was to come next. After some reluctance, the government authorities agreed to permit a ceremony of thanksgiving for the liberation of Paris. It was stipulated, however, that it should be held in Plaza Francia and not in the heart of the city. Plaza Francia is rather difficult to reach from downtown Buenos Aires, and wartime shortages had made transportation a headache in the best circumstances. It hardly seemed possible that enough *colectivos*, buses, taxi cabs and private automobiles could be commandeered to deliver any great numbers to the scene. But the Argentines are a resourceful people, and they do love France.

Women left home early and took their lunches and their children in order to be sure to be on hand for the celebration scheduled for the evening. Students skipped classes to get there. Most business houses let their employees out early.

Thousands streamed out of the center of Buenos Aires as if some plague had struck, and shops were either closed or deserted by 5 P.M., normally one of the busiest hours of the day. By 6 o'clock, over 300,000 persons had pushed their way into the plaza. The park was overflowing, and old timers said it was the largest crowd that had ever gathered anywhere in Argentina.

Few Colón opera openings had ever boasted such a distinguished attendance. Besides such renowned figures as Dr. Carlos Saavedra Lamas, the Nobel prize winner, there were stars from the theater and stage. General Arturo Rawson, the leader of the revolution, and the man who succeeded him, General Pedro Pablo Ramírez—both out of power—were there. So was Senator Palacios and many of his colleagues from the country's last elected legislative body. University professors rubbed elbows with artists who had studied in Paris and with ladies still wearing French gowns. Wealthy families who had lived and played most of their adult lives in Paris and on the Riviera arrived in mass, waving flags and singing the "Marseillaise" as lustily as any student. There were thousands of workers in the crowd too, but for the most part it was made up of middle class citizens.

The remarkable thing about the entire affair was its spontaneity. Unlike the government-sponsored demonstrations, which all employees on the public payroll were required to attend, nobody was forced to be there. And the few democratic organizations remaining intact hardly had sufficient time to rally any forces. It was a clear-cut case of the people showing their sentiments, not as representatives of any group or faction but as individuals.

But it would be a mistake to believe that love of France alone had attracted the tremendous gathering. Every "*Viva libertad!*" had a double meaning. A good many of the Argentines were shouting for liberty for themselves as well as for Paris. Some were openly and loudly anti-government, yelling "*Viva democracia! Viva democracia!*" and "*Democracia sí, Perón no!*"

After the brief ceremony conducted by the Francaise-Amerique Committee had ended, the crowd showed no inclination to leave, cheering first one and then another former public figure—Rawson,

Palacios and Ramírez. Any political complexion went as long as it was not in Casa Rosada.

All of a sudden, the cheers of the people were drowned out by police sirens, which seemed to come from every direction at once. Patrol wagons and armored cars skidded into the gathering from all sides, and police jumped out of their vehicles, clubs swinging. The people who fought back were clubbed or hit over the heads with revolver butts. Tear gas bombs were thrown into centers of resistance. Then into all this noisy confusion galloped the *cosacos*, their horses' hoofs clattering on the pavement. They rode straight into the crowds, sabers slashing.

Women and children were trampled. This so angered some of the men nearby that they tried to pull the police from their horses. Dozens of persons—both men and women—were packed into Black Marias and hurried off to jail. Some of the arrested persons had been cut by police sabers. Many of the other wounded and bruised were left to be carried off the plaza by shocked friends or even complete strangers.

Argentines who had witnessed the spectacle were so outraged that they hurried to their favorite bars and restaurants to repeat what they had seen. The symbol of protest was to sing the "Marseillaise," and soon it could be heard even louder than the night before. Some establishments where it was being sung were raided by the police. A free-for-all ensued when police entered the Boston Bar, traditional haunt of the American and British community, and it was finally cleared of its patrons and locked, but not before considerable crockery had gone flying through the air, most of it in the direction of police heads.

This new police activity was accompanied by another development. Groups of husky nationalist youths began to run through the streets screaming *"Viva Perón! Viva Farrell! Viva Soberanía!"* and *"Soberanía o muerte!"*

All of the flags were still up on the third day of the celebration. Until the liberation of Paris, I had been unable to recognize all of the government buildings in Buenos Aires. But it was easy now, for they were about the only ones, except German, which didn't have flags up. Argentines who had been unable to attend the big rally on the previous night journeyed to the Plaza Francia to place more

flowers on the already overloaded monument. Police were stationed
all through the park and around the statue, but there was no
repetition of the previous night's incidents.

La Prensa and *La Nación* had broken the shackles of the state of
siege to give a full account of the police aggressions and to place
the blame for the disturbance directly on the uniformed officers
who had interfered. They charged that women had been singled
out for especially harsh treatment.

The indignation was so great that the chief of police, then
Colonel Velazco, issued one of the few explanations in his official
career. He said that the women were "extremists," which meant, of
course, that tens of thousands of female "extremists" had suddenly
been discovered, where before there had been none!

Resentment of government brutality in suppressing the joyful
demonstration over the liberation of Paris was not sufficient for the
porteños to attempt to overthrow the military regime. However,
it does help to account for the malicious willingness of the Argentines to lend their ears and their tongues to the sensational and
much-publicized reports that the Nazis were planning to flee to
Argentina and there set up a base for a third World War. What
excitement that caused!

Besides a flood of newspaper stories regarding that possibility,
the *porteños* developed some ideas of their own. While official
statements sizzled back and forth from Buenos Aires, London and
Washington on whether Argentina would provide a refuge for
war criminals, some imaginative Argentines were repeating gleefully this bizarre story:

"Hitler come to Argentina? Nonsense, he's already here! Didn't
you know that he came on a Spanish ship? Well, he did. He was
disguised as a Spanish priest! And he just slipped in with all of the
padres here for the Eucharistic Congress."

Speculation went on for months. Many scoffed at the whole
idea of Hitler or any other high Nazi coming to Argentina. Among
them was General Orlando Peluffo, then the Foreign Minister,
who told the press: "It would be better to think that the refugees
will seek neutral countries, and not those, like ours, which have
broken off relations. Further, there are reasons of distance which
make it less likely."

However, others recalled their own government's sensational disclosures soon after the rupture of relations with the Axis. Then it was revealed that the Germans had surveyed a certain section of the coast of the province of Buenos Aires for the purpose of landing spies from a submarine.

It was a big day for the Argentines when, weeks after the war ended in Europe, the German submarine U-530 showed up in Mar del Plata. That was proof enough for a lot of them that Hitler had at last arrived, and witnesses hurried to claim that they had seen rubber boats sneaking away from the submarine. Finally another foreign minister had to issue an official denial that the No. 1 Nazi and his bride had entered the country.

Somewhat wistfully, *Crítica* advanced the theory that Hitler and Eva Braun might have reached Queen Maud Land, a few hundred miles from the South Pole, where another Berchtesgaden "is likely to have been built" during the German antarctic expedition in 1938-39.

It was a possibility no comfort-loving Argentine cared to investigate.

OPPENHEIM OPERA

I HAVE ALWAYS ENJOYED THE WORKS OF E. PHILLIPS OPPENHEIM, and I still do. But I realize now that a real situation can be far more menacing than anything cooked up by a master of the spy thriller. It was, in Argentina. From 1943 onward the atmosphere in Buenos Aires kept us wondering day and night what was going to happen next—and to whom. From the wings, we watched a real Oppenheim opera. The action on the stage was fast and hard on the nerves. One friend was clubbed by two well-dressed assailants as he walked home at twilight in a fashionable district. Another friend was whisked off to jail and deported. Still another was always plotting ways to needle the government. And one well-to-do lady actually propositioned us to run guns into Argentina. These events that flowed around us, however, were only a gentle swirl in the tides of excitement that swept the capital of South America's last remaining neutral.

The meaning of what happened was not always clear. One night we saw plain-clothes men and police officers seize a woman and take her away, screaming. Walking about the city at midnight we witnessed more than one little cluster of men suddenly battling with the police. Those were only the things we observed. Many other events were hidden by the size of the city and the muzzle on the newspapers. But rumor kept the air electric with tension which often became oppressive after it had gone on too long to be exciting. There was a popular escape from this, and that was the overnight and inexpensive trip by boat to Uruguay, where the air remained free and democratic. Hundreds of Argentines slipped across the river to evade the clutches of their police. Hundreds of others, less fortunate, were seized and clapped into jails, and eventually we were forced to revise our conception that it was a disgrace to spend time in prison.

We came to look on an ex-prisoner as an honored man. Those days we felt almost apologetic because the cop at our corner continued to bid us a cheery *"Buenos días,"* or a courteous *"Buenas noches."*

I take some pride in the fact that Leonard was once "escorted" to the dread Sección Orden Social of the Buenos Aires police station, the matriculation point for spies and counter-spies and the horror of horrors for Communists and other "conspirators" against the sovereignty of the *patria*. But he was back home forty-five minutes later, with nothing more exciting to report than a fatherly lecture from the head of the department.

This single brush with the authorities came over two years after we arrived in the country, some months after the military revolution had succeeded. There had been more than ample time for us to become thoroughly schooled in the lore of this true life cloak-and-dagger country where secret radio transmitters, microfilm in soap cakes, coded messages in walnuts, and filing cabinets full of fake identity documents were spoken of almost as casually as the weather or the football results. I always envied those Buenos Aires newspaper editors who became so blasé that when the Argentine government finally announced it had trapped a huge German spy ring—equipped with radio transmitters, many automobiles and thousands of pesos—they relegated the news to a routine head on an inside page.

My sophistication hardly reached that point. Take the case of the Hotel Viena, for example. Leonard and I had been strolling by it every day on our way to work, but we hadn't given it more than a passing glance, other than to notice the large marble statue in the dimly-lit lobby. It looked like any inexpensive establishment catering to genteel but impoverished elderly persons. Then one day, some months after Pearl Harbor, the Inter-continental Defense Committee issued a lengthy report on Axis espionage activities in Argentina. To our wonderment, the Hotel Viena, right in our own neighborhood, was named as a gathering place of notorious German spies. Not only that, certain young men of Teutonic appearance had felt so secure there that in signing the register they had listed their occupations as "parachutists." This so intrigued me, that I wasn't merely content to walk by this mysterious haunt at a snail's pace twice a day and gawk in at the elderly, white-haired desk clerk; I insisted on inviting friends over to tea and then luring them on a guided tour of the block on Calle Lavalle in which the hotel was located, while I recited which spies had been there and when, and to what evil purpose. My guests appeared somewhat less awed by this intelligence than did I, although I must reveal that in all the months that I "shadowed" the Hotel Viena, I failed to spot a single sinister character who fulfilled my ideas of what an enemy para-trooper ought to look like.

Not so the German bar located next door to our apartment building when we lived on Calle Tucumán. A tall and powerful blond man stood guard at the door each night and immediately became known to us as "The Stormtrooper." Every Sunday evening about 7 o'clock, some two hundred well-dressed men and women, accompanied by their children, used to spill out of its doors—not as if they had just tossed down a few beers and were ready to go some place else for dinner—but as if a meeting had adjourned. They were as sedate as any Parent-Teacher Association group. Leonard agreed that it wasn't natural for so many people to leave a bar at once, except at closing time. However, I never did succeed in convincing him that the singing in German we often heard drifting out from the bar was really the "Horst Wessel." The bar was, of course, out of bounds for the Allies.

The fact that we restrained ourselves from personally investi-gating such goings-on was only because our own spy complexes were relatively mild ones. By the time I arrived in the country in June, 1941, much of the German activity had gone underground.

No longer were German youths in uniform parading through the streets of Buenos Aires shouting "Heil Hitler" when we set up housekeeping, for President Ortiz in 1939 had banned the German National Socialist party from the soil of his country.

But two years later, there was shocking evidence that his orders had been obeyed in name only. The Chamber of Deputies Anti-Argentine Investigating Committee found 164 Nazi groups within the country masking as German cultural and benevolent societies. The members were under discipline from Hitler, the culture was furnished by Dr. Goebbels and the benevolence was supplied in reichsmarks. In those days, the methods used by committee members in swooping down on the German societies reminded me of nothing so much as an Oklahoma sheriff's force raiding a bootlegger's hideout.

The newspapers were full of the activities of the committee, and its findings were often the topics of hot debate in the Chamber of Deputies itself. On one occasion, an angry member hurled a cup of hot coffee into a fellow deputy's face. Luckily, it was a demi-tasse. And at least once a member of the investigating committee was called on to defend his convictions on the dueling field.

All such activity ceased, however, after Pearl Harbor, when President Castillo clamped down his state of siege. This in effect established control of the press, and the Argentine people were placed in the position of the famous three monkeys who are said to see no evil, hear no evil and speak no evil.

However, not even a couple of *yanqui* innocents could fail to observe the German influence in the country. It was virtually impossible to escape it.

When we finished work we liked to stop at a sidewalk cafe on Avenida de Mayo for a snack. It would have been necessary to wear blinders to have overlooked the big electrical sign of the German news agency, Trans-Ocean. The agency supplied news not only to the German language newspaper, *Deutsche La Plata Zeitung*, but to such Axis-financed sheets as *El Pampero*, *Cabildo*, *Momento Argentino* and any other publication caring to avail itself of the thousands of words sent daily from Berlin.

The streets of Buenos Aires echoed each evening with the cries of news boys vending their wares. Invariably heard above all the other din was the chant of "PAM-PE-RO! PAM-PE-RO!" It was always so loud and so frequent that it took some time to discover that this paper played a poor third fiddle to *Crítica* and *La Razón* in the afternoon field. The news boys only got a bigger commission for selling it.

Propaganda was only one of the many facets of the German penetration. There were German names on scores of business houses in the capital—although during the final year of the war many of the owners insisted they were Swiss. There were such giant enterprises as Siemens and Farben and also little candy and stationery shops. Their tea rooms and restaurants were always crowded, and all during the war, certain ones continued to print their menus in German, English and Spanish. Probably the most attentive and best educated waiters in the world were in Buenos Aires in the early 1940's. It was surprising to see so many blonds among them and so many who could speak to us in English, then switch to German at another table and into Spanish at a third. They were the most accomplished waiters I ever encountered, and so solicitous too. They always hovered near our table, presumably on the alert to bring another bottle of wine or an extra cup of coffee.

American sailors entering port were usually warned to stay away from certain restaurants in Buenos Aires because they were either enemy owned, had German waiters or many customers of known Axis sympathies. As a matter of fact, the Germans had developed such a penchant for waiting tables and tending bar, that before Pearl Harbor they were working even in the American Club. They never disappeared from many of the first-class restaurants and hotels, even after the American republics agreed to break relations with the Axis at the Rio de Janeiro Conference. They were in waterfront dives most likely to be frequented by visiting seamen, as well as in tea houses patronized by talkative ladies.

For a man willing to serve the Feuhrer as well as the customer, there was many a choice spot in Buenos Aires. An ideal one was a tea room and cocktail lounge on the top floor of one of the tallest buildings in town and located near the waterfront. The view was magnificent, and there were wide plate glass windows which afforded a sweeping picture of the great port area. There was also a wide balcony on which it was possible to get an even more detailed sight of ships being loaded or entering or leaving port. Leonard and I often visited there on our day off to admire the superb view. We could see ships miles out in the River Plate. A man with sharp eyes and ears would have had little difficulty in obtaining a fair idea of the shipping situation from that spot alone. The view from the German Embassy, likewise near the waterfront and in a tall building, was also said to be excellent, although Leonard and I never ventured there to find out for ourselves.

Then there was Tigre, a vast, middle-class Venice about eighteen miles out of Buenos Aires and one of the loveliest spots in the republic. This area is made up of thousands of willow-covered islands which form the great delta of the Paraná River. It is a most popular recreation area for white-collar workers, eager to escape to the seclusion of *recreos* (small inns) each occupying an individual island. Motor launches ply through the green maze of islands, picking up mail of the permanent residents and depositing visiting week-enders. Leonard and I were entranced with Tigre on our first trip. As we didn't know one island *recreo* from another, we decided that we would visit the Isla de Flores because it had the prettiest name.

We boarded a launch along with several other persons. During the course of the voyage, some of our fellow passengers began to speak in German. It took tremendous will power to avoid staring at them and speculating aloud over whether they were secret agents, escaped crew members of the *Graf Spee* or mere parachutists. They paid little attention to the scenery. In due time, the *capitán* of the launch stopped under the willows of one island which had great flowering plants of blue hydrangea growing along the banks. He told us that we were at the Isla de Flores. The returning boat would be there in an hour and a half. We hurried off the launch, our fellow German passengers right after us. I had the sinking feeling that maybe we were walking into a trap and wondered if my battered body would ever be found in this secluded spot. Or even if I would ever be missed. But Leonard and I ventured into the *recreo* and sat down at one of the few vacant tables. Families of respectable-looking blonds were all around us, a momentary comfort until I adjusted my ears for eavesdropping and found I couldn't understand a word—for all of the talk was in German. When the blue-eyed, light-haired waiter came to our table, we asked for a beverage—in bottles.

There was a stroll around the island, ostensibly to admire the flowers. Leonard accused me of really trying to find a radio transmitter hidden in the willows. He muttered something nasty about having married a "melodramatic snoop" and steered me away to the landing stage to await the first launch back.

But two years later the Argentine government confirmed my suspicions with the arrest of Bernardo Carlos Andrés Hingst, a fifty-six-year-old German, for operating a clandestine radio transmitter on his island in the Tigre. Only the vagueness of the police in failing to name the island kept me from attempting to trace it down, for in subsequent journeys to other islands on the Tigre we found many other *recreos* operated and patronized by Germans.

Unlike the British community which shrank as the war went on because so many of its young people volunteered for the various services, the German population gave every indication of growing. There was sound reason for this too. As the other American republics broke relations with the Axis, the various German agents in them found their health could best be preserved in a latitude between twenty and fifty degrees south, preferably east of the Andes.

By the time all of the Axis agents had congregated in Argentina, there were so many of them that they began to spy on each other as well as the Allies.

The British blockade in the Atlantic prevented the Germans from returning to their Fatherland in any great numbers. Apart from that, however, was the German conception that its colonies could be far more useful to gather information and spread propaganda in the foreign countries.

The United States and Great Britain, who were losing valuable shipping and many lives in the Atlantic because of the submarine tip-off system operating in Argentina, were forced to set up counter-espionage.

In February, 1943, Leonard and I ran into the first of several Yankee "newspapermen," better noted for their high standard of living than for their devotion to the typewriter. We met him while we were in Mendoza on vacation. He was staying at our hotel, eating in the best restaurants, and had already been there for weeks on assignment for a news service we'd never heard of before. When this handsome, young man introduced himself, we eagerly wanted to know just what kind of news he could be covering in Mendoza that would support him in such fine style. He was pretty vague about it, and for the next several days we hardly let the poor young man out of our sight in our eagerness to find out exactly what was happening in that wine-producing town so important that an American agency would find it necessary to send a correspondent down by plane and keep him there for weeks. Our suspicions were futher aroused when I asked him about some of the newspaper people in the part of Texas he said he was from. He didn't know any of the ones I had known. "There's more to this than meets the eye," we agreed, and there was. How much more we discovered when a friend of ours was arrested in Buenos Aires some months after our vacation and a short while after the military coup.

We had introduced the friend, a European refugee, to our mysterious young man in Mendoza and we learned eventually that we had thereby given aid and comfort to an American intelligence agent. This was confirmed when our young man of Mendoza left Buenos Aires hurriedly after the arrest of our European friend.

This episode brought the Argentine secret police to the door of our modest apartment on Calle Tucumán. Leonard had stayed home from the United Press that day with a bad cold, and when the doorbell rang I went to answer it. A little blond man demanded to see Señor Greenup and kept on insisting until Leonard came to the door in an old bathrobe.

The blond fellow asked Leonard if he knew Señor T——, our European refugee friend, and Leonard said that he did. Then Leonard was asked if he had recently lent our friend some money. Leonard immediately asked what right the blond man had to ask questions and was shown a leather booklet with "chauffeur" stamped on the outside and the man's picture and a cheap-looking badge inside that declared the holder to be an Argentine police agent. However, Leonard thought the badge looked like something that might have been picked up in the five and ten and courteously informed the blond that he would be ready and willing to answer all questions if the man would appear at the United Press office the following day with his credentials. The blond replied he would do that and left. We closed the door convinced that we had just been talking to a member of the German spy ring and that our poor friend from Europe must have fallen into the clutches of the local Nazis. Soon, however, the doorbell rang again and the little blond was back with a big policeman from the neighborhood beat, a strapping fellow in blue uniform and white arm bands. The policeman advised Leonard politely that the blond was an *agente* and that

Leonard had better get dressed and go quietly with him to head-quarters. I was nearly frantic. Everything that I had heard about people being arrested and disappearing in the jails, never to be seen again, came rushing in on me, and while Leonard was dressing I demanded to know the exact address and the department of the police station to which he was being taken. I also dashed out and called in our English friends who lived in the apartment across the hall. This man also questioned the police as to where Leonard would be taken and jotted it down carefully. I will never forget how I felt when Leonard marched angry and forlorn and half-sick off to jail. I was so excited that when the English neighbors gave me a water tumbler of sherry I drank it under the impression it was tea and didn't become aware it wasn't until sometime afterwards.

Meanwhile, believing that the time to spring my husband was now, before he had a chance to be forgotten and decay in Villa Devoto prison, I telephoned the night editor of the *Herald* who had many friends in the government. Leonard was back in less than an hour.

He had been taken by taxi to the Central Police Station and hustled into the office of the chief of the secret police. While waiting for the chief to appear, Leonard noticed the papers on the man's desk and was dumbfounded to see a dossier nearly two inches thick and labeled with the name of our refugee friend. Leonard wasted no time in explaining to the chief—who was a very suave character—that he had merely lent our friend some money to help him get established in a new job in a neighboring country. Thank goodness, Leonard has an honest face, and he was turned loose after signing a sworn statement. The chief, who was amazed that Leonard had no receipt for the loan, parted with a friendly admonishment that it was not good practice to lend money without having some record of the transaction.

Our friend remained in jail and we were so alarmed by the afternoon's proceedings that we expected our apartment would be raided the moment we left it. So that night we stayed home and built a bonfire in the bath tub. We had dozens of 9 x 12 negatives and prints taken during Colonel Perón's mountain army maneuvers on our vacation in Mendoza. We had excellent shots of Argentina's first ski troop units and some new light artillery. We decided that it might be difficult to explain to the secret police that these were nothing more sinister than souvenirs of our vacation. So into the bath tub they went and soon we had a blaze half way to the ceiling to the accompaniment of a whooshing, crackling sound as the fire spread to the negatives at the bottom of the pile. Black smoke came gushing out into the bedroom. We gasped for fresh air and our eyes watered, but we were afraid to open the window and let the smoke out and—most likely—the fire department in.

The days that followed were hectic. Twice we were visited by the wife of our European friend, who apologized for having been followed by *agentes* to our apartment and thereby putting us under more suspicion. But she just had to tell someone her troubles and explain what it was all about. She informed us that her husband had become involved in Allied intelligence work only after we had introduced him to the handsome young man in Mendoza. She admitted frankly that her husband had made a poor spy, he had been caught before he ever got paid. He should never have been a spy, she asserted, because he talked too much and liked to look mysterious as if he were carrying some enormous top secret. And he was always looking over his shoulder. We agreed that sometimes the unfortunate fellow did have the air of one carrying a bomb and also had a habit of peering around him suspiciously and then lowering his naturally loud voice to a conspiratorial whisper. But the local police considered him a spying menace so dangerous that he was kept locked in solitary confinement for a month, after having had his tie and shoe laces taken away so that he could not commit suicide.

All efforts by friends on his behalf ran against a stone wall of police silence, except for one influential Argentine who was warned that any further inquiries into the case would be ill-received. But our friend was luckier than most. He was let out in a few weeks and was escorted by police to a boat leaving the country.

Until then, the reports we had heard of wholesale arrests by the military government, the establishment of concentration camps and the formation of a real *criollo* gestapo in business suits had seemed too fantastic to believe. Things like that just couldn't happen in freedom-loving, civilized Argentina.

We knew, of course, that when the government was less than two weeks old the police had raided the Communist newspaper, *La Hora*, and all members of the staff had been jailed. But then Communists had been the whipping-boys in all of the South American countries for so long that this could hardly be classified as top news of the day.

One day an Englishwoman told us of seeing a strange sight at her suburban railway station. A train had stopped there briefly for water. She had first noticed armed police swarming over it, then she heard persons inside shouting and screaming. Some had tried to leap off and were clubbed. She saw two women lie down on the tracks in front of the train and then struggle wildly when men in plain clothes removed them. Later we learned that this was the first prison train of labor leaders and other opponents of the military regime bound for the dread Patagonian concentration camp of Neuquén.

Otherwise normal and sensible persons began to warn us to be careful of what we said over the telephone. They told us to listen for an unusual buzzing sound, and if we heard it we could be sure that the telephone was tapped. Of course, I heard it every time I picked up a telephone after that. But it was generally believed that telephone lines of newspapers, news agencies, journalists and some diplomats had been tampered with. One publisher, engaged in conversation in English with his lawyer, had been astounded when a voice broke in, also in English, saying, "Will you please refrain from criticizing His Excellency, the President of the Republic?"

Our Argentine friends said that a true gestapo had been created in the country, almost a carbon copy of the German, and that some of the leaders had actually been trained by Himmler's men.

They told us of men dressed in ordinary suits who sat on buses like any other passengers until they heard someone criticize the government. Then the critic was shown a badge and told to go quietly with the *agente*.

We heard of *colectivo* drivers stopping their miniature buses in front of uniformed police to "turn in" passengers who had spoken too loudly against the government. We were warned by well-informed Argentines to refrain from discussing politics in restaurants and bars, to avoid hiring any servant who seemed eager to work for less than the prevailing scale.

"Don't say anything in a taxi either," we were told. A movie man warned us not to applaud the Allied victories in the news-reels. "Some of the ushers are government agents, you know."

We heard of one ruddy Scotsman who had shouted "To hell with Hitler" in a very belligerent tone in his favorite bar. The words were hardly out of his mouth before he was tapped on the shoulder by a fellow drinker, shown a badge, and escorted to the nearest police station.

None of these little episodes ever got into print—because of the rigid control of the press by means of the state of siege—but news of them circulated from one person to another as fast as a news-paper rolling off a high-speed rotary press. We seldom met a person after June, 1943, who couldn't tell of some such incident he had witnessed personally.

Several times Leonard and I noticed little disturbances on the streets at night of several policemen surrounding one or two resisting persons. Invariably we searched through the newspapers the next day to see what the scene was about but were never re-warded with even the smallest police item.

Karl Marx must have gasped in his grave many a time during the next two years; so many and so varied were the bed-fellows he was given by the Argentine police. They ranged from Daily Worker red to Wall Street white.

Before the revolution, we had heard several conservative Argen-tines view with consternation the Communist menace in their country. But during the course of the conversation it usually developed that their idea of a dreadful proletarian world was one where all of the nation's housemaids quit their $20 a month jobs to work in factories, thus forcing the *señoras de las casas* to wash their own dishes.

The police conception of a Communist, apparently, was just as broad. Some months after General Ramírez came to power, the police announced that any person found distributing "communistic" propaganda or making uncomplimentary statements against the government by distributing leaflets, or writing on walls, would be arrested immediately and sent to confinement in the south

(Patagonia). Persons caught writing *"Viva democracia"* on walls were jailed as Reds. Any person printing any type of anti-government leaflet was a "Communist." A labor leader who led his union in a strike was a "Communist."

Naturally some bonafide Communist party members were arrested in the government's red purge, but they constituted only a fraction of those who merely opposed the military regime's policies and were picked up as Communists.

One of the most startling features of the military government was the rapid growth of the police power. Uniformed police became more conspicuous on the streets of Buenos Aires daily. Traffic police were everywhere, even on side streets which hadn't had an accident in years. One year after the revolution, there were 18,394 employees of the capital police department, of which 12,502 were uniformed, non-commissioned agents. This gave Buenos Aires a force as large as New York for a city a third the size. Besides the uniformed police, there were the plain-clothes men, estimated to number several thousand in Buenos Aires alone. One excited Argentine woman once said there were at least fifteen thousand of these "gestapo" agents operating in Buenos Aires in late 1944, but others, more conservative, thought a figure between three thousand and four thousand more likely. A new factor was the federal police with jurisdiction over the entire republic of Argentina.

One of our friends—an Allied intelligence agent—bragged one day that he could almost "smell out" a member of the Argentine "gestapo." Of course, Leonard and I were all ears to hear the secret of his remarkable gift. He told us and it was disappointingly simple. Our friend automatically became suspicious when he spotted a husky Argentine man in a loose double-breasted coat, for *porteños* prefer them almost form-fitting. Then if the man in the double-breasted coat loitered on a street corner without ogling or making remarks to the pretty girls who passed, it was almost a sure sign that he was out in the fresh air for other reasons than his personal enjoyment. If he seemed to take an undue interest in the pockets of the male passers-by, visually frisking them for guns or petards, he was virtually convicted in our friend's eyes, but not quite. However, if he saw the same man in the same place at the same time the following day, he could be pretty certain that he was a member of the *criollo* gestapo.

Equipped with this information, Leonard and I began to look over street corner loiterers with a knowing eye. Many times we weren't satisfied to stare in passing, but circled the block and looked again. Leonard began to accuse me of developing some of the mannerisms of our ill-fated refugee friend—I was peering over my shoulder too. That was the time to get out of Buenos Aires and into the restful atmosphere of a suburb. And so we moved to Olivos, fifteen minutes by train from the busy city.

We were relaxing in this undisturbed setting when Argentina ruptured relations with the Axis. Communiques began to fly thick and fast, and hardly a day passed without some new and sensational disclosure of German misbehavior on Argentine soil.

Colonel Enrique P. Gonzáles, the presidential secretary, held a press conference at which he revealed the existence of not one but two Nazi spy rings, one working under orders of the German Embassy, and the other operated by a private representative of Himmler.

Before the official fury had abated, General Friedrich Wolf, Military and Naval Attaché to the German Embassy, and Rear Admiral Katsumi Yukishita, Japanese Naval Attaché, had been placed under house arrest, both suspected of being the brains of the espionage setups for their countries in Argentina.

In the midst of all this activity, it caused some surprise when Colonel Perón, less than a month after his country had broken relations with the Axis, paid a social visit to Química Bayer—one of the biggest German enterprises—where he was tendered a luncheon by the workers.

The next day both General Wolf and Admiral Yukishita were released. It was explained that their detention had been lifted "because their freedom couldn't affect the current police investigations; because of their diplomatic character; because the acts of espionage they committed happened *before* rupture."

Within twenty-four hours, however, the Argentine government—through its own federal police force—disclosed that General Wolf had commissioned one of his underlings, Guillermo Otto Seidlitz, to survey the coast of the province of Buenos Aires for the purpose of finding a convenient spot to land two spies from a submarine.

A wealthy German landowner, Gustavo Eickenberg, had been contacted, and Seidlitz visited his seaside estate about forty miles south of Mar del Plata. He discovered several appropriate places near the German's ranch.

Seidlitz, the police revealed, had been thorough. He had finally decided on the best spot and in reporting back to General Wolf had even given soundings and approaches. The site of his choice, halfway between Necochea and Mar del Plata, had another advantage. The spies would be able to pass through the German's ranch, before reaching the road.

Police officials said they had proof for their disclosures but that their work had been hampered by the fact that the Nazi agents "had apparently been warned, or taken alarm."

During the course of their investigation, which began with the arrest of an Argentine diplomat, Oscar Helmuth, as a German agent by the British at Trinidad, they had discovered that two entirely independent organizations were working for Germany in Argentina.

One of these was under direct orders from the German High Command and known as the Abwher (Defence). By far the most sinister, however, was the second group—the S.S. Controlled directly by Himmler and known officially as the "Sicherheitsdienst," it had branches in the other countries.

The police then indirectly admitted that the entire German S.S. setup in South America had its headquarters in Buenos Aires. South America, the Argentine police revealed, had been divided into two zones, the East and the West. Juan Sigfrido Becker, a thirty-two-year-old German, with no visible means of support, was the chief S.S. agent in Argentina and director of the organization for the East. The West division was under the supervision of a Heinz Lange, but Lange's agents had forwarded their findings to Becker in Buenos Aires for transmission to Germany.

Becker had first arrived in Argentina in 1937 aboard the ship, *Monte Pascal*. Then, according to the Argentine authorities, he had been able to get back to Germany clandestinely in 1942. When he returned to Argentina a few months later, he had the rank of a diplomatic courier for the German Embassy. His real task, the police believed, was to organize German spy rings within Argentina.

Becker proceeded to divide the Himmler organization in the country into three groups, each acting independently. The mastermind himself headed one group, while maintaining liaison with the other two. He named Seidlitz to direct one of these branches. Prussian-born Seidlitz had lived in Spain until the outbreak of the Spanish Civil War, then he had moved on to Argentina to become representative of the Central European Tourist Agency. The third branch was headed by Hans Harnisch, an official of the German steel firm of Boker & Co.

In the course of their investigation, the Argentine federal police discovered that the three agents had divided their activities, or those of their junior agents, into four subdivisions. The first was purely military in nature. Police said they found documents covering the United States' war effort and details regarding the organization of the Army. The second activity was in the political field, and here again the police discovered reports regarding both the internal and external political situations in the American nations. The economic situation of the various American nations was appraised in one division, and in the industrial, full reports were found covering the possible and actual output of U.S. war industries.

The agents had obtained their information by listening to radio broadcasts from the belligerent nations and from special agents. And many means were utilized to get it from Argentina to Germany, the police acknowledged. When the Condor and Lati air lines were still in operation, these were used. And after that, agents relied to a great extent on secret wireless transmitting stations.

The police, however, said that stress should be laid on the important part played by "crews of the vessels of a certain neutral country, who acted as couriers between Argentina and Europe for the German agents, receiving payment on delivery to any German Consulate in Europe, from where the letters were forwarded on to Berlin."

The common man expressed cynical admiration for the police achievement in discovering in a single month what had gone officially unnoticed during several years of "neutrality."

Gilded statue of Christ on a quiet street in San Isidro

One of the cathedral towers in Córdoba

Leonard's buoyant newspapering friend B—— was not the least impressed by these disclosures on the part of the police. He boasted that he personally knew of more German agents than had been arrested—that there were between four hundred and five hundred operating in the country. Leonard and I often smiled indulgently at B—— when he confided that besides his bread and butter job he was doing confidential work for the United Nations. Behind his back, we remarked that no one endowed with such a marvelous and uncontrolled gift of gab in three languages should be burdened with a secret, state or otherwise. But we did have to grant that B—— had the impressive air of a man who knew more than he was telling, even when his conversation flowed forth with the fluency of a brook in the spring. It made good listening, and invariably he had an audience about him.

One day he called Leonard aside—and for once spoke in a low tone. His customarily high spirits had vanished. "Your house is being watched," he whispered dramatically.

Leonard greeted the warning with more amusement than concern. "Why should anyone want to watch my house?" he laughed.

"I don't know," his friend admitted soberly, "but they're watching my house too!" It wasn't necessary to explain that by the "they" he meant the secret police.

At dinner that night, Leonard took obvious delight in repeating the conversation. However, he did not need urging a second time to join me in walking around the block to check on our friend's report. The night was cool, and even in the bright moonlight we saw no sinister personage loitering near our home or even on a street corner.

We chuckled as we looked around the peaceful neighborhood then shook our heads regretfully that a man as young and promising as B—— should suffer such hallucinations.

I suppose the incident would have been forgotten by the next evening if we had not had an unexpected visitor—the sister of B——. After a hurried knock, she darted into the front room. Her voice was shrill and her eyes terror-stricken. She was too shaken to talk coherently immediately, but finally we calmed her enough to learn what had happened.

Her brother was in jail, she said. He had been taken there less than an hour before. A group of men had entered the family home and searched it thoroughly. One man had taken her shorthand notebooks to see if they contained anything subversive. The agents had looked at the books, questioned the family and ransacked the house from top to bottom. Then B— had been ordered to accompany them.

We didn't see our friend B—— for nearly seven months, for he spent more than half of the year behind Argentine prison bars without a charge ever being brought against him.

From then on, every time we heard the doorbell ring we had the sinking feeling that it might be the blond *agente* coming back for another visit and perhaps bringing some of his friends. We even acquired the habit of peering out the front door once or twice during the evening to see if anyone was watching the house.

Looking back, this behavior does seem to have been somewhat melodramatic, but in 1944 in Buenos Aires it was a simple case of doing as the natives did. The Germans in the country were almost forgotten in the preoccupation with another kind of gestapo.

The daily newspapers were permitted from time to time to carry brief items on the arrest of this or that person for being a "Communist" or for plotting against the military regime. But the story was far from complete, and we had to depend on the underground press and word of mouth reports for most of the news of what was happening inside the country.

This was an ideal set-up for a Walter Winchell. The catch was that any Argentine Winchell who dared tell what was going on— in print—would have lasted just one day in Buenos Aires before being rushed off to an unheated cell in the neighborhood of the Strait of Magellan. As a matter of fact, censors were careful not to allow Mr. Winchell's comments on the Argentine military government to be rebroadcast or reprinted in Argentina. Drew Pearson's unfriendly reports were also taboo. For many months, Sumner Welles was the only American columnist whose opinions on the Argentine situation were considered suitable for publication within the country. And if the Argentines wanted to know what the press of the outside world was saying against the military regime, they often had to turn to the underground newspapers that flourished as the censorship cracked down.

What we heard, as well as what we read in *El Himno Nacional*, the organ of Patria Libre, the chief underground movement embracing several political parties, was disturbing.

The arrests mounted. The Argentine League for the Rights of Man revealed in the middle of 1944 that there were almost 2,000 political prisoners confined to concentration camps, prisons and jails throughout the country—the great majority held without charges against them.

The experience was almost as frightful for the families as it was for the prisoners themselves. The man arrested in his own home was relatively fortunate, for then his family at least knew he was being taken to a particular jail. But the police sometimes resorted to the cruel practice of arresting a man in a bar, on the street, or in a bus, and then prohibiting him from notifying his family of his whereabouts. Legal counsel was often denied. He was simply whisked away. If his wife should call the police to ask if he was under detention, it was not unlikely that she would be told callously that they had never heard of her husband. Occasionally wives had to learn through the underground publications where their husbands were being held.

Labor leaders, Jews and Communists were singled out for particularly harsh treatment. And if they were in key positions to oppose the military regime—such as officers in important unions—their fate was sometimes the lonely Neuquén prison, 1,000 miles from Buenos Aires. This was said to be an old, semi-colonial establishment, which had not been repaired in more than half a century, and was said to be infested with vermin. There was no drinking water on many a summer day. The food furnished the inmates was so skimpy that prisoners had to augment their diet with supplies from a nearby grocery store which had a monopoly on prison sales and charged exorbitant prices. Three men were kept in a cell designed for one, and locked there twenty hours a day, forbidden to do any kind of work and not permitted to receive newspapers or magazines. Visits from close relatives were allowed only once a week and then for ten minutes at a time behind double bars and in the presence of a guard. Some of the prisoners are said to have gone insane.

No visitors at all were allowed in the island concentration camp of Martín García in the River Plate. Although the island was designed primarily as a military prison, civilians were held there after the revolution. I knew of one student who was kept there many months without once being permitted to see any of his relatives. Some 150 workers, students, businessmen, lawyers and doctors were placed in a 720-foot square area surrounded by a barbed-wire fence and a heavy guard—the first concentration camp established on Argentine soil.

These isolated prisons, however, were not by any means the only dreaded places of detention. Some of the worst torture chambers in the republic flourished in the big Central Police Station of Buenos Aires and in the station of the provincial capital at La Plata.

The *picana eléctrica*, a spur of electric current applied to the most sensitive parts of the body, was a favorite method of torture used to induce confession. The widespread use of this instrument was affirmed in 1945 by over a hundred former political prisoners who presented affidavits to the court in bringing torture charges against federal and Buenos Aires provincial police. They said the electric spur was only one of the many methods employed to "break" the prisoner; two others being the staging of mock executions and the application of lighted cigarettes to the body. Some of the tougher prisoners were given treatments of the *picana eléctrica* day after day, as in the case of Cesar A. Cabral, suspected of contributing to the underground newspapers, who was tortured for twenty-two successive days. A friend told us of one of his employees who had been administered the *picana* so often that he had lost the power of speech.

Some persons were said to have died in prison as a result of this treatment, while others were permanently disabled or driven insane.

Before constitutional government returned to Argentina with the election of President Perón, the jailing of substantial citizens such as university presidents, newspaper editors, former national deputies and wealthy landowners had become such a common occurrence, that some of the Argentines I knew had already figured out one way to take advantage of the circumstances. When a man felt the urge to stay away from work for a day or two, he could do so in relative security—especially in late 1944. All he need do on returning to the office was to report to his boss that he had been picked up by the police as an innocent bystander in one of the numerous roundups and had been forced to languish behind bars until his record was investigated. Few employers cared to question such a story, perhaps feeling that "There, but for the Grace of God, go I."

The man who got out of jail after some months, found himself not shunned but a social lion—so eager were his friends to get authentic reports of conditions inside the various prisons.

Such was the case of our friend, the buoyant B—— whose several months in prison had raised his stature in the eyes of his friends. It was some time after his release that Leonard and I had an opportunity to hear his story. The most conspicuous change in B—— was that he was continually looking back nervously to see if he were being followed. We noted that he was pale and many pounds thinner, although, he said, his treatment had been better than most.

At first he had been taken to the Central Police Station in Buenos Aires where he had been questioned hour after hour under powerful lights. He was accused of being an agent for first one and then another Allied nation. After days in the police station where he had been forced to sleep sitting up in a chair with the lights burning, he, along with several other prisoners, had been bundled into a long, black closed truck. They had been riding in the truck for some time when they heard the sound of water. Panic spread among the men. They thought they were being put on the *Penguin Special*, the notorious ship used to transport criminals to the sub-arctic wastes of Ushuaia in Tierra del Fuego, site of the prison from which few ever return.

They were almost happy consequently when they discovered they were only being moved to Villa Devoto prison. B—— said he found plenty of company there, for there must have been a thousand political prisoners crowded into this single establishment.

He was assigned a small cell, but with respectable company. There were seven others in the room with him, all suspected of intelligence work for the Allies. His cellmates included a Jew, a Mason, a Frenchman accused of working for the Free French and other Europeans.

Some of the petty annoyances of prison life came to his attention immediately. That first night in Villa Devoto he was badly in need of sleep. But the guard had kept tapping on the hot water pipe near the cell with his keys, until the men inside had each given him a peso to keep quiet. At other times, the prisoners were denied access to the near-by bathroom until the guard had been tipped properly.

The "Allies," as he and his fellow cellmates came to be known, were annoyed and jealous to see the favoritism shown the German prisoners, arrested when several Nazi espionage networks were smashed. He and his new friends were allowed outside for exercise only once every two weeks, and then for half an hour. The Germans, on the other hand, were given three exercise periods a week of an hour each.

And while B—— and his "Allies" were crowded into a single cell, the Germans had been alloted large ones with only two men in each. These were adorned with large, colored pictures of Hitler. B—— was especially impressed with the activities of the former chief of the Buenos Aires bureau of Trans-Ocean, the German news agency. He had been allowed a powerful short wave radio as well as a typewriter in his cell, and the Nazi journalist spent his days copying down broadcasts from Berlin, at intervals sealing the copy into envelopes. As he finished each envelope, he would summon the guard by shouting, "*Otro despacho!*" A guard would invariably hurry to the cell, take the dispatch and leave.

Some favored German prisoners were even permitted to leave Villa Devoto for week-end visits to their families or friends. Those who did remain inside the prison walls did not fare badly either, for German women of the various organizations in the country regularly brought in cakes and home cooked meals and kept the Nazi prisoners supplied with clean laundry.

The treatment of the Communists was in marked contrast. B—— said they had fared much worse than his own cellmates. Two large *cuadros* (rooms) were alloted to the Communists, and there were about two hundred men in each of them. But in spite of this, they had managed to achieve some of the little niceties. For example, two or three Communists were assigned to give shoe shines to other members of their *cuadro*, and teachers and professors gave classes. B—— said that during the time he was in prison, the Communists held daily classes in Greek. One teacher was delegated to offer daily gymnasium instruction.

Inmates of Villa Devoto relied largely on food from the outside, and the Communists had devised a system for this too. When friends or relatives brought parcels of foodstuffs, these were placed in the community "kitchen," to be shared by all. A corps of cooks, elected by the Communists, had charge of preparing all food in the *cuadro*. The Communists also engaged in another enterprise. From the scraps of paper wrapped around the food, they issued their own clandestine newspapers, with a lead pencil substituting for a printing press.

It was difficult to believe B——'s reports of flagrant favoritism to the Nazi prisoners, but they were reiterated by Dr. Augustín Rodríguez Araya, former national deputy, who was held in Villa Devoto at the same time as B——. Months later, the politician brought a court action against Colonel Filomeno Velasco, the Buenos Aires Chief of Police.

Dr. Rodríguez Araya, in charging Velazco with criminal complicity in Nazi espionage in Argentina, said the Germans interned had been permitted to keep alcoholic beverages in their cells, and not only had they been allowed leaves but "sometimes returned completely drunk." The case of Enrique Neiling, a German agent, was cited specifically. Neiling had been permitted to visit his wife in June, 1944, at which time she had conceived a child, born eight months later and registered with the authorities.

It might be supposed, from the torture methods of the Argentine police and their sympathetic handling of German prisoners, that the Argentine gestapo was an exact duplicate of the German. That is not true. The courteous and unpredictable *criollo* element still emerges in the most efficient Argentines.

Unlike the policeman who some years back carried sandwiches instead of a gun in his holster and once offered to share them with one of our American friends, today's officers are fully armed and highly trained. But the men inside the snappy new uniforms fortunately have not been wholly transformed. One man, caught in a mass roundup of suspected Communists in Dock Sud, a working class section of Buenos Aires, was held for several days and then released. The prisoner was deeply touched by the unique farewell he was given by a police official. As he was collecting his personal papers, the policeman handed him two pesos.

"What's this for?" the man asked.

"I thought you might like a little cab fare," the police officer explained, "and I hope you'll remember this when you Communists get into power and throw me in jail."

THE CONDOR AND THE BULL

T HE STRUGGLE FOR POWER IN ARGENTINA IS BETWEEN A
bird and a beast—the wild and rapacious condor from
the cold high air of the Andes and the bull pampered
on the fertile east central plains. In their native habitats, these
strange opponents would never meet; but in twentieth-century
Argentina they are symbols and they are engaged in deadly combat
to decide the fate of the nation.

The bull, highly bred, docile and incredibly fat is the trademark
of wealth and easy living of Argentina's landed aristocracy; the
condor has been adopted by the Argentines who do not own the
land, or the houses, or the factories. In one place, it is only a five-
minute walk from the bull to the condor. That is the beautiful
Palermo Park area, where the bull is enthroned in an annual ceremony in the landscaped pavilions of the Argentine Rural Society,
and the zoo near by, where the condors wait in sullen, watchful
captivity.

I saw the condors in a huge cage, high-domed and strong. A
sign warned visitors not to come too close, for the condor is a
bird of prey. They were huge, ugly birds, fantastic creatures which
I imagined might have sprung from the mating of a buzzard with
a red-nosed fighter plane. I learned later that the big ones were four
feet from head to tail, with a wing spread of ten feet. An attendant
threw large chunks of meat into the cage. It was a gruesome sight
to watch these birds, with their bald heads flattened on top and
red wattles on their featherless necks above a frill of white feathers,
ripping red flesh from bones with their powerful beaks. In the
Andes, these kings of the air soar gracefully at more than twenty
thousand feet, dropping down to attack sheep, goats and deer
without hesitation.

The mighty bird has two weaknesses, however: he eats too much, and when he is gorged with food he is sluggish and may be caught readily; he is also a heavy sleeper, and hunters are able to noose him in the trees. In these respects, he bears an ironic resemblance to the Argentine poor he represents, who perhaps eat more meat than is good for them, and who are known to have been lulled by extravagant promises. Yet the condor is a grim and awesome talisman of the less fortunate Argentine.

The several organizations which claim to speak for the under-privileged Argentine make liberal use of the condor as their symbol. Typical is the Alianza Libertadora Nacionalista, most of whose members wear miniature condors in their lapels and whose downtown headquarters is profusely decorated with big reproductions of the bird of prey. Evita Duarte, who married President Perón before his election, had a giant bronze condor with outspread wings adorning the wall of her apartment; and massive condors set off the vertically draped Argentine flags at important nationalist and government-sponsored functions.

It always gave me an uneasy feeling to see the condor in the lapel of one of our copy boys. I remembered how easily the condors in Palermo stripped the meat from bones, and I treated the youngster with some respect. I had read somewhere that the condor could go forty days without food, if he had to, but I wondered with some misgivings what would happen if our condor boy had to go hungry for a day or two.

Actually, the condor youth were well fed, but even so they were as fierce as the super-eagle of the Andes. If you can imagine what several thousand politically-minded "dead end" kids could do to turn Washington upside down, you have a picture of the condor youth in Buenos Aires. They were pro-Nazi and they were in operation in the grim days when it looked as if Germany was winning the war. I remember one big "neutrality" demonstration on an afternoon in 1942 when Buenos Aires appeared to have been transformed into a "Strength-through-Joy" settlement.

Column after column of young men marched past me in perfect military formation yelling for Enrique Oses, the editor of the Nazi *El Pampero*, and for General Juan Bautista Molina, who once had been the Argentine military attaché in Berlin. Standing on the steps of one of the big Catholic churches on Santa Fe "reviewing" the demonstration was Oses, raising his arm again and again in a Fascist salute which brought an answering Fascist salute from the army of young hoodlums marching by. The youth army massed around the statue of San Martín, and there were seas of Fascist salutes as Oses and Molina made strong nationalist speeches. There were yells against Great Britain and the United States. It was a memorable throng of young men, ranging in age from about fourteen to perhaps thirty-five, but mostly kids without education or opportunity and with malice in their eyes.

The young condors didn't hit their stride until the revolution of June 4, 1943. Then, in Perón, they finally found their man. When Perón was still no more than one of Ramírez' colonels, the "dead end" kids began yelling for him at every gathering; no public function was complete without their chant of PE-rón, PE-rón, PE-rón. The name was short and catching. Perón was the incarnation of the condor doctrines. He was the poor man's ideal, and the condors became his loudest-mouthed tools. One group acquired a headquarters on the second floor of a building just half a block from my office.

I was able to see into the main room of this condor office while passing on my way to work. The walls were painted a bright blood red, and on them hung big pictures of Perón. The kids used to stand on the balcony of their office and throw pamphlets into the crowd passing in the narrow street. I have a collection of their leaflets, crude, brief slogans in big type such as *"Patria sí, colonia no!"* (Our Fatherland yes, a colony no!) Others urged "good patriots" to read the Nazi-financed publications.

These "intellectual" activities were a minor part of the condor curriculum. The nationalist youth were better with their fists and stones, and they staged belligerent demonstrations which the police watched with benevolent eyes. They were anti-Semitic, they invaded the Jewish district, smashing store windows and starting fights with Semite youths. They terrorized known democrats, and when the condors swooped in the streets, their talons were long and ruthless, the beaks dangerous. The bird of prey, awakening, screamed hopefully of political and social justice.

For years they had watched, as helpless as they were envious, the gilded lives of the landed aristocracy; now, under the astute urging of Perón, they tasted the hot wrath and the determination that might change those conditions, improving the harsh circumstances of their own lives at the same time it dimmed the splendor of the nation's traditional overlords.

There were potent arguments. It was a fact, under the prevailing economic arrangement, that a humble-born youth could seldom hope to earn enough in his lifetime to own an automobile, a house or the gadgets that people in the United States look on as ordinary tools or comforts; this was true, no matter how smart he was, how hard he worked, or how assiduously he cultivated his economic betters.

For instance, our twenty-year-old copy boy in 1943 had a good salary—for a copy boy in Buenos Aires—of eighteen pesos or $4.50 a week. On this he was able to eat fairly well, because good food was cheap, but it required a wizard's management for him to appear as well dressed as he did. He confided once that he bought one modestly priced suit a year, paying for it in installments of about seventy-five cents a week. By the time the suit was paid for, it was worn out and he had the tailor make him another one, also to be paid for on the installment plan. It sounded like a dreary little rut, and he didn't see much prospect of improvement.

The lack of adequate housing is a desperate problem for the condors. Rents have always been out of all proportion to salaries, and many Argentines, including white-collar workers, can't afford a whole apartment; they live with their parents or move into a tiny room in a boardinghouse, and thousands of families are crowded dangerously together.

Laborers, both skilled and common, fare even worse than white-collar workers. In a decree setting up the Advisory Commission for Popular Housing on July 13, 1943, the revolutionary government declared that 80 per cent of the families of laborers in Argentina were living "in one room." A recent census by the Ministry of Education showed 67,233 cases in Buenos Aires where four to five persons were living in a single room; 10,346 instances of six to eight persons; and 594 cases of nine to eleven persons crowded into one room.

The noted Argentine economist and statistician, Alejandro E.

Bunge, says that from 140,000 to 150,000 laborers' families in Buenos Aires—the ninth city of the world—dwell in *conventillos* (the Argentine equivalent of "tenement"). Bunge adds that these families are "reduced to living in one room and to paying from a fifth to a third of their salary for it."

An article published in *La Nación*, July 2, 1939, on the eve of the meeting of the first Pan American Congress of Popular Housing, describes the dwellings of farm workers in bitter words: "The common farm dwelling really representative in our country is that of the renter or share-cropper, a farmer without pride of ownership in the land, a nomadic share-cropper; the gypsy-like dwelling of our farms is frequently without glass in the doors or in the windows, with a dirt floor, without trees, without shade. . . . The common dwelling in Santiago del Estero is frequently formed of two mud walls set at right angles, and a thatched roof."

Letters to the tabloid morning newspaper, *El Mundo,* asking advice on housing problems are just about as common as letters in our advice to the lovelorn columns. Here is a typical example:

"We are six children, my mother and old grandfather. We two girls rented the apartment and we want the rest of the family to live with us, but the landlord says they can't. The room is big, and besides we have a kitchen. And we pay 40 pesos ($10 a month). Can the landlord stop them from living with us if it is impossible for us to get other accommodations?"

The housing editor advised the girls to bring in their mother and brothers, also to be sure to insist on the 20 per cent rent reduction ordered by one of the first military government decrees in 1943.

Fuel being scarce and expensive, the poor usually rely on charcoal to take the chill off the air, and during the winter months the newspapers carry many a notice of deaths from the fumes.

Most Argentines dream of building a place of their own some day, but low wages, high cost of land and the lack of cheap, long-range financing all conspire to curb the desire. We knew of only two persons who owned their homes. One of the reasons for the great popularity of the lottery is that ticket holders always hope they will win and be able to buy a house. There is probably only one other way they'll ever manage it: Some real estate firms sell a piece of land and with the purchase price give the buyers enough bricks to build one room. The family builds the room, moves into it and then saves for several years to get enough bricks for the second room.

The overcrowding and monotony of the single rooms and little dwellings in which the lower middle class and poor Argentines live perhaps explains the popularity and prosperity of the coffee shops, tea rooms, bars and movie houses. In addition, this need for "escape" has provided Buenos Aires and a few other Argentine cities with the most elaborate—and least expensive—machinery for recreation I have seen anywhere.

Dozens of clubs for the middle classes have sprung up around the attractive and parklike outskirts of Buenos Aires. They are better equipped than most of the country clubs I have seen in the United States. Since most Argentines do not have automobiles, the clubs have to be built within easy reach of the city by train or bus. The Club Gimnasia y Esgrima, for example, is twenty-five minutes by subway and bus from downtown Buenos Aires. It is said to be the largest of all clubs, with a membership of perhaps fifteen thousand paying a monthly fee of $1.25 for the use of the following: A swimming pool; fields for football, field hockey, and baseball; tennis, basketball and handball courts. In the center of the sprawling establishment is a magnificent three-story club house, beautifully landscaped with trees, hedges, flower beds and green lawn. There is a basement restaurant where the youngsters can have beer and sandwiches and make all the speeches and noise they want. Upstairs is a well-appointed dining room where the more staid and prosperous members are served by uniformed waiters, at lower prices than they would have to pay in a downtown restaurant. It is an ideal place to spend a summer day. Gimnasia y Esgrima also has a club building in the center of the city, equipped mainly for such winter sports as swimming, bowling, basketball, handball and fencing. A big dining room here opens onto a roof garden, and there is a library. Both here and in the country club house there are fine ballrooms. The large membership makes it possible to operate these large establishments economically, but the club also has many senior and honorary members who contribute large sums for new construction or use their influence with the government to get substantial building subsidies. Even so, there are many city dwellers who cannot afford even the $1.25 a month required to use these facilities.

Wages are so low that it requires an amazing combination of thrift and guile for the Argentine underdog to keep his family well-fed and decently clothed, even though badly housed. The Argentine woman has a small monthly budget and does most of her thinking in terms of centavos, not pesos. When she goes to an open air market, she buys fifteen centavos worth of one thing, twenty centavos of another, and haggles long over the quantity she gets for the price. I've heard women argue and cajole for five minutes to persuade a flower dealer to reduce the price of a few poppies from ten cents to five.

Little economies are vitally necessary on all things—even cigarettes and movie tickets—because until the military government raised wages through a series of decrees, the average skilled laborer wasn't making over $45 a month. In November, 1944, the government issued a drastic decree that henceforth no bank clerk may start at less than $35 a month, he must make $80 at the end of ten years and after twenty-five years' service must be raised to $112 a month. Salaries were raised in general throughout business and industry.

In spite of the increases, which have come thick and fast since 1943, Argentine workers say they haven't kept pace with the rising cost of living. Take Juan, for example. He used to make 240 pesos ($60) a month working for an American company. On this salary he was able to feed his family, buy one bottle of vermouth a week, two suits of clothes a year for himself and decent clothes for his wife and small son. He and his wife went to the movies once a week and they were even able to buy dried prunes and peaches, considered a luxury in Argentina. He managed to put away a few pesos a month for a rainy day.

Today, Juan earns 360 pesos or about $90 a month—his increase in salary was ordered by the government to give Juan a better life. But now Juan can afford only one suit a year and his wife almost never gets a new dress. They go to the movies only once a month, never get any dried prunes nor put any pesos in the bank.

One Englishman wrote a letter to the editor of the *Buenos Aires Herald* and signed himself "POVERTY STRICKEN." He wrote:

"I might point out that even 500 pesos ($125) would be considered a fat salary by many good, sound employees, especially Argentines, who can never hope to attain this figure. Of course you will say, 'but they live much cheaper than the English.' Of course they do, because they are obliged to. There are no whiskies *'con soda,'* or gin *'con vermouth'* for them. They have to be content with a humble glass of wine or the still humbler *mate*."

In Argentina, even death doesn't provide escape from the installment plan. When a member of the family dies, the survivors often find it necessary to make small monthly payments on his funeral. Whether it be funerals or automobiles, the hard-headed American businessman learns that all is not gold that glitters in Argentina.

"You must never forget that the Argentine market consists of three and a half million persons—not 14 million," was the advice given by an experienced Argentine businessman to a group of visiting Americans looking to Argentina as a market for certain mass-produced products. In reality, some ten million or more Argentines have no purchasing power beyond the bare necessities of life.

A scrutiny of tax returns sheds some light on the living standard and purchasing power of the people. In 1940, there were 67,094 taxable incomes of under 5,000 pesos. Taking into consideration the exemptions already deducted, these 67,094 persons had total net incomes between 4,000 and 9,000 pesos, and averaging 5,551 pesos; but about half of them reported total net incomes of less than 4,000 pesos—or $1,000.

Above that income level, there were 20,089 taxpayers with taxable incomes of between 5,000 and 9,000 pesos; another 23,039 reported taxable incomes of 10,000 to 49,999 pesos; and 3,899 persons had taxable incomes above 50,000 pesos. More significantly, the analysis showed that the aggregate declared earnings of the 67,094 persons at the lower end of the income tax scale amounted to 372 million pesos, while the 3,899 at the upper end received 447 million. I was shocked to note that in a population estimated at nearly 14 million, only 114,121 persons earned enough to pay income taxes, and of this number approximately one-third reported net annual earnings of less than a thousand U.S. dollars. The mass— over 99 per cent of the Argentine people—still lower in the scale

Roses for sale that even the poor man
can afford, Buenos Aires Feria

Men of business, Buenos Aires Feria

Bare and rocky Andes in western
Argentina

Plaza de San Martín and Edificio
Cavanagh, Argentina's tallest building

is the raw material of the condor movement, the potential haters of the bull.

The lack of purchasing power, so evident among the condors and the condors-to-be, is not noticeable in the luxury-loving crowd that lives with the splendid bull; they have the wealth and the power.

I spent ten wonderful days at the Palermo Exposition in 1941 as the "official" livestock editor of the *Buenos Aires Herald*. My ignorance of the finer points of the purebred stock left me somewhat freer, perhaps, to observe and enjoy the over-all flavor of the main event.

On the afternoon of the Grand Exposition, I watched the bulls on parade and the Argentine women in their mink coats; and with amused astonishment and perhaps some malice, I jotted down points of superficial similitude: The expensive fur wraps of the high-born Argentine ladies found their counterpart in the splendid, shining coats of the bulls, both women and bulls appeared much pampered, exquisitely groomed and well-fed. It was obvious, however, that the women were genuinely interested in what was going on in the arena, while the bulls appeared politely bored by this coming-out party for their four-legged selves.

Even before the appearance of the bulls, it was a considerable spectacle. For the last hour a score of riders from the pampas, clad in the picturesque white and black and silver-gadgeted finery of the old *gauchos*, had been showing how clever they were. It was a little like a rodeo you might see in Texas or even as far north as Walla Walla. These modern *gauchos* would ride their trained horses into the middle of the area, stop and look around almost disdainfully at the twenty thousand or more spectators sitting in the stands. Then a *gaucho* would break loose, picking his leather lasso off the side of his saddle and starting to whirl it out ahead and to the side. Racing along, he would watch the looping lariat so carefully that it seemed he was doomed to crash into the railing at the side. But at the last instant he would skid his horse to a whirling halt, throwing a shower of fine sand into the ranks of standees beyond the rail; then he would streak off in another direction. The *gaucho* had no steer to lasso and throw, but he gave a masterly demonstration of his own riding skill, and many times escaped injury or death only by the split-second command he had over his powerful horse.

There were variations on this game, so exciting, all of them, that I remember wondering how the final event, the parade of the prize-winning bulls, could possibly rival them for the crowd's appreciation.

There was no violence, no wildness and no danger about the bulls. Yet, when Mitikile Roan Velvet 2 was led slowly out that afternoon, his coat magnificent and gleaming in the cold winter sun, he got more applause than all the daring riders. Mitikile Roan Velvet 2 was the 1941 Grand Champion Shorthorn of the Argentine. As such, he received the sort of ovation reserved only for the great popular figures and the President of the Republic. For the benefit of those who had not already seen and recognized the great bull when he entered the arena, the public address system solemnly intoned the words introducing "Mitikile Roan Velvet Dos," and the clapping continued loud and long. It was a great tribute to Argentina's bull of the year.

Mitikile Roan Velvet 2 seemed partly aware of this. He was only a little more than two years old, but he walked with the portly elegance of a bull who has known a thousand cows. In the shallow sands, already churned by the big horses of the gauchos, Mitikile Roan Velvet walked slowly forward, his short legs forcing him to roll ponderously as he came, step by step, to the reviewing stand where the Acting President of the Republic sat, flanked by his ministers, the silk-hatted diplomatic corps, and the cream of Argentine society.

His head was held high by the trainer who led him, and his eyes were hidden by his own curls and the mass of rosettes he had gathered in winning his way to the championship over four hundred other Shorthorn bulls. Mitikile Roan Velvet 2 was almost incredibly fat and blocky, and he carried an astonishing weight for his height and length and his two years. Those factors had made him champion, but they were not the extent of his elegance. Mitikile Roan Velvet 2 had had a bath that morning. His grooms had come to him where he stood up to his belly in clean straw in the Shorthorn Pavilion, and they had washed him with soap and water and anointed him with olive oil.

They had brushed his long, curly hair until it was clean and sleekly lustrous. They had lifted his tail and scrubbed there, too, until Mitikile Roan Velvet 2 was immaculate. Then the grooms had polished his short, perfectly formed horns, where the number of his registration in the Shorthorn Breeders' Book was indelibly burned. And, for the last loving touch, they had carefully curled and arranged the thick hair above the great one's eyes.

So there was elegance but no violence in Mitikile Roan Velvet's make-up. His attitude when he halted for the President of the Republic to admire him was one of genteel well-being on his own part and a benign complacence toward the watchers. Mitikile Roan Velvet 2 had been bred to be a pleasant spectacle. He was a blue blood, and he had been pampered almost from the day he was calved. He had never had the run of the ranch but had been confined in a small pen, sucking the milk from two cows, until he looked promising enough to be brought into the big barn and given a private stall, where he could be fed and groomed and watered in luxury, until he was big enough to enter competition. He was fattened on bran mash, liberally doused with molasses calculated not only to increase his girth but also to give a championship glow to his long, thick coat. His head was tethered so that he could not by some accident deform his horns or mar their tips; an expert with a file and polish kept the horns manicured, as well as his hooves. From the day he entered the barn, he was never turned loose, but was led out carefully each day to take a little sun and get the proper amount of exercise. A veterinarian kept watch over his physical condition, and his slightest indisposition was cause for alarm.

You heard the President of the Republic speak briefly, praising this year's achievements in the breeding of the bulls. The Minister of Agriculture discoursed for half an hour on the trends in the world meat market and the prospects for Argentine beef. Mitikile Roan Velvet 2 was complacent about this. It was as if he knew that some lesser *cabañero* than his owner would pay many thousands of pesos for him, and that he would have a private barn, would increase his girth and his length and would have hundreds of well-bred cows brought in to him in the proper season. That his calves would inherit the pampas and that he would be pampered to the end of his days.

Among the spectators in the stands, there were hundreds like Mitikile Roan Velvet 2. They were men and women who had been pampered from birth, who had been fattened and exercised, educated and groomed and watched over anxiously. There were more mink coats in evidence than on a winter's day at New York's Fifth Avenue and Fifty-Seventh Street. There were men in the best imported woolens, with expensive handmade scarves. All of them looking well-fed and full of *savoir-vivre;* people with the knowledge of power in their faces.

You knew instinctively that these people, like Mitikile Roan Velvet 2, had a high place in the life of Argentina. They sat here in the best seats in the winter sun: the richest, the most honored, the best educated, the most traveled, with the most elaborate houses both in the city and on the pampas, and the largest expanses of the best land in Argentina. They had security and a definite function in the land. They ruled it. With their money and their education and prestige they dominated the country's economy and ran the government, keeping the taxes low and their enemies powerless.

To them, there was nothing incongruous in the elegantly washed and manicured bull standing here for the President's inspection. Mitikile Roan Velvet 2 was no luxury; he was an urgent necessity to their way of life in Argentina. As long as the country continued to breed—and revere—bulls like Mitikile Roan Velvet 2, these people had little or nothing to worry about; they could continue their existence as magnificent nomads. They could maintain their houses and apartments in the capital, they could live in the mansions on their great *estancias* for a few weeks in the spring and the autumn, they could go to Paris and the French Riviera—barring the temporary "inconveniences" of the war—and there challenge the rich Americans and the Maharajahs of India as the world's most prodigal spenders of money.

I had heard a story of how one rich Argentine family distrusted the powdered milk of the ocean liners and the fresh milk of Europe; so when they journeyed to France they took their own cow with them. The cow was late arriving at the dock, so the big trans-Atlantic liner was delayed in sailing; long after the gangplank had been hauled up and the last visitor sent ashore, the cow was lifted carefully over the side, and only then did the luxury liner move out into the River Plate. After seeing this gathering in Palermo, I had no doubt the story was true.

It is difficult to gather statistics on the enormous land holdings of the Argentine aristocrats, for the simple reason that the landed gentry themselves have made certain it is a virtually impossible task. They would rather the people did not know exactly how vast a share of the land is firmly in the hands of a relatively few men.

Some writers have overstated the facts of the concentration of land ownership, but even the conservative economist, Felix J. Weil, estimated in his *Argentine Riddle* that three hundred indi-vidual and corporate persons in 1942 controlled 20 per cent of the land in rich Buenos Aires province and that a maximum of 3,500 persons owned almost half of the same province. These people owned the land in huge "properties" or *latifundios* which in many cases had been incorporated to avoid paying inheritance taxes that might conceivably have resulted in dividing up the land. In 1942, it was demonstrated that 259 individuals held land properties averag-ing 47,000 acres each, and 41 corporations (in many cases consist-ing of a single family estate) had properties averaging 63,000 acres.

The trend of the past twenty years has been for these large properties to become still greater in size—and consequently fewer in number—rather than to be split up. In spite of the optimistic observations of latter-day writers, there is no sign of the breaking up of the enormous *estancias*, and the chances of a small farmer getting a piece of land of his own are held to a minimum. The big owners are not interested in selling, and the economic and political system in Argentina has always been so much in their favor that they seldom have been forced to sell. That is why over 60 per cent of the 452,007 farms, ranches, orchards, and vineyards, listed in the national agricultural census of 1937, were farmed by tenants and share-croppers; and why from two-thirds to three-fourths of the wheat, corn and flaxseed produced in Argentina comes from farms run by men who do not own the land.

In the city of Buenos Aires the concentration of wealth in the hands of a relatively few persons is not obvious; there is a large middle class of businessmen and newly prosperous industrialists almost obscuring the opulence of the landed aristocracy but not yet challenging its dominance of "high society."

It is in the open country outside Buenos Aires, in the provinces of Buenos Aires, Entre Ríos and Sante Fe, that the lopsided organization of the Argentine economy becomes most apparent. You note that many railroad stations bear the names of the greatest *estancias* and that the stations themselves and their adjoining livestock pens and loading chutes were built to serve the large estates. The list of stations on some railroad timetables reads like a social register; the best landowning families are there. You see that nearly all of the highways run at right angles to the railway and are there as "feeder" routes to bring stock from the big ranches and take supplies out to them. The lack of good roads paralleling the railway is an indication of a policy planned to avoid the breaking up of the land into small farms.

The great plains are uncluttered, except for thousands of head of grazing livestock, occasional mammoth fields of wheat, corn or hay, and magnificent clusters of trees set well back from the right of way and sheltering great mansions in which the *estanciero* and his family almost certainly live only a small part of each year.

These park-like installations in the centers of the big estates are generally many miles apart. Their isolated presence here in the great sweep of the pampas—which are generally fertile and well-watered—must always amaze anyone who has driven through southern Kansas. The contrast between the wide and empty stretches of the Argentine countryside and the loose-knit communities of prosperous small farmers of the mid-western United States is as sharp as can be imagined. Although the annual rainfall and rich soil of Buenos Aires province are similar to that of Iowa, a large share of the Argentine soil is used for grazing, and the vast wealth of the land is concentrated in the hands of a few rather than being diffused among many thriving little farmers.

The opulence of the Argentine landholders becomes most evident when one inspects a typical large *estancia*, which may range in size from five thousand to fifty thousand acres (some are several times that large). The *estancia* is first of all a place to breed and raise cattle, and this work is done with great efficiency on the flat or slightly rolling grassy acres. The most spectacular aspect of the *estancia*, however, is the magnificent residence and the park of a hundred or more acres which surrounds it, both being designed and landscaped by artists. The family and the many guests they frequently bring with them can easily be swallowed up in the larger mansions, which are furnished in luxury and grandeur. Flower beds, lawns, gardens for outdoor eating and big shade trees complete the picture. Many *estancias* have swimming pools, billiard rooms, and there is always a host of servants. Interior furnishings are often French, many of the main halls have marble floors and statuary, with fine imported rugs vying for a place with the baronial splendor of large, beautifully-marked cowhides from the *estanciero's* own great pastures.

Also in the park-like central area is a six or eight room house for the *mayordomo*, the local manager and breeding expert, who generally takes his orders from the home administrative office in the city rather than directly from the owner. In spite of the fact that the *estancia* residences are themselves like country clubs, there are energy and money left over to build actual clubs where neighbors can get together for polo, golf, swimming, dancing and horse racing. These luxury establishments are also open to the *mayordomos*—the Englishmen, Scots, Irish and Basques whose education, good taste and usefulness to the cattle economy make them acceptable for social fraternization with the *estancieros* in the country, although they seldom qualify for such honors in the glittering social life of Buenos Aires.

In sharp contrast, the remainder of the *estancia* population lives in misery, or on the edge of it, according to the local conditions and the generosity of the *estanciero*. These are the tenants, the share-croppers and the peons. The latter are the most numerous and the worst treated of the farm laborers. They work long hours at hard labor, moving and branding cattle and sheep, tending watering troughs and fences, ploughing and sowing. Their lot has been a hard one for generations, the leading afternoon newspaper, *Crítica*, has complained in more than one bitter editorial, "because they cannot break the stranglehold of the big landowners."

As for elections, *Crítica* says, "They are made on the *estancias*, and the peons are lassoed like cattle. Schools? For what? The peon doesn't need a school, that's what they say. All he has to know is how to ride a horse and be able to stay out under the rain and wind and bad weather; and at night sleep on a board with his body numb with fatigue. And he is broken spiritually and physically.... The Argentine *estancieros* still want to live in the past century."

Curiously enough, the ignorant peon until recently has shown little resentment toward the luxurious way of life of the *estanciero* class or to the bull that is its trademark. When the *estanciero* makes his occasional visit to his property, the peon opens the gates and respectfully removes his hat as he passes. And he delights in the big collection of rosettes which the *mayordomo* keeps in his office to show for the years his bulls have competed successfully in the regional and national expositions. The peon will go to any amount of trouble to help a photographer get a good picture of his employer's bull—making sure the bull is posed in the position to show off his fine points to the best possible advantage. The peon has always taken pride in the traditions of his work and generally accepted the miserable conditions of his own life as being part of the natural pattern.

It is, therefore, understandable that the *estancieros* hated Perón when he recruited the peon into the army of the condor, thereby changing the traditional system under which the peons—through their awe of the *estanciero* and their real economic dependence on him—voted like slaves to keep the landowning class in power in Argentina. Perón was able to do this because he headed the Secretariat of Labor and Social Welfare, through which he issued a decree establishing minimum wages of $15 to $25 a month for farm laborers who had been accustomed to getting half that, and also because he had nothing to lose by promising to break up some of the great estates into parcels for smaller farmers; yet, there was a genuine and urgent need that these things be done.

In the presidential election of 1946 the *estancieros* lost their feudal control over the political force of their hired hands through a ruse as slick as any ever employed by a presidential candidate. Perón said, for publication, that if elected he would divide up some of the land; then employees in the regional offices of the Secretariat of Labor went to work on the peons. They visited key *estancias* and informed the peons that, if they would vote for Perón, they would receive a piece of land free. The peons were invited to visit the regional offices of the Secretariat and there were encouraged to select a choice tract from a chart showing the holdings of their employer. Many peons could not write, and in such cases their names were written in for them, with flourishes, on the acres they had chosen. So convinced were the peons of their impending good fortune, it was reported, that more than one simple-minded laborer went to his employer and tried to sell back to him the tract he (the peon) was going to receive after Perón was installed.

The success of this cunning political gesture, which assisted Perón to victory, should not be considered lightly. It was evidence of the great hunger of the little people for the land and for a better life. Whatever his motives, Perón had prodded the sleeping condor towards the economic revolution in which the bull and his class may lose their domination of Argentina.

Even before Perón's promises of social justice, a revolution against the bull was moving quietly but successfully through its first phase. This was the industrialization of the country. Between two world wars, factories sprang up in Argentina. Establishments that were "shops" employing a few skilled workers before 1914 expanded into factories later, and the number of manufacturing plants increased by leaps and bounds after the world depression of the early thirties reduced international trading. The beginning of the Second World War gave a new promise to industry inside the country, and again it burgeoned. German submarines and the conversion of the great Allied industries to war work reduced to a trickle the flow of manufactured goods reaching the River Plate, and the unprecedented demand for manufactured goods in Argentina assured fat profits and swift expansion to the new industrialists. They turned out chemicals, textiles, finished leather goods, refrigerators and radios in quantities unheard of in Argentina. And in 1942—for the first time in Argentine history—the yield of the factories exceeded slightly the combined value of livestock and all other farm products. For the first time, the bull and the fields of wheat and corn were overshadowed by the mushrooming factories. Argentina became the consumer's arsenal of South America; and an earthquake rumbled under the Argentine economy.

Since the First World War, Argentina had enjoyed the fruits of a carefully balanced agricultural economy. Her beef, mutton, hides, wheat, corn and linseed found a ready market in the industrial nations of the world. She shipped these raw materials to England, Germany, the United States, France and the Low Countries and in return received the fine textiles and rail steels of Britain, the precision instruments of Germany, the processed silks of France and Italy, the watches of Switzerland, the steel office furniture and automobiles of the United States. She bought these mass-produced articles cheaply, and she herself was able to supply the grains and meat produced on the pampas at prices lower, if need be, than any other agricultural country in the world. But to keep these prices low and to maintain the balance of this semi-colonial economy, the men who ruled Argentina before 1943 were certain they must do two things: First, they must not build too many factories to compete with the incoming flow of foreign manufactured products, otherwise they might not be able to sell their own raw materials abroad; second, wages must be kept low on the *estancias* and huge farms that turned out the meat and the wheat, otherwise higher prices for their raw materials would again make it difficult to sell them abroad.

The obvious penalties of this economy were that its success depended on the maintenance of a low purchasing power and limited consumption of goods among the mass of the people, not only on the farms, but also in the plants which processed the meat and in the offices which arranged the transportation and sale of the wheat.

This system could endure only in "normal" times and as long as the "bull" men were firmly in the saddle of the government. It could be—and was—upset by the war which cut off the European market, and by the military revolution which swept the "bull" out of Congress and Government House and left an opening for a man like Perón to harness the political force of the "have-not" condors. The opportunity was there to offer a new way of life to the Argentines, to liberate the peons, to build a great nation of a hundred million people dependent in large part upon themselves and their South American neighbors; there was a chance to raise wages and divide the land so that it could feed a larger population, to develop industry so that it could supply all the mass-produced gadgets, the necessities and the luxuries wanted by the people.

Perón—perhaps as ambitious for Argentina as he is for himself—made the grand promises, and the struggle between the condor and the bull was joined in all reality. It remains to be seen whether the bull has been defeated finally, whether the people he symbolizes will give up their battle. The bull may have been pampered too much and too long. Perhaps his manicured horns will be unable to reach and tear the underside of the condor as he soars out of his cage to end his captivity.

THE CASE OF THE CLEAN BALLOT

DEMOCRACY IS BOTH A COMMON AND REVERED WORD IN Argentina. It is like raising a flag to speak of democracy for all the Argentines like the sound and the theory of it. Yet in practice it is different. Where the word evokes the solemn expression and the hand over the heart, the putting it into practice brings out the cynical twinkle and the raised eyebrow.

Democracy is a masculine prerogative in Argentina, where the women are not allowed to vote and men are compelled to do so. Such is the compulsion of politics that thousands of men once left their graves every election to join the great procession to the polls. The presidential elections, held every six years, sometimes bore a considerable resemblance to the day of resurrection of the dead.

To most Argentines, "elections" is a weak word. The politician knows this, and he almost invariably strengthens the word by speaking of "honest elections." He promises that if he is elected, the elections from then on are going to be "clean." If it transpires that he was not elected, he cries in virtuous indignation that the election was not "honest." But if he is elected, the elections henceforth are not apt to be any more or less honest than he finds convenient to keep himself or his party in office.

Since Argentina won its independence from Spain in 1816 and set up a republic patterned after the United States, an outraged chant of "fraud" has swept the nation after many elections. The historians say that more often than not the complaint was justified, for not until the Saenz Peña Law was passed in 1911 did the country have its first free and reasonably representative elections. Throughout a century the Conservatives arranged things so that they had a virtual monopoly of "democracy," but in 1916 the large middle class Radical party voted Hipólito Irigoyen into the presidency in the country's first honest elections. Twice again the people's will prevailed, when Marcelo T. Alvear was elected in 1922 and Irigoyen was re-elected in 1928. But the Conservatives became exasperated with the new trend and overthrew Irigoyen in the middle of his second term with a military revolution led by General José Uriburu. They resumed their rule by force and fraud, and their chicanery kept them in power until the military revolt of 1943.

It is a curious thing that fraud and violence have played such a part in Argentine politics for on paper the election laws seem letter perfect. The vote is secret, each man is required to vote, and he carries a document to enable him to prove his identity at the polls. In addition, elections are held on Sunday to assure the largest possible ballot.

The Argentine electoral system is somewhat like that of the United States. The president, vice-president and senators are elected by indirect ballot through an electoral college of 376 members, proportioned among the provinces and federal capital on the basis of population. The election of the 158 national deputies, divided among the different provinces and the capital according to population, is by direct vote.

Although there is now a movement afoot to provide women's suffrage, women in Argentina have never been allowed to vote except in special and extremely irregular cases. One opportunity for feminists was provided by the former governor of a western province, whose illegal exploits in winning elections make him a contemporary legend. He was a fabulous character who ruled his province like an absolute monarch, even issuing his own currency. As a matter of fact, the only people in the provincial capital permitted to use regular Argentine money were the British railway employees who were paid by the home office in Buenos Aires; otherwise, you couldn't buy even a loaf of bread in the capital with anything but the governor's currency.

The governor invariably rigged the election machinery to suit the needs of the year. In 1934 he not only permitted women to vote in his province but actually required them to do so. Women known to be his strong supporters were allowed to vote as many as five times, in five different districts—always for him, of course.

Before a man may vote in Argentina, he must have a *libreta de enrolamiento*, which certifies that he is of legal age. This serves as an identification document, and he must present it when he goes to the polls, as well as when he pays his taxes and makes other legal transactions. When conscripts enter the army, they are required to surrender their *libretas* to the government and are not allowed to vote.

The governor found the "safe-keeping" of the *libretas* entirely to his liking. He handed the books out not only to women, but to two- and three-month-old babies as well. Then on election day, he sent police around to each home to escort entire families to the polling places. For thus stimulating the civic conscience, the governor was rewarded with impressive landslides.

Old residents of that province still like to tell of the manhunts that took place in that area immediately before election day among men known to oppose the governor. Police would stop such a man without any pretext and take away his *libreta*. When this was returned courteously to him (always after election day) he would see that it had been stamped, showing that he had voted. When the federal authorities stepped in to investigate at the end of 1940, they found five thousand enrollment books tied up in sugar sacks in the municipal buildings, where they had been kept and "voted" in various elections. They were the books that had been taken away from residents of the province and never returned. It was no idle figure of speech when the governor said he had five thousand votes "in the bag."

An Englishman who was closely associated with the governor for many years told us how F—— had come to power by a highly questionable maneuver after he had decided he wanted to be elected governor because he couldn't make enough money as a doctor. During a political tour, the old governor was killed by bullets allegedly fired by supporters of the ambitious F——.

About a hundred persons were rounded up in connection with the crime, and F—— was charged with being a ringleader. He was put in jail along with some of his followers. While F—— was still in prison, elections were run off in the province, and he was elected governor. Charges were still hanging over his head as the votes were counted, but thousands of his followers formed a

procession to the prison, broke down its doors, and carried F——
back in glory to the governor's seat.

In "fixing" elections, F—— stands head and shoulders above most
Argentine politicians, but there have been countless other cases
of colorful dishonesty.

Some of the methods were explained to us by one of our friends,
a former student of Cambridge, who enjoyed recounting his own
election experiences. He claimed that in one election in Córdoba
province, he had voted six times for the governor, using the *libretas*
of dead *ingleses* (Englishmen). Party workers supplied him with
one *libreta* in each of the six adjoining districts, and he was paid
so much for each vote. When a man dies, the family is required
by law to turn his *libreta* over to the government, and whichever
party happens to be in power, is in a position to use it in subsequent
elections.

There are many refinements of electoral fraud. An Argentine
newspaper man once explained to me that "it gets in the paper
when a gun is used at the polling place, but the other frauds don't."

The little town of Calera, in Córdoba province, provides a
sample of the idiosyncrasies of Argentine elections. When the votes
were tabulated there not so many years back, the election officials
were astonished to find more ballots than there were residents in
the town—this in spite of the fact that women supposedly were
not allowed to vote.

In the beginning, Ruth and I were inclined to believe that the
stories we heard did not present a true picture of elections in
Argentina and that by scraping around and carefully selecting
election scandals in the United States we could produce a reasonable
facsimile of the political corruption apparently prevailing in
Argentina.

Our views on this subject were dispelled, however, by the cynical
opinions expressed by our Argentine friends when the 1944 presidential elections approached in the United States. They simply
refused to believe that elections in our country were honest, or
even relatively so. They reminded us of Tammany Hall, and they
shook their heads in surprise when they learned that soldiers would
be allowed to vote in 1944.

One army man remarked in all seriousness just before President

Roosevelt's election for a fourth term, "Why of course, Roosevelt will be elected. There are eleven million men in the Army and Navy. They are all government employees and they will HAVE TO VOTE FOR ROOSEVELT."

Prior to the 1946 presidential elections, when Perón whooped up class feeling between the capitalists and laborers and between employers and employees, it was also inconceivable to our Argentine friends that an American farm laborer could vote one ticket and his boss another. You see, this had seldom happened in Argentina, where rich landowners traditionally collected the *libretas* of their workers and delivered them to the electoral board to be voted the Conservative way and stamped properly, later returning them to their owners. When we tried in 1944 to convince our Argentine acquaintances that an American hired hand was free to vote any way he wanted in the United States, they just looked at us with an expression implying, "Why, you poor dopes, you don't even know what goes on in your own country."

We once explained this, or tried to, to an Argentine man, who had been educated in England and traveled widely. He replied, "I might vote contrary to my boss's orders, but if I did I wouldn't be surprised if I were called in during the next two or three months and told I didn't work there any more."

Force has played an important part in Argentine elections for years. At times men going to a polling place have been confronted by armed men who handed them marked ballots and told them to put them into the box.

Thus, it was against a national background of politics traditionally studded with bribery, fraud, guns and knives that the Farrell-Perón government in 1945 announced that elections for president, vice-president, Congress and the provincial legislatures and governors would be held sometime in the future.

The people's gratitude for the coming elections was mixed with forebodings of unprecedented trickery and violence. It was predicted that Perón would be hopelessly beaten in an honest election, and the newspapers, aware of the ambitions of the man, could foresee nothing but the most dishonest elections in the history of the country. From both camps there came muttered forecasts of much bloodshed on election day.

The 1946 presidential election, and the months preceding, were unique for a number of reasons. They presented the almost magical contrast of one of the most violent, one-sided campaigns on record against an impeccably correct performance of law and order on the day of the balloting. They saw, for the first time, the major established political parties of the country uniting for no purpose other than to defeat a single man. It represented one of the few times in the history of the world that a "strong man" ruler has allowed the people a choice between himself and his opponents; by the same token, the candidate was able to carry out some of his campaign promises before he was elected and used the government's money and resources openly in his campaign. Finally, there was Spruille Braden's unique contribution to democracy in Argentina.

So much has been said about Spruille Braden in Argentina that it seems incredible he spent slightly less than four months in Buenos Aires as the United States Ambassador; it seems fully as fantastic that any one man—in particular an American—could have stirred a nation to such admiration and hate as the Argentines felt for Spruille Braden in the summer of 1945.

When Braden arrived in Buenos Aires in May, 1945, he was the first American ambassador there since Norman Armour was withdrawn after the United States and most of the other American republics had refused to recognize the Farrell-Perón clique, which ousted President Pedro P. Ramírez following his rupture of diplomatic relations with the Axis.

To most Argentines, Braden's arrival meant: The signing of the Act of Chapultepec at Mexico City; and the last-minute declaration of war on Germany by the Argentine military government had convinced the government of the United States that it must come to terms with Perón. And the United States' insistence that Argentina be admitted as a charter member of the United Nations at San Francisco heightened the impression that the U.S. government had decided to accept Perón and his associates and to do business with them as a government.

In the months before these developments, there had been growing in Argentina a considerable opposition to the military government. It had expressed itself to a limited extent in the jubilant celebration of the liberation of Paris and more pointedly in the celebrations of the Allied capture of Berlin and the surrender of Japan. But it was largely an underground movement with no well coordinated leadership and no public voice. It had been suppressed so brutally that it had in fact never had the chance to crystallize. In part it had depended for encouragement upon the supposed support of the United States (even when that consisted mainly of scoldings administered to the military regime by Cordell Hull and President Roosevelt); and now, with Roosevelt dead and Hull out of office and the United States again sending an ambassador to Buenos Aires, the opposition felt its moral support abroad fading away.

Braden hastened to correct the impression that the United States preferred to deal with a dictatorial government rather than with a democratic government. His bags were hardly unpacked before he was declaring, for all to hear, that it would be a mistake to think that Americans were expending blood and treasure so freely upon the battlefields of the world to wipe out dictatorships, only to welcome fascism among their neighbors. The United States, he asserted, wanted to see democracy everywhere in the world.

Braden continued to sweep aside ruthlessly the cobwebs of Argentine misunderstanding. When Vice-President, War Minister and Labor Secretary Juan Domingo Perón asked Braden for planes, tanks and guns to re-establish the "equilibrium" of armed might in South America, Braden bluntly replied that the military government must first show its good faith by complying with the democratic and anti-Nazi commitments it had assumed by signing the Act of Chapultepec. When Perón wanted American correspondents to soften their critical reports about his government, Braden suggested that Perón could have a better press in the United States if he released political prisoners and freed the newspapers of Buenos Aires from censorship. That also was in the Act of Chapultepec.

Personal and diplomatic relations between Perón and Braden started with warm *abrazos* at their first formal meeting but chilled when the strong man realized the United States Ambassador was not bluffing in his demands for complete Argentine compliance with the Chapultepec agreements. Perón did grant absolute freedom from censorship for American correspondents in Buenos Aires and even allowed the Argentine newspapers to reprint the critical reports the correspondents sent out; he also released over a thousand political prisoners. However, he failed to deal effectively with German-owned business firms and industries, which the Argentine government was in fact patronizing heavily in spite of American protests.

The release of political prisoners and the new-found freedom of the press in Buenos Aires—even if only partial—served to recharge the energies of Perón's opposition, which also found in Braden's "undiplomatic" speeches an inspiring tonic.

Braden's presence had a catalytic effect on the opposition to Perón inside Argentina. Students, the middle class, the dormant political parties, professional groups, industrialists, businessmen and a certain portion of organized labor came out in the open to demand the return of constitutional government. Braden spoke frequently and scathingly—in public and private gatherings—of the weaknesses and vices of dictatorial governments but refrained from referring specifically to the Perón-Farrell regime. His office was always open to anyone in Buenos Aires. Student leaders and politicians came to see him. When Perón protested, Braden explained that he was the United States Ambassador to Argentina—which included the Argentine people—as well as to the Argentine government.

As a spokesman for democracy, Braden was becoming a real rallying point of the democratic elements whose activities in turn became a threat to the life of the military regime. Presumably that was the reason for a campaign launched in July to vilify the American Ambassador by connecting him with the disaster in which hundreds of lives were lost in one of the mines of the Braden Copper Company in Chile. Posters suddenly appeared by the hundreds on the walls of Buenos Aires. The heading on the posters was "Crime" with this legend: "Workers, unite against Wall Street imperialism. Braden means exploitation and crime in Chile." It was an obvious and clumsy effort to lead the Argentines to believe that Braden was the owner of the mine, with which he was not and never had been associated. Some persons charged at the time that the Secretariat of Labor and Social Welfare was printing and distributing the posters, but this was not proved. However, it was true that the police made no effort to interfere with their distribution or to remove the posters from the walls until weeks after they first appeared. Police likewise did not intervene during a public demonstration which had been arranged to discredit the American Ambassador.

Neither the public attacks nor threats telephoned to the United States Embassy dissuaded Braden from his policy. On one occasion, Perón protested vigorously to the American Ambassador against his speaking activities and issued a thinly-veiled warning. Among his followers, the strong man said, were thousands of *fanáticos* who adored their leader so blindly that Perón could not control them, and in consequence he could not accept responsibility for what they might do to "anyone" whom they thought was blocking Perón's path. Braden replied firmly that the lives of Argentines in the United States were protected by his government, and Perón must do the same for American citizens in Argentina, including American correspondents who had been threatened with physical violence.

At no time did Braden express publicly his condemnation of the Argentine government by name or single out any of its personalities for criticism. On August 28, however, following his appointment as Assistant Secretary of State in charge of Latin American Affairs, he addressed a meeting given in his honor by all Argentine and American cultural institutes, and there was no one in the overflowing hall who failed to realize that his subject (still unnamed) was the Argentine military government. Braden spoke about "the typical characteristics of what we could call the ways and means of evil life under fascist regimes."

"One by one," Braden said, "there appear...all the elements used by fascism in its stupid stratagems since the day of the so-called march on Rome: Subversion and disorder, organized by the government itself and using paid assassins under an honorable disguise... calculated and underhanded use of violent methods...violation of the law of hospitality which forbids any treacherous attack on him who is sheltered under the same roof...use of intimidation and threats against the precise persons whom that Government was under obligation to protect and respect..."

Braden received a tremendous ovation when he concluded: "Let no one imagine that my being transferred to Washington means the abandonment of the task I have undertaken. The voice of freedom makes itself heard in this land, and I do not believe anyone will succeed in drowning it. I shall hear it in Washington with the same clarity with which I hear it in Buenos Aires. I will know it is the voice of the Argentine people—their authentic voice."

What Braden had done in Argentina was not to engage in revolutionary plotting, or to offer arms and ammunition or dollars to promote a revolution, or to organize the resistance. That was not necessary, and he had not done it. All he had done was to speak fearlessly to let the people know that the United States approved democracy and abhorred dictatorship.

The voice of freedom was loudest in Buenos Aires a few days before Braden's departure in September when several hundred thousand Argentines took part in a gigantic March of Freedom, which the military regime could not interpret as anything but a rebuke for itself and the expression of a desire for a return to constitutional government.

A few days after Braden had gone, the government re-imposed the state of siege, arrested hundreds of students and political leaders, and clamped down so brutally that the indignant reaction forced Vice-President Perón to resign.

However, Perón was able to stage a spectacular return to power, and the nation again moved toward elections, which President Farrell had promised some months earlier.

The government openly violated President Farrell's promise, made at the annual Army-Navy banquet, that his regime would not support any candidate. Perón had the full backing of the Secretariat of Labor and Social Welfare. The Secretariat had branch offices in all principal cities and towns throughout the country, with large funds and a propaganda organization that a presidential candidate in any country would envy. The Secretariat used its resources of manpower and funds in Perón's campaign and among its lesser functions distributed pins, handkerchiefs and other small articles bearing pictures of Perón.

The remainder of Perón's support came from the Catholic church and two hand-tailored parties: The Labor party (organized by the Secretariat of Labor) and the Radical Civic Union Reorganizing Committee (*Unión Cívica Radical Junta Reorganizadora*), both of which were created specifically to back his candidacy. The local hierarchy of the Catholic church overwhelmingly favored Perón, who emphasized that his policies for the people's social welfare were based on encyclicals issued by various popes on this subject. A Pastoral Letter instructing Catholics not to vote for any organization advocating separation of the Church from the State was a direct blow at Perón's opponents, among whom were the Communist and Socialist parties.

The foregoing were powerful vote-getting organizations, but Perón was not content to test his strength with them alone. Two months before the election, Perón bought and wrapped up the presidency with his famous *aguinaldo* decree of December 20, which gave a general increase in wages to workers throughout the country, in addition to a flat "Christmas bonus" of an additional month's pay at the end of the year. The workers could have no doubt that Perón was responsible for the decree, the signature of which he had announced the day he left the government, and the campaign promise made along with the decree was that it was only a token of the things to come if Perón were elected. It was also made known that Perón favored a profit-sharing plan, not included in the decree. The benefits which did appear in the decree were in themselves spectacular: The wage increases ranged from 10 to 25 per cent, extending to all workers and employees except domestic servants, government employees and public service employees.

It was a tremendous bid by Perón for the presidency, because the decree purchased the support of tens of thousands of underpaid business, agricultural and industrial workers, probably more than enough votes to swing the election throughout the nation.

From the standpoint of the opposition, the decree was disastrous, for it left almost nothing for *them* to hold out to the voters. Of what use for them to campaign for "social justice" when Perón was already ladling out millions of pesos to labor?

Perón's opponents—the Socialist, Radical, Communist and Progressive Democrat parties—had heavy going from the start. This coalition movement, the Democratic Union, was born in violence. Police tear-gas squads invaded headquarters of the powerful Radical party November 14 and dispersed some five thousand persons awaiting a Radical decision whether to join the Democratic Union.

This did not thwart a favorable decision by the Radicals, and six weeks later the national convention of the Radical party selected Dr. José P. Tamborini as its presidential candidate and Dr. Enrique P. Mosca as its vice-presidential candidate, which other members of the Democratic Union agreed to support.

The democratic candidates were able, useful men. Tamborini was a physician, Mosca a lawyer. Both had served in the national Chamber of Deputies, and Tamborini had been Minister of Interior in the cabinet of President Alvear from 1925 to 1928. But they were "compromise" candidates, selected more for their ability to maintain harmony in the ranks of the Radical party than for outstanding vote-attracting qualities. Neither had they the crowd appeal or the personal magnetism of Perón, and they were in no position to match his sweeping platform promises of gains for labor. Their main plank—a return to democratic government—was designed for its intellectual appeal to the middle class rather than for rabble-rousing.

Added to that, they never had a fair chance to present their program. Police and armed thugs yelling for Perón took turns attacking and attempting to break up political rallies of the Democratic Union.

On their tour of the northern provinces in January, the Democratic Union's candidates were victims of an organized attempt to sabotage their campaign. No sooner had the candidates announced they would visit the Province of Entre Ríos, than the Federal Commissioner there published a decree forbidding all political meetings.

Stones were hurled repeatedly at the train on the journey from Buenos Aires to Santiago del Estero in the north. Between Santiago del Estero and Salta the train was attacked in Güemes, where numerous shots were fired into the train and some persons wounded. The candidates complained that wherever they stopped the police permitted small bands of young thugs wielding clubs and pistols to attack or disturb their meetings without making an attempt to intervene. They claimed their *peronista* attackers followed them from town to town in trucks, stirring up trouble wherever they attempted to hold meetings.

When the train bearing the Democratic Union candidates returned from its tour of the provinces, it bore evidence of a journey through fear—smashed windows, bullet holes and a burned-out baggage car. By contrast, Perón's tour of the country was remarkably free from violence.

An unknown number of persons—variously estimated at from thirty-five to one hundred—died in attacks by police and Perón supporters on gatherings of the Democratic Union. Police protection was virtually non-existent for Perón's opponents.

Four months before the election, the government announced the lifting of all restrictions on political parties by abolishing a decree issued by President Ramírez in December, 1943, which had dissolved all political parties. In theory the new decree left the parties free to function, but in practice the government still maintained the state of siege under which it could break up any political meeting and arrest the participants. The state of siege remained in effect until forty-eight hours before the elections.

Two weeks before the election of February 24, 1946, the U.S. State Department exploded a bombshell in the hemisphere by publishing its document known as the "Blue Book," officially entitled *Consultation among the American Republics with Respect to the Argentine Situation*.

The "Blue Book" was a thoroughly damning indictment of the Argentine military regime and the Castillo government that preceded it. Based on a study of German and Italian documents and interrogation of German and Italian officials who handled "activities in and with Argentina," the "Blue Book" listed these main charges:

"1. Members of the (Argentine) military government collaborated with enemy agents for important espionage and other purposes damaging to the war effort of the United Nations.

"2. Nazi leaders, groups and organizations have combined with Argentine totalitarian groups to create a Nazi-Fascist state.

"3. Members of the military regime who have controlled the government since June, 1943, conspired with the enemy to undermine governments in neighboring countries (Bolivia, Brazil, Chile, Paraguay and Uruguay) in order to destroy their collaboration with the Allies and in an effort to align them in a pro-Axis bloc.

"4. Successive Argentine governments protected the enemy in

economic matters in order to preserve Axis industrial and commercial power in Argentina."

Other highlights of the "Blue Book" were: "Solemn pledges to
cooperate with the other American republics were completely
breached and are proved to have been designed to protect and
maintain Axis interests in Argentina. The policies and actions of
the recent regimes in Argentina were aimed at undermining the
Inter-American system. . . . By its brutal use of force and terrorist
methods to strike down all opposition from the Argentine people
the military regime has made a mockery of its pledge to the United
Nations 'to reaffirm faith in human rights, in the dignity and worth
of the human person.' "

The State Department noted that on October 3, 1945, it had
begun consultation among the American republics and that all of
them had agreed to participate in consultation with respect to the
Argentine situation. "The information in support of these charges
is respectfully submitted to the Governments of the American
republics for their consideration in relation to the Treaty of Mutual
Assistance to be negotiated at the forthcoming conference at Rio
de Janeiro. . . . The question is whether the military regime, or any
Argentine government controlled by the same elements, can merit
the confidence and trust which is expressed in a treaty of mutual
military assistance among the American republics."

This 131-page document was diplomatic high explosive, and
news agencies worked feverishly around the clock broadcasting it
to the hemisphere. Newspapers in Buenos Aires printed the accusations textually, some of them even giving it half their precious space.
In spite of the newsprint shortage, editions were enlarged and
street sales swelled by the hundreds of thousands. *Porteños* grabbed
the papers so eagerly that the over-size editions sold out every copy,
except the ones the editors needed for their archives.

Citizens of Argentina, even though they had known long where
the sympathies of their military rulers lay during the war, were
amazed by the scope and the careful detail of the "Blue Book"
accusations. They were also stunned by the manner in which the
United States had laid the Argentine case before the hemisphere.
Crítica commented on "the profound consternation and stupefaction" resulting in all the countries of America. The important

morning tabloid, *El Mundo*, said in an editorial: "The Blue Book produced in us a feeling of confusion, stupefaction and shame. In view of the impression caused by these revelations, we cannot hazard a guess about what sanctions public opinion will decree against those who wished to deliver our country to the enemies of humanity. What is certain is that we are being stigmatized abroad for the faults of those who, blinded by the totalitarian mirage, compromised the prestige of our country." Other pro-democratic newspapers commented in a similar if more restrained vein.

For some time to come, it may be debated whether the purpose of the "Blue Book" was to influence the outcome of the Argentine elections or to restate clearly and unequivocally to the other American republics the policy of the State Department, which had previously shifted erratically its position regarding Argentina. Its dramatic appearance just two weeks before the elections convinced many that it was intended to alienate Argentine voters from Perón. However, the politicians had all but concluded their campaigns. James A. Farley once laid down the political axiom that what happens during the last thirty days of any campaign has little weight, for by then the voters have already made up their minds on how they are going to vote. The political effects of the "Blue Book"—if any—probably were confined largely to Buenos Aires. The bulk of the newspapers of the interior, where the election was eventually decided, lacked the resources to reprint the text of the "Blue Book," and the persons who subscribed to the great dailies of Buenos Aires were most likely the type of landowning or professional groups who already were unalterably opposed to Perón on the basis of his record inside the country. For most of them, as well as for the Argentines who worshipped Perón, the issue had always been simple: Perón the man, Perón the exponent of "share the profits," Perón of the *aguinaldo*; not Perón the internationalist.

Perón was astute enough to realize this. He had concentrated his campaign artillery on domestic issues. His ventures into the international field had been entirely defensive, and his views on international matters were mostly designed for export to his neighbors. He had assumed the pose of a man being "persecuted" by the Democratic Union and Spruille Braden; in public, he had always interpreted United States' opposition to him as not the sentiment of the people or the government of the United States, but the result solely of Spruille Braden's "hatred" of Perón. It was a policy mainly designed not to win votes but to keep from losing them. It was typical of the candidate that he did not change his tactics as the result of the "Blue Book." His reply to the "Blue Book" was a "Blue and White Book" which was a careless, undetailed and un-inspired statement that the "Blue Book" was a pack of lies cooked up by a single man who hated Perón. As one of the more observant political commentators in Buenos Aires immediately noted, the "Blue and White Book" was a "low caliber" document which did not show the imprint of the "first-class brain" that Perón undeniably possessed. It could be assumed, therefore, that Perón had not even taken the trouble to draft the "Blue and White Book" himself or to concern himself with it very seriously.

Perón's personal reply to the "Blue Book" was made in a speech February 12, on the occasion of the "official proclamation" of his candidacy for the presidency. In a double-barrelled attack on Braden and the Democratic Union, Perón told his supporters that "Braden gave shape, courage and directives to the amorphous political organism that opposes us. He implacably and systematically depreciated the revolution of June 4, 1943, its men, and myself in particular.... Braden is the inspirer, creator, organizer and true head of the Democratic Union.... Braden wished to establish in Argentina his own government or a puppet government, and for that purpose he began to secure the cooperation of all the available quislings."

Perón also spoke of Braden's "active, deep and insolent intervention in the internal politics of our country." Then, putting the finishing touch on his portrait of a poor *criollo* boy fighting single-handed against the "Colossus of the North," as represented by the former American ambassador, Perón said that in return for Braden's "powerful" friendship, all the Argentine "quislings" had to do was to make a "declaration of hate for my humble person."

This was good politics. It has frequently been smart political practice, in the majority of the Latin American countries, for a candidate to shy away from an entangling friendship with the United States and better still to denounce "Yankee imperialism," "economic strangulation by Wall Street," and other vague threats of domination from the north. So there was nothing new in Perón's denunciation except the Braden twist. This time, Braden was the perfect symbol, a big and fittingly "tough" incarnation of "Yankee imperialism."

The leaders of the Democratic Union, meanwhile, felt that in spite of all the obstacles thrown into their path by the police, the government and Perón's hooligans, they had succeeded in reaching the people with the message that they must choose between "dictatorship" and "democracy." They were convinced that the people, if they had a chance in honest balloting, would repudiate Perón and his ideas by an overwhelming majority. Significantly, however, they were almost certain that there would be widespread violence at the polls and fraud in the counting, and that in consequence the outcome would be amply discredited before the rest of the nations of the hemisphere.

At this point, in stepped General Carlos von der Becke, Commander-in-Chief of the Argentine Army, to reiterate the Army's promise that the elections would be orderly and honest. Von der Becke, as chairman of the Electoral Coordinating and Executive Committee, assigned the bulk of the army, navy and air force troops to preserve order at the polling places, asserting that their guns would assure the sanctity of the will of the Argentine people. He kept his promise to the letter. Soldiers with fixed bayonets paced up and down outside each polling place, and more soldiers with rifles stood inside.

There was no violence on election day. By evening the soldiers had carried the sealed ballot boxes through the quiet, almost deserted streets and deposited them in legislative halls for safekeeping. Then to the Argentines came the stunning realization that they had just taken part in completely honest balloting.

This phenomenon so overjoyed the leaders of the Democratic Union that they put their full seal of approval on the elections, claiming that they had won in a landslide; in fact, the first few thousand returns indicated that they were well ahead. Dr. Tamborini told reporters he was sure he had won, and one leader of the Radical party confirmed, "There has been no fraud today." The influential democratic daily, *La Prensa*, observed in awe that the election had been "perfect"—a phrase seldom if ever used before by a responsible newspaper in describing any Argentine election. Other papers, both pro- and anti-Perón, gave a similar verdict.

When the returns trickled in slowly in the days that followed, Perón was shown to have won the presidency by getting approximately 55 per cent of the total popular vote; and of the country's 376 electoral votes, he received 304 against the Democratic Union's 72. It was said to be the greatest electoral vote landslide in Argentine history. Perón supporters won the governorships of all provinces, a majority of 109 to 49 in the Chamber of Deputies and all 30 seats in the Senate. The Socialist party, formerly one of the strongest political forces in Buenos Aires, was eliminated from the Congress for the first time in 34 years, and the Communists likewise failed to win a single seat. The Radical party, once the most powerful in the nation, was relegated to the lower-house minority with 44 seats.

To all the criticism that had been levelled at Perón and the military regime by opponents both at home and abroad, this sweeping victory for Perón seemed to supply the perfect answer. In any case, after the results became known, it was too late for the Democratic Union to resist or to claim "fraud." Its leaders had given the election a clean bill of health on the night of February 24, when they had overlooked the constant violence against themselves during the campaign, as well as the skilful manner in which Perón had loaded the dice with his *aguinaldo* decree, and the government's flagrant support of the colonel. They had thoroughly burned all their bridges behind them. The colonel had become the constitutional president of the Argentines.

The mystery of how the veteran leaders of the Democratic Union came to commit political suicide on election night may never be cleared up fully. There is, however, a story of a priest who once went to the polling place, which may contribute valuable evidence. The election board official refused to give him a ballot, saying, "But father, our records show that you have already voted."

The priest, astonished but polite, replied, "I beg your pardon, but that is impossible because I have not been here before." But the official stuck to his position that the priest had voted some hours earlier.

The clergyman, finally realizing that the men on the election board had already used his ballot for the candidate of their choice, shrugged his shoulders in defeat and left the table. As he passed through the door, he was heard to say in a voice of wonder, "Well, I've been a priest in this town for twenty years and I have seen many strange things. But this is the first miracle in my life."

Likewise, perhaps, the opponents of Perón had been blinded by a miracle—an honest ballot in Argentina.

PERON, LATIN SUPERMAN

ARGENTINA, LIKE MOST SOUTH AMERICAN COUNTRIES, HAS been swept off her feet in times past by strong, chieftain-type leaders known as *caudillos*. Men of action and strong personal leadership, rather than refined oratory and finesse, have captured the people much as the old-time *gauchos* robbed meek and civilized men of their wives and daughters and carried them off on their saddles to live like nomads on the unsettled plains.

For a time in the twentieth century it seemed that the day of the *caudillo* had ended, and that Argentina had settled into the routine of legal government and colorless leadership. But the new trend reckoned without Juan Domingo Perón.

The man embodies the greatest success story in Latin America today. He got what he wanted with fabulous swiftness. Perón came out of nowhere in 1943 as a colonel, by 1944 was strong enough to run the military government, and then wooed the nation to win the presidency by a great landslide in 1946. The man came up so fast that his story sounds almost unreal, like an accident in history. Of course it wasn't. Perón planned it that way.

The qualities that have intrigued the biographers of Perón have been his charming manner, his gift of gab, his endowments as a politician, his ruthlessness and his enormous physical energy. Yet his most spectacular asset is his flair for showmanship. It was a supremely valuable tool in building himself up for the presidency. The only way he could get and keep what he wanted was to sell himself to the people.

One of the greatest disasters Argentina has ever known gave Perón's genius for press agentry a heaven-sent opportunity. That was the San Juan earthquake in early 1944. Even before it became known that thousands had perished in the wreckage of the city, Perón was on the radio appealing for aid for the stricken inhabitants, and he kept up his pleas until the generous Argentines were contributing clothes, beds, food, medicine and millions of pesos to help the colonel's campaign. Perón departed far from tradition to help put his appeal across. With an actress on each arm he walked down swank Calle Florida to solicit contributions, knowing that even though he was doing what no staid member of the government would dare, his picture would appear in hundreds of newspapers. The San Juan catastrophe almost came to be known as Colonel Juan Perón's earthquake, and the publicity was worth more than a million pesos of advertising.

Perón's genius extended to organizing political and labor demonstrations, and he was accused with some justice of hiring young men to stand near the microphones at government rallies to chant his name so that it would be heard again and again over the radio, leading the listeners to believe that Perón had a giant following and would bear watching. Needless to say, he would.

One of Perón's greatest achievements in the field of exhibitionism saved his political career, if not his life. This was in October, 1945, when opposing army, navy, student and professional elements decided that Perón must be eliminated before he became a real menace. The *coup* forced Perón's ejection from the offices of Vice-President, Minister of War and Secretary of Labor in the Farrell government. Perón himself was arrested and taken to the isle of Martín García in the River Plate, where he was held while the leaders of the opposition forces set about organizing a new regime. While the new government was struggling over the hurdles of reorganization, Perón got back into Buenos Aires through pretending that he was seriously ill and required complete medical treatment. Once in the hospital, he quickly rallied his forces about him, and labor leaders under his spell called their men into the streets. The laborers, perhaps fifty thousand strong, gathered in the plaza in front of the Government House that afternoon and demanded to see their leader, Perón. They threw stones at the Government House and kept yelling in a frenzy so impressive that it was finally deemed advisable for Perón to leave his "sick-bed" in the hospital and appear on the balcony of Government House, along with other members of the Farrell regime, to reassure the workers. Perón capitalized on this to the full, even reminding his followers that it was only his loyalty to the "sweaty masses"—in which he included himself—that had persuaded him to leave the hospital. To top off this impressive scene, Perón ordered the workers to stage a general strike the next day, which was done with sufficient violence to discourage anyone rash enough to plot against his regained freedom and health.

In his campaign for the presidency, Perón indulged in practically all the tricks known to the American politician—from kissing babies to drinking cheap wine and soda with the workers in smelly, third-rate bars covered with soggy sawdust. In the past three years, he probably has shaken as many hands as did James Farley as Postmaster-General.

He personally inaugurated maternity wards, which is a little outside the usual ken of the Argentine politician, and even got down into ditches to dig real dirt, a procedure that is practically unknown to the Argentine government official. Perón also had pictures taken of himself talking with real working newspapermen, and on important occasions in wintertime wore the white coat of his summer uniform to distinguish himself from the rest of the crowd wearing regulation garb. Not content with breaking all the traditions, he also began speaking of himself as "Argentina's first soldier," "Argentina's first worker" and "Argentina's first airman," all depending on whether he was addressing a group of fellow army officers, a labor meeting or some of the officers of the air corps. Transparent as this strategy was, it served to lift him out of the ordinary run of army politicians, and got his picture printed and his name mentioned much more often than any press agent would have dreamed possible.

Perón's personal appearance was one of his greatest assets in winning fame and fortune. He is a handsome man, well and massively built, tall but so broad-shouldered that he seems of medium height unless you are quite close to him. If he has a slight paunch, he keeps it well concealed by his carefully tailored uniforms and street clothes. His carriage is military and erect. In a sports shirt he looks like a he-man. His strong, white teeth flash often in a smile, and one Argentine woman told me that if he was ever defeated in politics he needn't worry, he could make plenty of money posing for toothpaste ads. Another woman, perhaps among those who had fallen for the Colonel's charms but could not quite digest his politics, observed that surely Perón must dye his hair black, that it was against all the laws of nature for a man his age to look so young and vigorous.

The comparatively vigorous military life Perón has led and his rough-and-tumble days as a youth in the country probably account for his rugged physique. Perón was born October 8, 1895, on a farm owned by his father, not far from the little town of Lobos, sixty-five miles south of Buenos Aires. When Perón was five, his father moved to the flat, rather barren territory of Santa Cruz, later acquiring a sheep ranch near the town of Comodoro Rivadavia. This cold and desolate land of Patagonia, one of the most thinly populated areas on the globe, gave Perón the son an active life. At the age of ten, when his family moved with him to Buenos Aires to enable him to complete his primary studies and go to high school, he was already a strong boy. He later became an excellent horseman and was an outstanding recruit for the Argentine Military Academy, from which he was graduated as a second lieutenant at the age of eighteen. Passing through the usual military channels, he became a full lieutenant six years later, at the end of 1919, when he entered the Sargento Cabral Officers School. Here he concentrated on sports. He became a champion fencer, an expert boxer and crack pistol shot. His physical prowess tended to obscure his tremendous mental energy and achievement, and even down to the present time there has been a widespread misconception that Perón is little more than a gifted talker and lucky fool. He stayed in this school six years, leaving it as a captain in December, 1924. The following year he entered the Superior War School, and after completing a course of study there he was assigned in 1929 to the General Staff of the Army, Operations Division, remaining until September, 1930, when he was appointed to a post in the Ministry of War. A few months later he was named professor of military history in the Superior War School, while remaining in the War Ministry. It was in this period of study and instruction that he wrote four military books and started a fifth which he never had time to finish.

In 1936, while serving as Military Attaché in Chile, he was promoted to a lieutenant colonelcy. He was sent to Europe early in 1939 to study mountain warfare in the Tyrol region. He was in Europe observing the war for nearly two years, touring France, Germany, Hungary, Albania and Spain. When he returned, he was sent to direct the Mendoza mountain troops detachment, becoming the inspector of mountain troops and being named a full colonel on June 30, 1942, less than a year before the 1943 revolution which he and other colonels helped direct to success.

In the thirty-two years between his induction into the military academy and the 1943 revolution, Perón was a thorough-going student of military history and theory. When he was not studying it, he was teaching it, and sometimes both processes were going on simultaneously. And, because of the traditional orientation of the Argentine Army on the lines of the German military machine, Perón was exposed to the leading German military and political theory of that day. This shows in his writings, which are all liberally studded with quotations from the best German minds of the late nineteenth and early twentieth centuries.

Yet Perón the intellectual was not bogged down in a mass of technical military tactics and strategy. On the contrary, Perón in his impressionable years learned that it was the "leaders" who had won the great battles of history. He believed that without the "leaders" the untutored masses of armies might never have succeeded in altering the course of history. Having accepted the "leader" principle, Perón ruthlessly broke down the personalities, the minds and the training of some of history's greatest military men to learn what constituted their genius. In his *Notes of Military History*, written in 1934, Major Perón's admiration for Alexander the Great is undisguised. His description of Alexander the man is an interesting study of what Perón considers the physical equipment of a great leader. This "most accomplished leader of Greek antiquity," says Perón, "had all the qualities for it. His great eyes shone with extraordinary limpidness; the nose aquiline; his head slightly inclined toward the left shoulder, giving him a majestic aspect." I have seen more than one picture of Perón with his head turned slightly and inclined to the left, perhaps with the idea of giving himself that same "majestic aspect."

Perón's analysis of leadership went deeper. He noted that Hannibal "was not bound by iron rules, but always moulded himself to fit the circumstances." Napoleon "comprised in his gigantic personality the highest qualities of the leader, an iron character, constant perseverance, an unlimited audacity, a profound mind and a high sense of responsibility.... His natural energy was combined in physical activity and a capacity for work that permitted him to manage personally the affairs of State during the actual conduct of his campaigns."

It did not escape Perón that most of his military heroes of the past were also gifted with political ability, and he became convinced of the inseparability of politics and military affairs. Perón advocates "the necessity of a permanent collaboration of politicians and military men, because of the relation between politics and war. The political factor has... capital importance in the preparation and realization of war."

From this historic viewpoint of the intermingling of politics and militarism, Perón studied thoroughly the rise of fascism in Italy and naziism in Germany and the New Deal in the United States; and in the two totalitarian and the one democratic systems he saw various elements that could be put to work for Perón in Argentina. Because Hitler and Mussolini lost the war, Perón has never publicly described himself as being like them, but he has vigorously fostered the legend that Perón is a Latin Franklin D. Roosevelt, and his wife, Eva, has been presented to the public as being a second Eleanor Roosevelt.

Making all allowances for the relative size and importance of Argentina and the United States, there are many likenesses between Perón and the late President Roosevelt. The rich people in Argentina refer scathingly to Perón as "that man" in Casa Rosada, much as American industrialists spoke bitterly of "that man in the White House." And there are people who swear by Perón's great new ideas for bettering the poor man's lot in Argentina and raising the stature of the nation.

Perón and Roosevelt shared other qualities: Immense personal charm, spontaneous wit, agile minds, boundless confidence in themselves and their ideas, a wide appeal to the masses of their respective countries and an amazing aptitude for coining phrases that stick.

In lieu of the "forgotten man," Perón raised up the "*descamisados*" or the "shirtless ones." Perón also has an iron determination, political savvy and plenty of sheer courage that shows up best when he is confronted with what is seemingly an insurmountable set of circumstances.

It is about there, I believe, that the comparison between Perón and Roosevelt must end. For the two men, both magnificently equipped to serve as leaders of men for the furtherance of their nations, were as unlike as night and day in their methods of getting what they wanted.

To Perón, his own word was law, and he did not hesitate to use brute force to impose it; his gangs of thugs often went into the streets to beat and intimidate his opponents, thousands of whom were arrested or exiled. Perón paid lip service to the democracy of Roosevelt in an attempt to win the approval of Latin America and the world, but his regime made real use of the Hitler and Mussolini techniques. It was under him that the federal police was organized into a huge Perón organization useful in crushing civil liberties and capable of facing the Army in a fight, if that ever became necessary. And under Perón, independent labor unions were broken and forced into organizations modelled on Mussolini's syndicates. It was Perón's idea that a branch of the military government—the Secretariat of Labor and Social Welfare—use the taxpayer's money to help elect him "legally" to the presidency and that the universities must be "reorganized" (regimented) to produce the type of educated youth he needed for his work of government. And under him the Argentine economy was forced into a mould as rigid as that in Germany and Italy.

It is extremely difficult to be objective about Perón. Few Argentines can. Either they hate him as a rabble-rouser, a demagogue and a complete but dangerous fraud, or they admire him with a feeling almost of worship. Either Perón is Satan himself, or he is a saint leading Argentina to the green pastures of a new social order.

People are drawn to—or repelled by—Perón, depending largely on their economic levels. In general the rich fear that he will take away their wealth and traditional political power (he has already defeated them decisively in the political field), while the poor see in Perón the Messiah to raise their standard of living beyond their wildest dreams.

A good share of Perón's ability to win friends, however, is his penchant for adapting himself to the viewpoint of whichever group he happens to be courting at the moment. Thus one day he can speak soothingly to the magnates of industry and agriculture, then the following day raise the hopes of labor with promises of sharing not only the profits but also the wealth of the country. And entirely apart from his political and economic ideas, Perón has a personal magnetism that draws people overwhelmingly to him.

For example, what the late President Roosevelt called the "wolves" of the American press, on junkets to South America, have been almost invariably enchanted by Perón on first sight. And not until a correspondent has been in Argentina for some time is he likely to write anything unfavorable to the new Argentine President.

Much of Perón's charm is nothing more nor less than sex appeal. I have seen many women and girls tossing flowers in his path, and on one occasion I was simply flabbergasted to see Argentine women—many of them staid matrons—climbing trees or sitting perched in branches awaiting a glimpse of Perón in the parade that was soon to pass. Perhaps such goings-on would have caused no excitement in the United States, but in Argentina, where women have not even the right to vote and are in general relegated to a very dignified and modest position in life, the sight caused a real sensation.

Perón's almost hypnotic powers were in evidence during his campaign for the presidency. In Rosario, women fainted by the dozens in a huge square where Perón was speaking, and girls of the bobby sox age chased his train as it moved slowly along the campaign route. Perón has never attempted to deny his manly charms. At the height of the talk about his romance with radio actress Eva Duarte, Perón issued a statement for publication. "I am accused by my enemies of associating with women," he said. "Of course I do.

"What do they expect me to do," he demanded, "go around with men?"

As a matter of fact, Perón is admired and envied by a great many men, and the widespread rumors of his virile powers certainly did him no political harm. Mobs of workers eager to shake hands with Perón almost crushed the candidate's party during his campaign tour through the industrial cities. Perón, every inch a he-man, has a warm smile which is accentuated by the numerous horizontal lines around his eyes. The "bags" under the eyes serve to make his face more interesting. He has a ruddy complexion, probably traceable to his Scottish grandmother, but this is no novelty or handicap in Argentina, which racially is "whiter" than the population of the United States. In other ways, being mainly of Italian descent, he is completely satisfying to the nationalistic Argentines. He is absolutely at ease in any gathering, whether in a mansion of some industrialist or in a lowly bar in the Avellaneda slaughterhouse district.

Perched happily alongside Perón on the top rung of the Argentine ladder is his helpmate and former protégé, Eva Duarte de Perón, who also knew what she wanted—and got it. Eva, more commonly known as Evita, or "Little Eva," is less than thirty years old, younger and more glamorous than any first lady in Argentine memory. She and Perón make an extremely handsome couple.

Evita also is notable for her ability to flaunt the conventions. In the first place, she had virtual public recognition as Perón's lady love long before they were married, and the conventional folk of Argentina were scandalized at the prospect of Perón's becoming president without legalizing their relationship. The political convenience of a wedding played into Evita's hands, and a few months before the election they took their vows in a church ceremony. Evita also received the Pope's blessing for the marriage, which was an enviable achievement considering she had been the most gossiped about woman in many a year.

When Evita first came out of obscurity in the early days of the revolution, she had dark hair worn in a rather long bob. She was good-looking even then, but not in the smoothly dazzling way she is as the President's wife. Evita has become a blonde, her hair done in an elaborate up-sweep style. Her clothes are designed by some of the most exclusive French houses in Buenos Aires, and she is said to own at least a dozen fur coats, including ermine and mink. Her jewels are spectacular and she is fond of displaying them. All this from a girl who a few years back earned $35 a month as a part-time radio actress.

The story of Evita's meteoric rise is as fabulous as that of her husband. And Evita is just as audacious, just as ruthless and ambitious and courageous as Perón. Like Perón, Evita has found her looks a great asset. She is slightly taller than the average Argentine woman, with a Lana Turner figure and beautiful legs.

Stories vary on how she met Perón. One version is that they met at the big benefit rally for the San Juan earthquake victims. Evita was there in her capacity as a radio artist. Perón, then one of the powers behind President Ramírez, was there with Libertad la Marque, the noted tango singer. Evita, anxious to meet the handsome Colonel Perón, insisted that Libertad la Marque sing for the crowd. Libertad sang so well that the crowd applauded again and again for encores, with Evita leading the clapping. But while Evita was applauding, she took the chair that Libertad had vacated at the side of Perón, and there began a long and profitable friendship.

Another version is that Evita's desire for luxury was always getting her into debt and that in the early days of the revolution Evita was called to the posts and telegraph department, where her permit to perform over the radio was in danger because of bad debts amounting to several thousand pesos. She first met the secretary to the head of the department and immediately charmed him. He in turn introduced her to the departmental head. He likewise found Evita fascinating. It never hurts a rising and ambitious politician to know a beautiful woman—especially in Argentina—so the head of the department introduced her forthwith to Perón, who also was captivated.

Friends who knew her when she was struggling in the poorly paid radio profession, tell how she used to put her head between her hands and say over and over, "I will be somebody. I can just feel it, I will be somebody some day."

Evita was shrewd enough to recognize that her best chance of being "somebody" was to hitch onto the rising star of Perón. All the talk and criticism that this set off was probably a hindrance to the colonel's career, but Evita worked hard to make up for the disadvantages.

One of her early activities was to organize the artists and radio workers into an industry-wide union. She did this with the full approval of the Secretary of Labor and Social Welfare—Perón—and then paid him for the privilege of bossing the industry by using radio to boost Perón to the almost complete exclusion of other members of the military government. Perón began to be presented to the people as a sort of Latin superman, the most intelligent man in the military regime. Perón was the hero of her "Toward a Better Future" program, and the propaganda during her half-hour broadcasts was so undisguised that other members of the government threatened to revolt unless Perón ceased monopolizing the publicity. This opposition forced Evita into eclipse for a few weeks in the middle of 1945, but she was soon back dictating to radio again, with the Spanish equivalent of "You can't keep a good girl down."

It turned out that nothing could keep Evita down, not even the temporary ouster of Perón as Vice-President, War Minister and Secretary of Labor and Social Welfare on October 9, 1945. True, the officials of Radio Belgrano, Argentina's leading radio station, gleefully fired her within an hour or so of Perón's resignation, for they were tired of her dictating to them. Evita, showing plenty of courage, went down to the boat with Perón when he was arrested and sent off to the isle of Martín García then immediately set about conniving to bring him back to power. Evita called in leaders of various groups of *descamisados* and union leaders, and outlined to these "shirtless ones" the strategy for the frenzied gatherings that enabled Perón to regain his position. Evita is said to have helped engineer the whole big demonstration in Buenos Aires that brought Perón back to power.

After that, the pair was married and Evita campaigned at Perón's side for the presidency. Her presence on the campaign train marked the beginning of a new political way of life for the Argentines, who are accustomed to their first ladies being gracious and entertaining but completely removed from political activities. Evita blithely kicked over the traces of such tradition and became one of her husband's closest political advisers, sitting in at conferences and helping the new president divide the spoils of office among his henchmen. She began going out on her own to the working districts and inspected factories, housing projects, and made speeches in behalf of the new government of Argentina. She was installed in an office of her own and did not hesitate to call cabinet members into her headquarters to administer tongue-lashings or to distribute largesse. And while Perón was known as a "strong man" abroad, some Argentines suspected that at home he was a hen-pecked husband.

Evita's frequent excursions into the political field are certainly unorthodox, but no more so than the manner in which she makes them. Evita doesn't dress in sack cloth and ashes when she goes out among the working class. She wears her furs and her jewels and they love it, probably because it gives them hope to see another working girl who has made good. They take real pride in Evita's beauty. Paradoxically, the only group that seems to approve of the luxury-loving Evita is the working class.

The respectable middle and upper class families are aghast at the phenomenon of Evita, who still isn't entirely acceptable to high society and has therefore proceeded to make her own. One of her earliest conquests as the First Lady was the diplomatic corps. Evita presented the wives of many diplomats with gold bracelets and other jewelry, all of which is supposed to have improved considerably Argentina's international relations.

This move followed one of her most spectacular social indiscretions, her appearance at the presidential inaugural banquet in a glittering evening dress with one shoulder bare. The dress was sensational and beautiful, but custom had it that at all such functions the First Lady should appear with a neckline not too décolleté. But Evita sat with her bare shoulder next to the Cardinal—the highest Catholic official in the country. Photographs of the function showed Evita perfectly poised and lovelier than ever, but the Cardinal's eyes were averted as if in prayer.

Persons who have visited the presidential palace say that never in the history of the country have a chief executive and his lady lived in such luxury—amid crystal, fine silver, religious paintings and brocades. Some observers see in Evita's love of finery the clue to what may happen to Perón's high ideals about social and economic reforms, for Evita's own ideas on politics are a great influence on the new president. This may be a handicap. Evita can't tolerate opposition and is satisfied to have "yes" men in the highest government posts. She is also known for her spiteful nature. Evita has compiled a "black list" of persons who have gotten into her bad graces, and she awaits her opportunity to get even with them, to engineer their fall from power or influence. When she accomplishes this, she scratches off the name, and is ready to eliminate the next one on the list.

Although Evita has a German secretary and several German friends, there is no evidence that she is pro-Nazi or pro-Fascist. She seems to be merely pro-Perón or pro-Evita. Some persons complain that when she makes a speech she does not address people as "Argentines" but as "*peronistas*" or "*mujeres peronistas*." Her only political philosophy is said to be that of opportunism. One version has it that she was one of the first to urge Perón to cooperate with the United States.

"Remember, the United States is a strong country, and we have to get along with her," is said to have been Evita's practical advice.

The Argentines have never seen anything like Evita. Most educated persons laugh at her attempt to pose as a Latin edition of Eleanor Roosevelt, and one of the opposition newspapers constantly pokes fun at the antics of "The Lady President" in Argentina. It does require a lively imagination to find in the youthful, glamorous and bejewelled Evita much resemblance to our own former First Lady. Evita's talent lends itself mostly to intrigue. She hasn't had much education but has a quick wit and thinks on her feet. Yet to many Argentines, Evita is an enormous joke. The idea of a big, dashing fellow like Perón being hen-pecked is supremely funny. As one Argentine lady said, "We have a very fine sense of humor."

The outline of Perón's rise to power shows that the new president has more than sex appeal in common with his opportunistic wife. His later years are a brilliant blend of long-range planning and immediate acceptance of sudden opportunities. Long before the rise of Hitler in Germany, Perón had convinced himself of the supreme value of the "leader" principle, and in communicating these ideas to the students under him at the war college and to his fellow army officers he was creating the demand for a real leader in the Argentina of the future. Perón says that when he visited Italy he studied and discussed the Mussolini state and also inspected the Italian economic system, with particular attention to the labor "syndicates." In the 1939-41 period Perón watched the Wehrmacht overwhelm Poland, the Low Countries, Yugoslavia and France. He was impressed with the striking power and efficiency of the German Army, as well as the organization of the National Socialist Party which made it possible for Germany to fight a total war.

It was the Second World War, perhaps, that crystallized Perón's driving ambition to do things for himself and for Argentina. He began, among the younger officers of the Army, a crusade for "spiritual renovation," a crusade that is said to have led to the GOU. This organization, known variously as the *Grupo de Oficiales Unidos* and *Gobierno, Orden, Unidad*, was a sort of elite military "lodge" comprising the most militant, idealistic and reactionary elements among the colonels and the younger generals. It was the fountainhead for most of the ideas of the military government installed in June, 1943, including its pro-German "neutrality" and the repressive techniques required to secure complete domination of Argentina.

The first months of the revolution were Perón's time of greatest trial, danger and opportunity. He was actually unknown outside the Army, and there were men in the government with far greater military and social prestige. But generals and admirals learned quickly that their naval and military manuals did not supply all the answers to the problems of running a government—finance, economy, labor and public opinion were more difficult than logistics.

In October of 1943, strikes were breaking out all over the country as labor opposition to the Ramírez regime began to crystallize. A widespread strike was in progress in the vital meat-packing industry, and the threat of a general strike menaced the military government's position. Labor unrest stemmed largely from the government's prior dissolution of the left-wing faction of the General Confederation of Labor, comprising about half of the organization's 330,000 members. Labor, also shorn of its right to bargain collectively, was preparing to strike back before its position became hopelessly weak.

This dangerous situation was made to order for Perón's talents.

On October 27, 1943, he was named head of the National Labor Department and promptly went to work. He brought to bear on these difficulties not only the techniques of the corporative state unions he had observed in Italy and Germany, but his enormous reservoir of charm and know-how in getting along with people. He went directly to the laborers themselves in many personal visits to the factories. The workers were amazed to discover that Perón could talk their language, swap stories and enjoy drinking with them in the neighborhood bars they frequented. Perón won converts to his person by the thousands and laid the foundation for deals between his department and some labor leaders. He learned which others he could not hope to win to his cause and promptly sent these independent characters off to Villa Devoto prison or to concentration camps in Patagonia. He worked so swiftly in disorganizing the independent unions and winning others to his cause, that the general strike was called off. The department was reorganized as the Secretariat of Labor and Social Welfare, and Perón was named its director in recognition of the fine job he had done. That gave him a firm foothold in the new government. Perón was recognized by many then as a man who could get things done.

Most men would have been content to deal effectively with the labor troubles and let it go at that, but Perón saw a chance to fashion labor, through his new Secretariat, as a means for winning popular support to further his own political ambitions. He was aware, however, that labor and mass publicity were long-range political projects and that the Army remained the key to getting immediate power in the military government. Army politics was a dangerous game, for older officers were jealous of their rank and influence, and the younger officers of Perón's rank were just as anxious for power as he. There was always danger of a rising man being taken out of politics and "exiled" to some small and remote garrison post.

Obstructing Perón's path at this time were several army officers who held higher posts than he, and who were closer to President Ramírez. After Ramírez broke relations with the Axis, Perón rallied sufficient support to oust him as well as some of Perón's rival officers. General Edelmiro J. Farrell, whose friendship with Perón was of many years standing, was installed as President and Perón was sworn in as the Acting Minister of War.

In this post, Perón was able to consolidate his grip on the armed forces by accelerating military expenditures to new record totals— from 298 million pesos in 1941 to 1,428 millions in 1945, over 50 per cent of the government's annual expenditure. He created a new division—the seventh—in northeastern Argentina, established new garrisons in the northern zone and re-distributed garrisons in the eastern zone. These activities enabled him to send some of his rivals to distant posts where they no longer could be contenders for the presidency. Perón also stepped up the production of army equip- ment in Argentine factories and in general overhauled the Army, strengthening it in a way that was gratifying to the commanders under him. Proof that he was getting results for the Army, which naturally throve on expansion, was seen in the giant display of tanks and other military equipment being manufactured in the country for the Army, which Perón put on display in Buenos Aires on the anniversary celebration of the first year of the revolution.

True, General Farrell remained in the presidency, but Perón had nothing to fear on that score. He and Farrell remained fast friends. Farrell had never liked the job, being a man with little ambition and a considerable propensity for drinking. General Luis Perlinger, a leading rival for the presidency, was left by the wayside when Perón on July 8, 1944 was appointed Vice-President of the nation, a post both Perón and Perlinger had long coveted because it was the stepping-stone to the presidency. Perlinger resigned as Minister of Interior a month later.

It was time for Perón to branch out for the kind of support that he hoped would end the "provisional" nature of his regime and put it on a permanent basis. Now that Perlinger had left the interior ministry, which controlled the federal police, it was advisable to build the police into a first-class weapon. Police personnel was stepped up to something over thirty thousand, theoretically sufficient to handle the big Campo Mayo army garrison if the officers there ever turned on Perón and Farrell. At the same time, Perón courted the working masses of the country constantly and openly. This was accomplished partly through hundreds of decrees pro- viding pensions, better working conditions and higher wages for groups ranging from newspaper men to peons working on the vast *estancias*. Perón, in speeches and press conferences, also trumpeted the need for ending speculation which was raising the cost of living and said it was the aim of the government to assure all of a decent standard of living. Perón wooed labor thoroughly and successfully. It was his labor and police following that saved him when he was ousted from all three of his government posts in October, 1945. The situation was also bolstered by Perón's deft tailoring of two parties to support his candidacy—the Labor Party and the dissident section of the Unión Cívica Radical, Argentina's great middle-class party.

The clincher for Perón's victory was the government's decree in December granting a wage bonus of one month's salary to all Argentine workers in private industry at year's end, along with wage increases ranging from 10 to 25 per cent. This measure, as workers saw it, was but a promise of things to come with Perón as President.

Perón won the election by the greatest electoral landslide in the history of Argentina, getting 304 of the 376 electoral votes and also winning a completely pro-Perón Senate and a whopping majority in the Chamber of Deputies.

For the first time in his meteoric career, Perón appeared to be firmly in the saddle. He had the popular support necessary to win approval or at least acceptance of his regime abroad; he still held the support of a considerable portion of the Army; through his friend, General Filomeno Velazco, he controlled the federal police; and he had the *descamisados*, or shirtless ones, as a final block of worshipful support, to counter any combination that might attempt to unseat him. The *descamisados* comprised some labor, all the have-nots and malcontents and strong backs who believed fanatically in Perón and would shed blood to keep him in power.

On the other side of the ledger, but by no means offsetting his strength, were a number of weaknesses. Perón, like the Napoleon he admires, likes to run the whole show himself, and hence tends to handle too many details and to name "yes" men and incompetents. Also he had promised to labor, either directly or by implication, a great deal more than he could hope to deliver. This was true of political spoils, which the Labor party resentfully had to share with the much less important "rump" Radicals. It was also true of his promises to curb inflation, to rush massive workers' housing projects, to divide the land and share the profits of business and industry. Perón had promised all but the millennium, if he were elected. Now he was elected, and Argentine labor was not yet in paradise. Perón has a gifted tongue, and the charm of hearing his own voice sometimes leads him into extemporaneous exaggerations. It has been said that Perón talks too much.

There is an odd likeness between Perón and two of the outstanding figures of Argentine history: The great dictator Juan Manuel de Rosas and the strange but democratic Hipólito Irigoyen.

Perón's critics have often likened him to Rosas and there are some grounds for the comparison. Both came to power with wide mass appeal, especially among the poorer classes. The handsome young colonel of over a century ago commanded the respect of the men under him because he could throw the *boleadoras*, break horses and lasso along with the toughest of his hardened army of followers. And a hundred years later, another ambitious and handsome colonel found skill at sports helpful in gaining a following among the younger officers. He could out-fence, out-ski and out-box the best of them.

As Rosas took over the reins of government he was elevated from a colonel to a general, just as was Perón prior to becoming president. Both assumed office with all of the trimmings of legality, Rosas by means of a plebiscite, and Perón through election.

The techniques by which Rosas arrived at and retained his power are a familiar story to any student of Argentine history, and Perón is one of the most diligent. Rosas had found it helpful to maintain an elaborate espionage network to keep him informed of the plots of his enemies, and he also assured a friendly clergy by granting many favors to the church.

The revolutionary government, of which Perón was a key figure from the very beginning, found it expedient to utilize some of the same techniques. The secret police became a powerful arm of the new government, and the Catholic church was courted with a fervor seldom seen in this hemisphere in modern times. From the first, the hierarchy of the church was well disposed to the military government and especially so after the Ramírez regime decreed

Catholic religious instruction in the schools, which subsequent administrations have been reluctant to erase.

The university and higher education have been a painful thorn for both men. Rosas virtually destroyed it in his day, and Perón has sought to curb student political activities.

And probably not since the days of Don Juan Manuel have the citizens of Buenos Aires been so familiar with the likeness of their leader as today. While Perón has not gone to the lengths of Rosas, who had his portrait placed on a cart and then required some of the leading citizens to act as beasts of burden to draw it through the city, today's president has been far from shy about showing his face either in person or by placard, and often both simultaneously. Giant reproductions of his smiling countenance have come to be standard equipment for government rallies and other appropriate occasions.

Even their home lives bear some similarity. While Evita Duarte de Perón has been compared with Eleanor Roosevelt, persons familiar with Argentine history say she more nearly resembles Doña Encarnación Ezcurra y Asguirel de Rosas, the wife of the dictator. Doña Encarnación was as spectacular a figure in her day as is the lovely Evita in hers.

While other women were content to remain in their humble abodes, Doña Encarnación was recognized as an acute and cunning strategist. When her husband left to fight the Indians, she was able to look after his affairs at home, even to directing his band of followers. Her visits, along with her husband to the poor Negro districts, had their counterpart over a century later when Señora Perón began to interest herself in the activities of women workers, inspecting their factories and acting as their counselor. And just as Doña Encarnación cut a dashing figure in red satin evening dresses, so has Evita in her revealing gowns.

There are more striking resemblances, however, between Rosas of the 1830's and 1840's and Perón of the 1940's. One of these was the ability to inspire their followers in giant gatherings to a frenzy of unquestioning faith. Rosas was one of the greatest rabble rousers ever produced in Argentina, and Perón has the same gift. And both leaders organized bands of fanatic followers who would stop at little or nothing.

In 1833, during the administration of Balcarce, an institution known as the Mazorca was created to spread the views of Rosas, the man who was to rule Argentina some years later under the bloodiest, most criminal, barbaric and terroristic regime of personal government the country has ever known.

The Mazorca was a sort of private army recruited from the lower classes which took the law into its own hands, with little or no discouragement from Rosas. It terrorized the streets of Buenos Aires, yelling for the "restorer of the laws" (Rosas), shooting, ambushing and murdering the men whom they were told opposed him.

The reign of terror and despotism enforced by the Mazorca extended even beyond the capital, and Argentine historians estimate that several thousand persons died at the Mazorca's hands.

It is true that the Mazorca included many decent and well-meaning persons, but the brotherhood also numbered among its members the worst rascals and assassins who ever placed their whips and their daggers at the services of a dictator. There is a grim likeness between the Mazorca and the *descamisados* who support Perón.

Like the Mazorca, Perón's crowd includes many sincere men and honest crackpots and those of the lower classes who have been really ground under by the vested interests in Argentina; it also provides a refuge and a profession to hundreds of the vilest sort of thugs who with knives, guns, clubs and stones beat and intimidated the opponents of Perón, smashing heads and destroying property and making a tragic farce of the 1946 electoral campaign.

As for that other figure, Irigoyen, Perón himself has found it flattering to make the comparison. Irigoyen in the early part of this century offered a new way of life to the Argentines, as Perón is doing now. Irigoyen instilled a sort of blind, unswerving faith in his followers. With his own magnificent hypnotism, Perón has built the same kind of following among the down-trodden masses of Argentina, who have been kicked and disillusioned by their rulers so often that they are willing to obey blindly this magic new voice in the industrial age. Yet there are differences. Irigoyen, twice elected president and ousted in his second term by the Conservative interests he so bitterly opposed, was not a ruthless political scientist, but a dreamer. He was also a democrat, through and through, in his political thinking. Perón is neither a dreamer nor a democrat, at least not in the Anglo-Saxon sense.

Perón has often expressed his faith in democracy but had only contempt for its results in Argentina, sneering at the "fraud, lies, exploitation or social injustice" of earlier regimes. The revolution, he said, sought "the total moral recuperation of the people, which would automatically be followed by full internal political liberty." Thus Perón conceived of democracy as something to be permitted only when other matters had been properly arranged. In many speeches to his followers and political helpers, Perón has intertwined democracy almost inextricably with the leadership principle. And the "leader" he endowed with a mystic ability to grasp and visualize the over-all national and international picture, "which others cannot see." This leader was to stand at the apex of an enormous mass movement, ruling with inflexibility but wisdom through the lower echelons of command, much in the manner of an infallible general commanding his army.

As Perón saw it, in a New Year's speech he made in Santa Fe shortly before his election, the leader "has two or three disciples so that when he dies there is always someone who will continue in time and space. Behind those come the General Staff of the party, which has eight, ten or twenty specialists or technical men for each great branch of State.... And there is not a problem, however insignificant, that within their province they do not dominate... so that when they reach office they open the drawer of their desk, take out their plan and order its immediate execution."

The leader of this form of democracy, of course, was Perón. "I am a leader of the true democracy, born of the people to govern the people for the people."

The Superman had found a substitute for the Divine Right of Kings. As early as December, 1944, long before his hat was officially in the presidential campaign ring, Perón was asked by a group of Chilean journalists visiting Buenos Aires if he was prepared to govern the country as its president. To this Perón replied, "In these things, I am one of those who sustain that there is no man who can escape his destiny. If destiny obliges me ... but they will have to ask me; and I am not going to take any step in that direction."

Where is Perón taking Argentina?

Part of the answer to that is that Perón believes in the "destiny" of Argentina just as he believes in the "destiny" of Perón. The two are intertwined, and it is evident in many of Perón's speeches that he believes there has been a great lag in fulfilling the destiny of Argentina. This should be remedied, he is on record as saying, by intensifying the industrialization of Argentina, raising her standard of living, increasing her population, and strengthening and modernizing her armed forces so that the nation's potentialities of greatness can be realized.

There are many Argentines, sound statisticians and writers and economists, who have been advocating part of this program for many years. They have said that a land of Argentina's vast resources and area could profitably support a population double or even quadruple the present fourteen million inhabitants, even though it would mean revamping completely the nation's economic system from a semi-colonial to a mainly industrial status.

What the economists consider a desirable theoretical possibility, Perón deems a necessity in the development of the nation's "destiny," a word that he has used time and again in referring to the future of the Great Argentina. In speaking of "destiny," Perón is appealing to the deep-seated conviction of the Argentines that they are the greatest people in South America. One who has lived in Argentina for any length of time knows that the Argentines—with or without the encouragement of Perón—consider it the nation's right and duty to assume the leadership in South America. And it is a sore point with them that the balance of power on the continent was upset during the war not only by the industrial growth of Brazil but also by the quantities of Lend-Lease planes, tanks, guns and armored vehicles supplied to Brazil and Argentina's other neighbors by the United States.

In considering the means whereby Argentina is to recoup and perhaps improve on her position of dominance in South America, it is not to be forgotten that the background of her new leader is definitely militarist-authoritarian in nature. Perón has always emphasized the use of force or the threat of armed activity as the keystone of any nation's foreign policy. Thus he was understandably surprised at the cries of shocked outrage that came from the press and the diplomats of the United Nations when he said, in a speech inaugurating the foundation of a chair of national defense at the University of La Plata in 1944, that "war is an inevitable social phenomenon." He had said the same thing in his military history in 1934 and no one had noticed or protested, the difference being that in 1934 Perón was an unknown major, while in 1944 he was recognized as the main pillar of the military government and the likeliest future leader of Argentina.

Perón, by 1934, had accepted the Prussian concept of "total war," which he said "makes it necessary to take advantage of the last vital physical, material and spiritual energy ... to bring together all the material and spiritual forces, seeking active or passive allies, creating the best conditions for the operations, forming a movement of opinion favorable to the end sought."

The modern concept of total war demands, Perón wrote, complete preparation of the entire nation in peacetime. This is true regardless of whether it is to be an aggressive or defensive war. Nothing must be left to chance. In the case of Argentina, which in 1934 had an undersized industry incapable of supporting the nation in a major conflict, Perón emphasized that the country's financial credit abroad must be kept at a high level, while at the same time home industries (especially armaments) must be developed swiftly. He called for "the creation of numerous plans (economic, industrial, financial, etc.) that form part of the war plan ... in the form to serve, in the best way, the armed forces of the State in the operations of war."

As for war doctrine, Perón declared himself in favor always of "a vigorous offensive and swift blows," and he subscribed to the German view that it is better to fight the war on the soil of the other nation. He devotes far more space in his military history to offensive than to defensive strategy. He spoke disparagingly of defense as being suited only for very special cases and for "weak armies. Defensive strategy is bad for morale. It is useful to avoid defeat, but not to attain victory."

To Perón, war is the means whereby a nation keeps what it already has, or acquires what it needs and cannot get by peaceful methods. In peacetime a nation must prepare for war—either to defend its possessions or to build up the military strength to insure the achievements of its objectives as laid down by its leaders. Military strength is useful in the latter sense either as a threat of military force or for actual resort to war if the threat proves insufficient to secure compliance with the demands of policy.

In the international field, Perón has sought to rebuild the prestige of Argentina, which suffered drastically in South America because of her pro-German "neutrality" and the increased strength of surrounding powers through Lend-Lease. During the war, the Argentine military government cooperated with the German Nazis to set up the "friendly" Villarroel government in Bolivia and carried on a vigorous but unsuccessful campaign to install similar anti-U.S. governments in Chile, Paraguay, Uruguay and Brazil. Paraguay, a small but necessary unit in this anti-U.S. "southern bloc," gratefully accepted tokens of friendship from both the United States and Argentina.

In these manipulations, "a principal leader of the Argentine conspirators was Colonel Juan D. Perón. A successful coup d'etat springing from these sources did take place in Bolivia, just when one was also believed by its perpetrators on the point of fruition in Chile. Concurrently, Perón spurred on the Brazilian Integralists, while similar efforts were directed toward Paraguay and Uruguay." The U.S. State Department, making these accusations in its "Blue Book," said the main reason the plot failed was that other American countries became aware of the attempt and combatted it diplomatically.

Perón's diplomatic strategy shifted quickly and successfully in 1946, when the rather crude attempts at subversion of neighboring governments had been largely abandoned. By establishing relations with Russia, Perón brought pressure for better relations with the United States, and he hastened the thawing of his impasse with the "colossus of the north" by the startling declaration that if the United States were to fight the Soviet Union, Argentina would be on the side of the United States. He also had Congress ratify the Act of Chapultepec for Inter-American collaboration and in so doing dispelled some of the distrust of Argentina that prevailed in the United States and the other American republics.

The suave new diplomatic process was coupled with an aggressive campaign to expand Argentina's trade and influence with her neighbors—as far north as the Río Grande. This was possible only because of the war, which had familiarized Latin American countries with the *Industria Argentina* mark when their supplies of manufactured goods from other countries were curtailed or cut off entirely and which had also transformed Argentina from a debtor to a creditor nation. At the end of the war, Argentina had plenty of money to lend—well over a billion dollars in gold bullion and dollar and sterling balances. In late 1946 and early 1947 she began lending it.

The loans, made by the government controlled Banco de la Nación Argentina rather than by private enterprise, were tied up with trade treaties and financial agreements which promised to operate to the mutual benefit of Argentina and the other contracting countries.

Chile, which was desperately short of food and foreign exchange, borrowed about $175,000,000 from Argentina, with which she agreed to improve highways and railways linking the two countries, develop her waterpower resources and expand her mining of nitrate, copper, iron, coal. Argentina's Five-Year Plan would absorb increased production of Chile's raw materials. In turn, Argentina would receive the right to use Valparaiso as a free port outlet to the Pacific and would establish a branch of the Bank of the Nation in Chile.

The Moríñigo government in Paraguay was bolstered by a $2,500,000 loan from Argentina, and agreement was reached in principle for a customs union.

In quick succession, Argentina signed trade agreements with Peru, Ecuador and Brazil, in each case using the government controlled surpluses of food—mainly wheat and meat—to drive the bargains. Argentina was accused with some justice of withholding shipments of food to her neighbors to win trade concessions. One of the concessions she desired was to establish branches of the official Argentine bank in other countries of the hemisphere. In 1946 she won permission to set up branches of the bank in Chile, two in Ecuador, and in 1947 Argentina was planning to extend them also to Brazil, Peru and Bolivia.

In 1947 the outlines of Argentina's trade expansionism were becoming clear. Argentina wanted to become the leading banker in

Latin America, and through her state controlled air lines and fleet of trading vessels she hoped also to become the No. 1 trading nation south of the United States.

The plan was much more ambitious than was at first apparent. It extended beyond Argentina's immediate neighbors and even beyond the South American continent. The battleship *Rivadavia* late in 1946 made an extended good will cruise of the Caribbean area. More important than the cruise itself was the diplomatic and trade mission it brought to Mexico to attend the inauguration of President Miguel Alemán in December. The mission, headed by big, hearty Senator Diego Luis Molinari, toured Central American and Caribbean republics for nearly three months. Molinari and his advisers visited Mexico, Guatemala, Panama, Venezuela, the Dominican Republic, El Salvador, Costa Rica, Haiti, Cuba, Honduras and other countries, sounding out the businessmen and governments on an Argentine plan for hemispheric trade cooperation. The Argentine blueprint included a merchant marine of one hundred vessels, a big commercial air transport network, and a continental banking system dependent on the official Argentine bank. Molinari said he had received assurances from the governments of Mexico, Cuba, Haiti, the Dominican Republic, Venezuela, Panama and Guatemala that they accepted the Argentine plan "in principle" and were willing to sign agreements to carry it it out. Presumably a first step would be to establish Argentine branch banks in the capitals of some of the countries named, and through the banks to lend money which eventually would broaden the basis of Argentina's influence, both financial and political.

Observers who saw Perón embark on this new policy of investing money with his neighbors, recalled with misgivings the "Economic Action" section of his "Nation in Arms" speech in La Plata in 1944, in which he said, "Countries in time of peace try to submit the economies of the countries who are their most probable adversaries to certain vassalages and critical situations, preparing real time bombs to be exploded at the desired moment."

At home, Perón gripped the entire nation's economy in a totalitarian-type control fully as rigid as anything achieved by Hitler or Mussolini. In the last few weeks preceding his inauguration as president, the government nationalized the Central Bank, placing loans, interest rates, foreign exchange and the opening of branch banks under government control. It also created a government monopoly of re-insurance, which previously had been handled mostly in London and New York, and approved government regulation of insurance operations. State monopolies in the grain trade were established. Perón's Congress soon passed a law, ostensibly adopted to facilitate control of prices but actually giving the government broad powers to step in at any stage in the production or distribution of goods, including control of "all raw materials and manufactured goods, foodstuffs, clothing, housing, construction, lighting, heating and any others affecting living or working conditions and the transport of such things." Among other things, the Executive Department was authorized to "establish rationing regulations, regulate manufacture, transport, supply, use, distribution and consumption." A measure of the powers conferred on the presidential office is seen in the paragraph in the law calling for the "creation of registers of persons or entities covered by the dispositions of the law; the establishment and verification of stocks; verifications of origins and costs; making forcible entries; demanding the exhibition of books and papers."

With export prices already being set by the government in many lines, the new law passed by Congress gave Perón power to lower or eliminate customs duties, so that the government may in effect eliminate certain industries and favor others by its arrangement of tariffs. Industry had already seen which way the wind was blowing when the government withdrew the legal status of the Unión Industrial Argentina (the equivalent of the National Association of Manufacturers in the United States). Perón wants industry to operate under the absolute direction of the government.

The regimented future of industry is indicated by what has already happened to labor. Perón wooed and won the labor vote with glittering promises in the 1946 elections, but long before the balloting he had labor completely under his thumb through the conversion of labor unions into official groups controlled by the Ministry of Labor and Social Welfare. He had also eliminated collective bargaining, with government dictating to both employer and employee groups in labor disputes. Speaking to the Stock Exchange in September, 1944, Perón had warned the nation's wealthy class of the dangers of communism in Chile, Bolivia, Paraguay, Uruguay and Brazil and said that the best way of fighting the Communists in Argentina was to assure social justice to Argentine labor. Referring to labor in a subsequent speech to the nation's leading manufacturers in the Unión Industrial Argentina, Perón stressed that the "only dangerous mob is an unorganized mob." He assured the manufacturers that the labor masses were being organized and that "in due course it will be found that the employers are controlling their workers through the unions" which the government then was organizing. A little more than a year later, Perón closed the manufacturers' organization and now controls *both* the industrialists and their workers.

In early 1944, when Perón was first generally recognized as the real head of the military government, his program, his ideas and his acts went on trial before the people of Argentina and the hemisphere. His ideas and what he had so far accomplished were approved by more than half of the Argentine voters in the presidential elections of February 24, 1946. The Argentine people may not soon have another opportunity to pass judgment.

The majority of the other American republics promptly announced they would respect the results of the elections, which even Perón's opponents admitted had been cleaner, at least at the polls, than almost any in Argentine history. This did not mean, however, that the other republics—and especially Argentina's near neighbors—proceeded to erase the question mark after the name of Perón. Notwithstanding the return to "normalcy" of Argentina's foreign relations, Perón the President remained just as much on trial as Perón the strong man had been. His acts at home were still subject to careful examination for a clue as to where Argentina was really heading.

The Argentine scene was not entirely reassuring to the other republics. It became apparent that the powers accorded by the constitution were not sufficient for Perón.

One of the obstacles that the elections had not cleared from his path was the Supreme Court, which had consistently withstood his rule by decree under the military regime. Perón decided that the old court must go and instructed his supporters in Congress to impeach the justices. The men to be impeached were Chief

Justice (retired) Roberto Repetto, Antonio Sagarna, Benito Nazar Anchorena, and Francisco Ramos Mejía, and along with them Attorney General (fiscal) Juan Álvarez. The charges against them were unparalleled, to put it mildly. The court, it developed during the impeachment proceedings, had been guilty of: first—recognizing the de facto government of General José Uriburu in 1930; second—recognizing the de facto government of General Pedro P. Ramírez in 1943 (of which Perón was a leader); and third—having "placed obstacles in the path of the (Farrell-Perón) de facto government by declaring many of its decrees unconstitutional." The Chamber of Deputies promptly approved the impeachment measure and passed it along to the Senate, whose every member is a *peronista*.

This process had not been completed when Perón took his next great stride, the introduction of his enormous Five-Year Plan. This was a blueprint for the new and greater Argentina that Perón had written about (as a major) in 1934. It was a scheme to raise the economic and industrial potential of Argentina. If carried out it would give her a place among the major powers of the world.

Even the Argentines, who supposedly had become inured if not entirely agreeable to the grandiose ambitions of Perón, were startled by the size of his newest scheme. Taken as a whole, it would mean more power for the state (and for Perón) in an Argentina that would be stronger in its armed forces, in its industry, transportation and even in population. The individual would live in conditions of greater health and prosperity, but in exchange for this the State would exercise new controls over his life. The plan was so big that it had to be broken down for analysis.

By 1951, if the section on industry were followed through, Argentina would be producing 43 per cent more manufactured goods than she did in 1943, would have a third more industrial workers receiving half again as much wages and salaries; and power installations would be increased 50 per cent. New industries "necessary to national defense" would be encouraged and sheltered from competition. Industry would be decentralized and factories would be built far from Buenos Aires, nearer the sources of hydroelectrical energy and natural gas.

Labor, besides receiving higher wages as the result of industrialization, would be encouraged to share in ownership. Perón promised "economic advantages" to a wide range of enterprises—agricultural, livestock, forestry, commercial and industrial—if they permitted their workers to share in ownership. All profits above 5 per cent earned by companies participating in this plan would go into "workers' stock" to replace capital stock. To assure a larger supply of skilled labor, the plan provided for new technical and industrial training schools.

More than a billion dollars would be spent on public works, including reorganization of the country's entire transportation system by the construction of new railways and highways and improvements in harbor facilities. Hundreds of thousands of workers would be required for projects stretching from one end of the Republic to the other. Some of these—such as free recreational centers for workers—would represent substantial social gains, and there was little doubt that the nation's physical well-being would be advanced. Under this part of the plan over $150,000,000 would be spent building hospitals and clinics, and medicine would be virtually socialized. The State, if it so desired, could move doctors to outlying areas where it appeared their talent could be put to better use.

Where it was deemed necessary, economic power would be extracted from the individual person or private business enterprise and transferred to the State. As Perón expressed it, "We are not putting into effect a directed economy but rather an orderly and ordered economy. Under the plan, the State becomes a competitor, not a director. It takes products and sells them in the manner that it considers best suited to the interests of the nation." As a matter of fact, Perón already exercised vast control over the nation's economy and only needed to consolidate and put into use the powers he had arrogated to himself.

The Army's sinews would also be strengthened. Argentina would build airplane factories and in them produce her own military planes. A reserve of air-minded men would be created in the glider schools and clubs and through the extension of the Argentine State Merchant Air Fleet to North America and Europe. Undisclosed but presumably vast sums of money (entirely independent of congressional appropriations) would be used in the complete modernization of the Army and the construction of military factories. The Armed forces would be reduced "quantitatively but not qualitatively"—which means mechanization.

More hands would be required to build and support the bulging new Argentina, and the plan called for fifty thousand immigrants a year. Some of them would participate in colonization and irrigation of areas now largely unsettled. Those skilled in other lines would be welcomed in the development of a national fishing industry and the exploitation of mineral deposits.

Government itself would be reorganized and "streamlined" to provide greater authority at the top. Powers would be shorn from the legislative and judicial branches and handed to the executive branch—Perón. Ironically, Perón asked his Congress to pass laws which would divest the parliamentarians of some of their prerogatives. He asked for complete control of the educational system. The Congress' most treasured authority—the power to appropriate funds—would be largely suspended once it had written a blank check for the $1,665,000,000 which it was estimated the Five-Year Plan would cost the country; and the blank check did not include all military expenditure. The Argentine Army staff, as well as Perón, would have the authority to spend money for equipment and construction in strategic areas without requesting the permission of Congress.

Taking into consideration Perón's repeated declarations that a nation must at all times be prepared for war, and the Five-Year Plan's general purpose of mobilizing the political, economic, industrial and human resources of the nation, it could only be assumed that the sums to be spent on secret military preparations would be generous.

Perón also requested authority to reorganize the federal judiciary system. He would establish career posts extending from justices of the peace to justices of the Supreme Court.

Thus Perón would alter vastly the system of checks and balances set up by the Argentine constitution without ever bothering to tamper technically with that document or putting his amendments to the test with his people. He would emerge, undisputed, as the most powerful man in Latin America—and one of the most absolute rulers in the world—in control of the entire political, economic and military life of his nation. A man with a tremendous grip on the masses of his country and with a determination to make his country great.

His neighbors in America would watch this great new experiment in strong government and socialization for guides to their own future. If Perón succeeded where others had failed, there would be men in Latin America to emulate the valuable features of the plan. But if Perón's Argentina took the direction of European experiments in national socialism, which were unable or unwilling to live within their own borders and insisted on their right to expansion, the New World would become a dangerous place.

Understandably, all eyes were on Perón.

In one of his speeches as Vice-President, Perón said, "In my optimistic dreams, I often see a nation economically powerful, and within it a rational and balanced State by which the economic, social and political needs for the happiness of all Argentines would best be served."

I would not venture to predict how far Perón will get with this task or exactly where he will lead Argentina. But I have no hesitation in saying the coming years will be a real adventure for the nation, a time as colorful, as dynamic and as exciting as Juan Domingo Perón. And that is saying a great deal. An assassin's bullet or bomb, a civil war, a military *coup* are ever-present possibilities in the life of the Latin American ruler—whether he be strong man or president. A man who zooms to the top in three years can be pushed out in a day in Argentina. But there is one thing certain about Perón—he will never die of boredom. And, as long as Juan Domingo Perón is in the saddle, neither will the Argentine people.

EDUCATION FOR PERON

A SCHOOL TEACHER, NEARLY SIXTY YEARS IN HIS GRAVE, IS one of the most controversial figures in present-day Argentina—most respected by democrats and most hated by the elements which have been in power since the June, 1943 revolution.

Domingo Faustino Sarmiento left an heritage bitterly opposed to totalitarian rule, therefore it is his name that has been most often used as a banner in the struggle against military government. It also explains why the educational system, and in particular the universities, have fought against Perón and his ilk.

Sarmiento was a president, but first and foremost he was an educator. Proof of this is that he built a thousand new primary schools in Argentina at a time when there were fewer than two million inhabitants. He also brought teachers from the United States to instruct the young men and women who were to teach in the new buildings. Sarmiento believed that literacy and a knowledge of the world would help make his people great.

He did more to educate the Argentines than any other man. In 1869, before he became Minister of Education, seventy-seven out of every one hundred persons were unable to read or write; but in 1895 when his efforts were beginning to bear fruit, nearly half the population could read and write; and in 1943 the Ministry of Education estimated that only 16.6 per cent of all persons above the age of fourteen were illiterate. In South America this is a remarkably low figure. Only Uruguay can compare with it.

There have been other great educators in Argentina, but most of them took their inspiration from Sarmiento. He is indirectly responsible for the fact that in recent decades Argentina spent more money for education than all the other countries of South America together; that until recently there were two school teachers in Argentina for every soldier; that until the military *coup* of 1943 Argentina was one of the few countries that spent more money on her educational system than she did on her Army, Navy and Air Force.

The educational system in Argentina has not changed a great deal since the days of Sarmiento, except that the schools have become larger and more numerous. The basic standards that Sarmiento set for education of the people have not changed much— perhaps not enough. The standard requirement for compulsory attendance is for three years in the schools supported by the federal government and two years in schools financed by the provinces. The primary schools still maintain six grades, and there are far too few secondary schools to take care of students who could and should advance beyond the primary schools. In 1942 the Ministry of Education estimated that out of the approximately two million students in all the nation's schools, only one out of eleven reached high school and one out of forty-two attended an institution of higher learning. An indication of "improvised" education is seen in a 1944 report stating that the rich Argentine nation had only four thousand buildings constructed especially for schools. The national educational authorities were renting eleven thousand of the fifteen thousand structures used in the country as schools and even by renting still did not have enough room to give each child a desk.

As for instruction, teaching is still by rote and recitation and is largely "academic," with little emphasis on preparing the students for any life other than a "cultural" or strictly professional one. There is scant industrial or specialized instruction, which is a serious lack at a time when Argentina is changing from an entirely pastoral era to a mixed economy of agriculture and industry.

But the fact that Sarmiento was responsible for the present educational system and the construction of one-fourth of the buildings expressly raised for primary schools does not account for the hatred felt for him by the totalitarian forces—the ones who have arrested teachers for merely reciting speeches he made nearly a century ago.

To them it is the ideas of Sarmiento that are dangerous—in

particular his belief in democracy and his open admiration of the United States. These concepts of Sarmiento lived on in the schools. That is why peace fled the classroom with the advent of military government in Argentina, and desks and chairs, the blackboards and buildings marked the field of battle for the opposing ideas of Sarmiento and Juan Domingo Perón. Ideas fought ideas, and sometimes blackboard erasers went into combat with tear gas bombs. The struggle was as unequal as bare hands against a saber. With brute force the military regime and its followers were able, at any chosen moment, to muzzle the democratic spokesmen in the primary and secondary schools. Through mass discharges and suspensions of teachers and threats against others they extracted lip service for their creed in the classroom. And they implanted authoritarian doctrines through at least one special "orientation" school for teachers which is, fortunately, inoperative at the moment.

The only pillar of the educational structure which consistently has repulsed the totalitarians is the university hierarchy. The university students constitute one of the few elements which viewed the 1946 presidential elections as a battle between fascism and democracy. That is why Perón and the *peronistas* hate the universities and are "reforming" them.

It was not surprising that the military men who seized power in Argentina should attempt to revamp Sarmiento's educational system into a new mold for the young. They had seen the carefully indoctrinated youth of Germany and Italy become enthusiastic and useful slaves of fascism in those countries. And the Argentines set out in more or less efficient fashion to duplicate the performance. Teachers were told what to teach and which things to ignore— which of the great Argentine statesmen should be passed over lightly in history classes, and which others should be held up and glorified in the eyes of Argentine youth. As in Germany, the emphasis was shifted from the great but unspectacular values of culture, philosophy, art and the sciences to glorification of military history and super-citizenship.

Not by accident did we learn of the perversion of education in Argentina and the heroic struggle of the university students against it. Ruth and I never had a chance to forget it, because of Albert, a gay, intelligent nineteen-year-old who liked to drop in on us and talk. We liked to have him come. Albert always brought a little gift—sometimes just a few chocolates, fifty centavos worth of cakes, or some garden flowers for Ruth.

But one night he came flourishing a bottle of French champagne. The dust was still on the bottle, and it was years old.

"Albert, you shouldn't have done this," I protested mildly. I didn't think a student could afford such luxuries.

Albert grinned, waved my protest aside as if even champagne wasn't good enough for his friends.

"But we're going to celebrate," he said. "Besides, the father of one of my friends gave it to me because of what we did to the German chargé d'affaires today. He was invited to speak before our law class.

"Well, it was like this," Albert continued, "when our professor brought the German into the classroom we clapped our hands and cheered. The German liked it. He smiled at us and bowed. Then, we started clapping our hands together harder and harder and yelling, 'Bravo, bravo.' After we had kept this up about ten minutes, the professor motioned for us to be still. But we kept right on applauding and applauding. Finally, the German sat down, but we kept on cheering him. We didn't stop for the whole hour and he never did get a chance to say a single word."

Ruth and I were impressed so much by the cleverness of Albert and his classmates that we asked him if he would take us to visit his school, the University of La Plata, on our next day off and Albert agreed.

When we arrived at the law school building the following week, we were greeted at the door by a committee of students who ushered us into a conference room, where we were seated in high-backed leather chairs around a big oval table. All of the law students were dressed in correct dark business suits and their mustaches were neatly trimmed. Clean-shaven Albert looked strangely like a plump brunette cherub among his somber classmates. They were older and more serious looking than university students in the United States.

I didn't see any bobby soxers and asked about the status of women in the university. The students told me that there were a few women in the university but not the large proportion of coeds found in the United States.

One young man, whom Albert introduced to us as the president of the La Plata Federation of Students, informed us that unlike the United States, the students of Argentina were a real political force. They were either Fascists, Conservatives, Democrats, Socialists or Communists. They took their politics as seriously as Yankee students took their college football.

As for rights, Argentine students were far ahead of their colleagues in the United States. Compulsory class attendance, for instance, had been abolished many years ago, and students found nonattendance an extremely practical way of eliminating professors who were inefficient or whose politics they didn't approve. For example, if one of the law professors started teaching Fascist doctrines, students who disagreed could simply stay away from his classes. He couldn't go on teaching to an empty room forever, so the students would eventually have a professor more to their liking. They even had a voice in choosing the dean of the law school.

Another boy explained that the school was now in the midst of a student election with the party lines sharply drawn between Fascist and Democratic students. The issue in the coming election was not who would be the campus beauty queen but whether Argentina should remain neutral or join the Allies. They then explained their alliance with students of other universities throughout the country and told how it had helped to bring about better conditions for students, as well as greater influence in national politics.

After our conference with the students, Albert took us in to meet his dean, a gentle little man, who served us coffee in his office. Ruth asked him to comment on the legality of President Castillo's state of siege. The question obviously distressed him and instead of replying he went to one of his book shelves and took out a manual on democracy he had written several years earlier for distribution among the armed forces. Then we asked him if he would discharge a professor for criticizing President Castillo or his policies. The dean promptly replied that his professors were free to criticize—that is, as long as they confined their criticisms to the policies of the government officials and did not attack the men personally.

The law school dean told us that many professors were also senators and representatives and that one of the surest ways to become president of Argentina was to get to be a college professor first.

Ruth and I left the University of La Plata that afternoon feeling ashamed of ourselves and other Americans because we knew so little of the fine institutions of learning in that land.

The revolution came two months later.

I had not particularly noticed the school children before then. I knew, of course, that they all wore white cotton pinafores which made the rich and poor look alike. And I had sometimes been amused to see little girls wearing fingernail polish and lipstick. Otherwise, I hadn't thought much about the school children of Argentina.

But almost overnight, it looked as if the country had been taken by an army of white pinafores. I guess I noticed them for the first time at the big Flag Day celebration just a couple of weeks after the military coup. There were thousands of them out that day. Row after white row walked through the streets, and behind and in front of them marched the soldiers. Many of the students were only seven or eight years old. It was a cold, windy day and I wondered how any mother could be foolish enough to let her child out of the house in a thin cotton uniform, bareheaded and without gloves. They shivered and their hands and faces turned blue with cold while they listened through the long nationalistic speeches.

The next day, a friend complained that her children had been given a holiday from school but were ordered to attend the celebration. Their teachers were required to be there to take the roll, and the principals were there to watch the teachers.

After that, no one could overlook the school children in their white pinafores. They were in every newsreel paying homage to one general or another. They lined the streets in parades and threw flowers at General Ramírez, later at General Farrell and still later at Colonel Perón. But they were always there, as ever-present as the blue and white Argentine flag.

Ruth and I used to go to all kinds of demonstrations after the military government came to power. We watched anti-United States meetings, nationalist students' rallies and the government holiday celebrations. The children were at all of them.

Ruth came home from visiting a friend one day with an alarming report. The friend's eleven-year-old daughter had wanted to show off before a visitor so she sang the June 4 revolution song—every word of it. Then she told Ruth that she "just loved to march." We knew then what was happening in the schools.

We knew one Argentine teacher—whose family had cherished liberty for generations. Her mother had been taught by some of the American teachers brought to Argentina by Sarmiento and she recalled the experience with obvious pride. The daughter also hated the military dictatorship but was attending every parade and demonstration. It was that or her job, and she needed the money. But out in the fresh air dictatorship wasn't so bad, she said. In the schools it was worse. She told us of the wholesale dismissal of every teacher in her school with a Jewish name. "Couldn't it have been for some other reason?" I asked.

"No," she replied, "only because they were Jews. Among them were some of the best teachers we had. Some had been at the school for ten and fifteen years."

But long before these dismissals began, the totalitarian teachings and the pattern of the Argentine school system had already become apparent.

One of the first acts of the new government was to modify the hitherto autonomous Universidad Nacional del Litoral. The pretext for so doing was that the school was "communistic," and to make sure that students would be taught no more "advanced (democratic) ideas" the well-known pro-Nazi, Jordan B. Genta, was named the interventor. To the astonishment of his students, he informed them that he had been sent there by God for the good of the country.

This self-proclaimed apostle, however, was greeted with boisterous irreverence by university students all over Argentina. Albert and his colleagues staged a demonstration in La Plata, the highlight of which was turning loose a pig bearing the name of Genta in big letters.

It was Genta's faith in Hitler, rather than in God, which forced his removal by the Minister of Education, Colonel Anaya. So great was the rejoicing in Santa Fe, the home of the university, that citizens rang church bells throughout the city.

The students' triumph was short-lived, however. Anaya's courage cost him his job. Genta was rewarded for his services at Litoral by an appointment as *interventor* in the National Teachers' College, where he was in a position to do far more damage to the democratic cause without being in the public eye. And to replace Anaya as Minister of Education, the government selected Dr. Gustavo Martínez Zuviría. Under the pen name of Hugo Wast he had written the most vicious anti-Semitic books in all South America. His works against Jews and democracy were in almost every Latin American bookstore, and his claim that fascism was the only means of world salvation was well known to most of the Argentines.

Just a short time before Zuviría's appointment, a group of some 150 prominent Argentines, many of them educators and professional men, had signed a manifesto asking for the restoration of constitutional government and for Argentina to break with the Axis. The new Minister of Education issued a decree ordering the immediate dismissal of all university professors who had signed the document.

This statement of the government's intention to remain friendly with the Axis and at the same time to liquidate academic opposition, caused great indignation in educational circles. Various university presidents resigned immediately rather than permit the expulsion of their pro-democratic teachers. Among them was Dr. Alfredo Palacios, the President of the University of La Plata and the grand old man of Argentina. A Socialist senator for many years, Palacios had been responsible for more liberal labor and social legislation than any other man. No man in public life was more respected by the people. Palacios' stand was that he would resign the presidency rather than oust six of his professors for signing the manifesto although he planned to continue teaching in the university.

When Dr. Palacios presented his resignation to the five-member faculty council, all but one of the others resigned rather than accept the post. The fifth council member, who then became president, was promptly burned in effigy by the students and at least once his image, labelled "Quisling," was found hanging by the neck from the highest flagpole.

The purge continued. The University of Buenos Aires lost seventeen professors, including such noted figures as Samuel Bosch, Rafael Augusto Bullrich, Mariano R. Castex and Bernardo A. Houssay. Twelve leaders of the University of Córdoba were discharged; the University of Litoral lost eight; the University of La Plata, six; the Ministry of Public Instruction, six; and the National Council of Education, one. Houssay and Castex immediately fled to Uruguay to escape arrest, as did several other of the manifesto signers.

Zuviría was only beginning his strangulation of education in Argentina. He outlawed the powerful Federación Universitaria Argentina, the national association of university students, branding it "communistic."

The democratic federation retaliated with a nation-wide student strike. We saw a lot of Albert and his friends during those days and they told us of the arrest of many of their classmates. Students who had part-time jobs in the government were warned that if they supported the strike they would lose their jobs. If the father of a university student worked in a public office, he was visited by a government official and told that unless his son returned to the classroom he would be discharged. No pressure was too big or too little to be brought on the students. Some of the student leaders were called in by government officials and offered soft jobs at high salaries if they would fall in line with the new regime. Albert was offered a job at $125 a month—which is a princely sum for a student—if he would use his influence to get his friends back to classes. Albert refused. About that time, the students began to take up collections for a clandestine paper. Albert stopped smoking so he could use cigarette money to help buy newsprint and pay printers. He walked instead of riding a bus, thereby saving two and a half cents.

As was to be expected, a few of the students liked the new government and found it profitable to inform on their democratic classmates. But Albert and his friend, Arturo, took effective steps to muzzle one group of pro-Fascist students who lived together in a large house in La Plata after learning they had made overtures to the army leaders. One evening Albert and his cohorts mailed a large quantity of leftist literature, as well as several dozen copies of the student underground newspaper, all addressed to students in that house.

Then they watched cautiously while the postman delivered the package. After allowing a reasonable time for the students to open it, Albert telephoned the La Plata police with the anonymous tip that a group of Communists were living at the address of the Fascist students. Then Albert and his friends sauntered over to that neighborhood to watch their project bear fruit.

The police were prompt and a few moments later Albert saw them dragging out half a dozen young men who were loudly protesting, "But we're Fascists. We're not Communists, we're Fascists!" The young men and the literature were taken together to the central police station. It took about three days for the students to establish proof that they were actually Fascists and therefore entitled to continue their studies unmolested. By planting such evidence, Albert had shown a keen understanding of government policies regarding education. Every repressive measure was taken under the guise of fighting communism, even though communism is a negligible influence in student life in Argentina.

We learned something of what Zuviría ordered teachers to stress and ignore in their classrooms from a friend who worked part time as a teacher and part time as a journalist. He had been warned by his superiors to ignore certain sections in the primary school history books and in particular to skip lightly over the section dealing with the life and works of Sarmiento. He had been ordered to emphasize and glorify Rosas, the Argentine dictator and bloody tyrant of a century ago.

Meanwhile, a mother reported to us how her daughter in kindergarten was being indoctrinated even before she knew how to read and write. On the child's return from school one afternoon, the mother asked what she had learned that day. "Oh, we learned about the other countries," she answered. "And what did you learn about them?" the mother asked.

The little girl promptly recited, "We learned that the other countries are our friends, but the United States is our enemy!"

From his exile in neighboring Uruguay, Dr. Gumersindo Sayago, one of the professors ousted from the University of Córdoba for signing the manifesto, charged that in primary schools and high schools an "unfortunately large number of totalitarian teachers install a false concept of sovereignty by exalting the hate of the foreigner, especially the North American."

It was about this time that Zuviría issued his swan song on the task of education in Argentina:

"The country must be Christianized in harmony with its history and constitution. The birthrate, rather than immigration, must be increased .... The doctrines of hate and atheism must be eradicated .... The revolution was carried out under our one and only flag and under the sign of the Cross."

To help along his "Christianizing" process, Zuviría made two important appointments in the educational field. José María Rosa, Jr., was named Director of the Board of Education in the province of Santa Fe, and Julio Sanguinetti was given a similar post in the province of Buenos Aires. Both had been previously identified with the Axis-financed press.

Another appointment was that of an army officer to the chair of educational philosophy in a normal school. He was given the job after Zuviría and his associates decided that the teacher who had held the post for many years, a Jew, should not be entrusted with a position in which it was possible to mold the opinion of future teachers. Thus the army officer was induced to take the position. The students shortly began to ask their new teacher questions. Unqualified as he was, he could never answer them. One day he became infuriated by their questions, began pounding his desk and shouting, "Will you stop asking me questions! I don't know anything about the subject. I'm only here because it is my duty!"

An Argentine educator friend of ours told us at a cocktail party one night of his own experiences with the military government. The man, a school inspector, had been one of the first to lose his job under the new regime because he had always been an outspoken friend of the United States and of democracy. His greatest hero was Henry Wallace.

He described how he had become friendly during the previous summer's vacation with a navy man and how they always exchanged warm *abrazos* when they met on the street, in true Latin fashion. On their last meeting, some weeks past, the naval man proudly informed our friend that he had just been appointed second in command of a battleship.

The previous day, he had been surprised to get a telephone call from the navy officer. "Can you help me out?" he was asked. "But I don't know anything about battleships," the school man confessed. "Oh, it isn't that," he was told. "I've been named the head of a division in the Department of Education and I don't know anything about it."

Our friend reached for another San Martín cocktail and beamed as he recalled his reply. "I just said, 'Well, I don't think I should. You know what is happening to collaborationists in France these days.' "

Meanwhile Zuviría, an ardent Catholic, continued to cultivate the church in a move to get its wholehearted support for the new government. And on December 31, 1943, the day that all political parties were dissolved, the government issued a sensational decree— Catholic religious instruction for all public schools. The decree stated that the Department of Religious Instruction, under Zuviría, had been created for the purpose of controlling the teaching of the Roman Catholic religion.

Parents could request that their children be excused from religious instruction, the government promised. In practice, however, this was seldom considered advisable. A father holding a government post, or being in any way connected with the government, automatically put his job in jeopardy by making such a request.

An overwhelming majority of Argentines are Catholic, but religion has been separated from the schools for generations. The decree met with mixed reception from Catholics, some of them believing that religious instruction should be confined to the church and the home. But those who held such sentiments seldom dared express them, as government statistics later showed. The Ministry of Justice and Public Instruction announced that 91.1 per cent of the pupils under the ministry's jurisdiction had chosen to take the courses of religious instruction, and the remaining 8.9 per cent favored moral instruction. The percentages of pupils who had been exempted from religious instructions in eight of the provinces were: Buenos Aires, 2.05; Catamarca, 0.00; Córdoba, 0.60; Corrientes, 0.05; Entre Ríos, 4.36; Salta, 0.40; San Juan, 0.09; and San Luis, 0.10 per cent.

Ruth and I watched education go farther and farther down the totalitarian path, with practically every issue of a Buenos Aires newspaper printing short filler items about teachers being discharged for "communism," for obstructionist tactics, for "indiscipline" or equally obscure offenses. At the end of the first year of the revolutionary government, the National Board of Education announced it had dismissed 348 teachers and others considered "unworthy of the honor of being teachers in Argentine schools or forming part of the administrative staff of the board." Of the total, sixty-four were discharged for "Communist activities," fifty-four for "immorality," forty-six for "disorderly conduct."

Argentina's rupture of relations with the Axis came early in 1944. Many Argentines believed that their schools would soon be allowed to revert to the liberal tradition of Sarmiento. Support for their optimism came with the removal of Zuviría, the most frankly pro-Nazi member of the cabinet, less than a month later.

But later events proved them too trusting. President Ramírez was almost immediately ousted and Perón soon came to the fore as the Argentine "strong man." The hated Zuviría was replaced in the highest educational post in the land by Dr. Alberto Baldrich, a political adventurer who had been known as a Communist but had since "matured" into a nationalist and rabid anti-*yanqui*. Baldrich had recently distinguished himself by expropriating certain American interests while serving as federal commissioner of the province of Tucumán. The street car company had been taken over, and Tucumán street cars were seen proudly flying the Argentine flag on the trolley rope and displaying posters which read, "This Car Argentine."

In his new post, Baldrich received a full-page tribute from the Nazi-financed *El Federal,* on the first anniversary of the revolution. The newspaper, which had appeared under the name of *El Pampero* until the rupture of relations with the Axis, said that the universities were now in good hands. Also praised by *El Federal* was Dr. José Ignacio Olmedo, the head of the National Council of Education. *El Federal* rejoiced over the fact that Olmedo had been given the responsibility for molding Argentine children into the nationalistic ideology.

Dr. Olmedo came up to the newspaper's expectations by ordering all teachers of children from the third through the sixth grade to hold special classes for three days during the revolution celebration and giving the teachers a list of nationalistic slogans which they were ordered to keep on their blackboards during the period. Among these were:

"Our Fatherland exists by the free determination of its people and by the victorious strength of its sword."

"We are a free and constitutional nation, therefore have the inalienable right of carrying out a great function in America."

"It is not enough to be an Argentine, you must know how to prove it."

"To be Argentine does not constitute a peaceful, contemplative or literary position. To be Argentine is a dynamic and essentially active condition."

Special slogans were issued for the girls. Among them were:

"One son more is a new sentinel of sovereignty."

"The new Argentina wants healthy, strong and heroic women."

"The Argentine woman must know how to fulfill her natural obligation with zeal."

A short time later found Baldrich enlarging his scope to advise soldiers in the *Gaceta Oficial* that "when the sword of the military is unsheathed it is not merely a piece of shining metal but a materialization of the spirit in which is present nothing less than the Fatherland itself. For this reason, to have a Fatherland and to be its soldier is one and the same thing."

The same warlike note was reflected in the July, 1944, issue of the Bulletin of the Ministry of Justice and Public Instruction, which stated, "The State is an order that is at once warlike and cultural . . . it is a society that is by definition an army whose arms are prepared for battle and whose souls are prepared for flight (dying)."

Only four days after his appointment as Minister, Baldrich ordered all pupils to write a composition based on the principles expounded by General Farrell at a special Pan-American Day address during which the President complained that "Argentina is not understood" by the other countries of the Americas.

When one pupil, Martha Grinberg, a fifth year student, received her copy of the Farrell speech, she tore the copy into small pieces before the other students and her teacher.

When the incident reached the attention of Baldrich, he promptly expelled Martha from school and announced that she also would be prohibited from attending any other school in the Argentine republic. Furthermore, the principals had been entirely too lenient with Martha, and for that they were ordered suspended from their posts for fifteen days.

Martha was soon to be joined by other grade school pupils.

Bernardo Wolnivch, a Uruguayan, and sixth grade pupil, was expelled from his school and prohibited admission to others for being an "unworthy and bad foreigner." Bernardo had at the end of a patriotic ceremony torn his national rosette from his pinafore, thrown it to the ground, and spat on it.

Similar measures were taken against Bernardo Schievitch, a pupil of an adults' school, who, upon being reproached for not having attended a patriotic ceremony, replied that he could not be "forced to love" his country's flag.

Juan Moroz, an eight-year-old Russian, also was expelled when it was reported that he had "used offensive words with regard to the person of His Excellency the President of the Republic." A like fate befell Moses Levy, age fifteen, when it was charged that he caused a disturbance during a ceremony held in homage to the Argentine flag. Another boy, Antonio de Simón, was expelled for derisive whistles during a lecture on Flag Day.

During this period, Argentina was in a diplomatic quarantine, unrecognized by most of the countries of the world. Soon President Farrell's government began to make a few token gestures toward democracy, and with these came the "resignation" of Dr. Baldrich.

These moves apparently fooled no one inside the country, least of all the nationalist students. For days before the Día del Estudiante celebration, sound trucks paraded the streets announcing the Marcha de Antorchas or torchlight parade, sponsored by the pro-Nazi Sindicato Universitario Argentino, much smaller than the democratic Federación Universitaria Argentina, but noisier.

On the day of the parade the streets were flooded early with pamphlets attacking such men as Doctor Palacios and other democratic leaders, but the students waited for dusk to fall before beginning their march from the closed Congress building to Plaza de Mayo. Their torches cast a red glow over the crowds as they marched in almost military formation down the avenue shouting such slogans as *"Mate sí, whisky no,"* and *"Sanciones, ha! ha! ha!"* The reference to sanctions was made at a time when there was much talk of the United States imposing economic sanctions against Argentina for her failure to live up to her treaty commitments.

The nationalist students stopped along the line of march to throw stones into the plate glass window of the democratic newspaper, *Crítica*. To our astonishment we found an American friend in this crowd, carrying a torch and shouting nationalist slogans in Spanish. When the police took away the youth who had hurled the stone, our friend followed behind them, and later reported to us that the young man had been quietly turned loose on a side street a block away. After a pause in front of the Axis-controlled newspaper, *Momento Argentino*, to pay tribute to it for its support of "neutrality," the students massed in the beautiful plaza, directly in front of the Government House.

What I saw in the plaza was both impressive and sinister. The nationalist students had rigged up a tremendously large Argentine flag. It was draped vertically with a big condor of metal on top of it. Then there were smaller flags, also hanging vertically. Hundreds of blazing torches and mounted police with glittering trappings all around made us feel as if we had stepped somehow into the middle ages. The smoke from the torches cast a stinking haze through the whole plaza. It was one of the weirdest sights I had ever seen.

The speeches followed the usual Nazi line, favoring neutrality, the Perón-Farrell government, and opposing cooperation with the democracies.

About this time Doctor Palacios, who had been under constant police supervision since he resigned as president of the University of La Plata, made his escape by night across the River Plate to small but intensely democratic Uruguay.

Albert woke us up early the next morning to tell about it. Doctor Palacios, as we knew, was one of the most easily recognized men in Argentina. His handlebar mustaches, broad-brimmed black hat and long-flowing black cape made him an easy figure for the police to watch, and he was followed everywhere he went. It had been impossible for him to leave the country as his house had been under observation at all hours.

Then, according to Albert, one of the educator's favorite students had an idea which was communicated to the proper channels, and the necessary preparations were made. One night the student went to call on his old professor. Some time later, "Doctor Palacios" was seen leaving the house and the plain-clothes police naturally followed the figure in the black cape and wide-brimmed hat. Meanwhile, the real Doctor Palacios inconspicuously left by the back way to take the secret route to Uruguay. Behind him, he left a letter of resignation which further damaged the prestige of the military government.

"Educators," said Doctor Palacios, "are the soul of the nation; they study its problems, scrutinize its ways, and strengthen its sentiments . . . . But now I cannot teach with dignity because I have not liberty. I do not see any way of filling the chair, under police vigilance. . . . I am leaving the country with great grief. . . . Taking away our liberty means denying our traditions."

In late 1944 and early 1945, the military regime began to show unmistakable signs of shifting towards the democratic processes in education. It was the eve of the Mexico City Conference when the Farrell-Perón government was anxious to appear in a good light abroad and thus win long delayed recognition from the other American governments.

In February, 1945, the cabinet met and voted to reinstate all university professors who had lost their jobs for signing the pro-Allied manifesto eighteen months earlier. Special pains were taken to point out that the dismissals had taken place during the regime of President Ramírez. The government press office announced that President Farrell had "interrupted his convalescence" to attend the meeting.

Perón, also seeking a seat in the "democratic" bandwagon, called on the Minister of Public Instruction that same day, and the Minister later revealed that Colonel Perón had urged him to call university elections and thereby restore autonomy to the universities.

The decree was then issued ending intervention at the Universities of Buenos Aires, Córdoba, Tucumán, Cuyo and Litoral. Elections were called for March to select university governing councils, which in turn would select the deans and delegates to the supreme councils.

The elections were held and the democratic forces again gained control. The honeymoon lasted for some six months—from shortly before the Mexico City Conference where Argentina obtained continental recognition to after the San Francisco Conference where she was given a seat with the United Nations.

Argentina's delegates to San Francisco hardly had time to return to Buenos Aires, unpack their suitcases and sit down to *bifes*, however, before the conflict between the democratic educational forces and the totalitarian government was resumed.

This time the students took the offensive, and for the first time in twenty-seven years, all of the universities in the country were closed in a twenty-four-hour nation-wide strike to demonstrate the opposition of the entire student population—leftists and rightists alike—to the military regime and to demand the return of democratic, constitutional government. Some thirty thousand students of all political complexions were called out by the university federation. The students were mainly incensed by the government's international double-dealing.

For even though Argentina had joined the United Nations and declared war on the Axis, pro-democratic forces attempting to celebrate the fall of Berlin had been fired on by the police.

And when the Japanese surrender came, some two hundred uniformed troops, led by their non-commissioned officers, invaded the streets of Buenos Aires shouting, "*Viva* Hitler! *Viva* Mussolini! *Viva* Perón! Down with Democracy! Death to the Jews!" and "Long Live Germany!" When bystanders refused to proclaim their support of Perón, they were beaten. At the end of two days' rioting, four persons had been killed and more than a hundred wounded, many of them students.

Secondary school teachers of the nation then proposed a period of mourning and the suspension of classes for two days to show their "repudiation of the vandalistic deeds committed by totalitarian and retrograde movements." The government immediately dismissed by decree the twenty-four high school teachers, including fourteen women, who had signed the original manifesto. But most of the high schools remained closed, and those that did open were shunned by teachers and students alike.

The greatest wave of terrorism and retaliation in recent Argentine history followed the giant "March of the Constitution and Freedom," a pro-democratic demonstration, in September, 1945. The abortive military uprising led by General Arturo Rawson in Córdoba a few days later gave the authorities an excuse to re-impose the state of siege and punish their critics.

Within twenty-four hours, educational and cultural leaders were crowded into jail cells all over Argentina. Among them were all six presidents of the country's universities, along with many deans and professors. Three of the presidents, those of the Universities of Buenos Aires, Córdoba and Litoral, had signed a declaration asking the military government to surrender its powers to the Supreme Court. The head of Litoral University had been even more blunt. He had signed his name at the top of a list of some one hundred professors petitioning the Supreme Court to withdraw its recognition from the regime.

The university students answered with a nation-wide program of civil disobedience. They barricaded themselves inside university buildings in the heart of the capital, as well as in the universities located in the provinces. Embattled students in the engineering school of the University of Buenos Aires were only a few feet away from Colonel Perón's stronghold, the Secretariat of Labor and Social Welfare.

As soon as the students of the University of Buenos Aires took over the engineering, law and social science buildings, large squads of armed police attempted to storm the buildings. When the students still held out, thirty armed men walked across the street from the direction of the Secretariat of Labor and fired on the students, wounding two.

A day later masses of police, accompanied by the local fire brigade, surrounded the University of La Plata. First they broke down the great door and then hurled tear gas bombs while the firemen turned fire hoses on the students trying to hold them back. From classroom to classroom the battle raged. With tear gas and truncheons the police fought against students armed with the only weapons they could find—chairs and benches, blackboards and school books. When the battle ended, eleven students, including women, had such severe police saber cuts in the head that they had to be rushed to first aid stations. And of the 250 students and professors arrested, at least 50 were injured.

Police in the capital were just as ruthless as they had been in La Plata. They broke into the University of Buenos Aires buildings, and arrested between 1,500 and 2,000 university students and professors, including 200 girl students and professors' wives. The women were thrown into cells with prostitutes.

Similar drastic action was taken to evict students barricaded inside other universities.

A people aroused by the needlessly harsh treatment of its students was one of the factors which swept Colonel Perón temporarily from power in October, 1945. It is significant that one of the first acts of the new two-man cabinet was to issue a decree re-opening all Argentine universities.

But Colonel Perón and his cohorts were able to regain power and brought back with them their totalitarian ideas of education.

However, the university students continued to oppose Perón strongly through the campaigning for presidential elections. His election was a severe blow to them. The votes—cast in freedom and counted honestly—knocked out a main prop from student opposition to military government, their argument that the regime was "unconstitutional." It also gave Perón a free hand to enforce his will on the universities. Promptly the students announced they would return to their classrooms, "enriched by the experience" of fighting Perón, and that there would be no more student strikes such as that in September, 1945.

Some men might have been content with this declaration that the students were abandoning their greatest weapon, but not Perón. On May 4, a month before his inauguration as president, the government again sent *"interventores"* into all six of the nation's universities, with orders to eliminate "politics" and to recommend "reforms" in their teachings.

Perón still had not completely silenced the opposition to him in the universities, but in his Five-Year Plan, presented to Congress in October, 1946, he sounded the death knell for free education. Under the plan, the new President would control the educational system; Perón would appoint a National Council of Education to choose teachers and select the curricula, and he would also name the president of each one of the universities.

It was obvious that teachers and professors who defended anti-government attitudes must either be "converted" to the cause or lose their jobs and in some cases their freedom; and those students outspoken against their "constitutionally elected" president could expect expulsion and possibly arrest. Their disappearance from the top rung of the nation's educational ladder would hardly be noticed, for soon there would be plenty of students with the officially correct views moving up from the secondary schools to replace them.

Perón's "purge" of both educators and students in the universities proceeded rapidly in late 1946 and early 1947. Several hundred university professors hostile to Perón's doctrines were dismissed or resigned voluntarily in protest. Scores of students barred from Argentina's universities for their continued opposition to the government sought higher learning in neighboring Uruguay and Chile. Others with smaller financial resources were forced to abandon their university training.

When Perón leaves office five years hence—if he does—it seems likely that his type of instruction will by then have snuffed out the flame of educational freedom which had been lighted by Sarmiento but a few decades ago.

The next few years will open up new opportunities for thousands of young Argentines. There is great need of technicians and skilled workers to supervise operations of men and machines. Perón's Five-Year Plan called for a vast expansion of industry, and it also outlined a system of State schools to prepare Argentine youth for a place in the industrial Argentina. Many students will be encouraged to abandon the classics in favor of the monkey wrench, blueprints and industrial charts.

Our friend Albert will not like this. There will be limited room for him in the new Argentina. For with the shining new gadgets in the laboratories will go regimented flag-waving, over-doses of super-nationalism and deification of the leader. All this will be repulsive to Albert, who reached intellectual maturity before the revolution of 1943. But Albert has a little brother. He already knows how to march, and he has learned to like it. He has many years remaining in the classroom. And it is in his school days—not Albert's—that there will be education for Perón.

WE MEET THE PEOPLE

I N A WAY, MY FRIEND A—— IS A THROWBACK TO THE FIERCE, wild and cantankerously proud *gauchos* who roamed the Argentine pampas a century ago. She would be the first to ridicule that idea, of course, for today A—— is a middle-aged and highly intelligent spinster, with plenty of money and an elaborate house in Buenos Aires. But amidst the gilt and silk of her home dwells an Argentine rebel, an individualist as rugged in her way as the vanished *gaucho* was in his.

The black eyes snap as A—— talks about "that man" in Casa Rosada.

"Aren't those kerosene lines a disgrace?" she asked me one day, referring to the queues of persons waiting to obtain fuel for their stoves. I remarked that they were unfortunate, but that Argentina had been lucky in feeling the war so little, that a shortage of kerosene seemed a small price to pay for peace.

"Nonsense," A—— interrupted, "we have plenty of kerosene here. It isn't that at all. It's just that man Perón, trying to humiliate us. He's trying to wound our *dignidad* by making us wait in line. He knows that if he can get us to do that, sooner or later he will be able to regiment us on the big things."

I assured her firmly that if ever regimentation came to the Argentines it would surely be in the distant future, long after she had gone to her resting place.

I have seldom seen an Argentine wait for anything, other than his old age pension.

Attempts to shackle the *porteño* with some of the supposed conveniences of modern civilization have ended mostly in dismal failure. He likes the gadgets, but he defies the hindrances. For instance, efficiency experts have succeeded in installing traffic lights in Buenos Aires, but they have never been able to keep them there; *porteños*, pedestrians and drivers alike, welcomed the go-ahead of the green light, but they stormed at—or ignored—the command of the red; eventually they ignored both colors, and traffic resumed its happy, chaotic normalcy; the lights were mercifully removed.

The city fathers still shake their heads when they recall the sudden death of another and supposedly *porteño*-proof plan. In an attempt to impose discipline at the busy Boston Bank corner, they posted signs saying, "Please do not cross the street until a policeman instructs you to do so." To make sure the new rule was enforced, uniformed police were spread liberally around the corners of this intersection, and another was placed in the middle to direct traffic. But the crowds disregarded them. Finally the police, angered by this disrespect, began blowing whistles and shouting. When that also failed, they grabbed wayward pedestrians by their collars and began hustling them back to the curb. But while they were busy, dozens of other *porteños* took advantage of the fracas to cross the street unmolested. The next day the signs were removed, and to this day crowds are only mildly restrained by the policemen in the centers of the intersections. In fact, I heard of one traffic officer who found his duties so light that he installed a charcoal brazier in his lofty, parasol-covered traffic stall and proceeded daily to cook *puchero* there for his evening meal.

Unregulated Buenos Aires at the close of the working day bears some resemblance to New York at the rush hour, but it has more the earmarks of a cattle stampede. The Argentines themselves have been quick to see this, and their most devastating insult is to call each other *animales* in sharp, piercing voices, while they too proceed to shove the unfortunate one nearest them.

When a *señora* or *señor* walks down a street he goes full-steam forward, and woe be to the passers-by not fleet of foot enough to step aside. I had been stepping aside for years, when one day my spirit of adventure got the better of me. I wanted to see what would happen if I did not. I was in front of Harrod's on Florida and a portly, well-groomed matron was bearing down in my direction with all of the determination of a two-ton tractor. But I didn't flinch, I kept walking straight ahead too. The matron also refused to budge and of course, we collided. The repercussion was sudden and violent, and shoppers in a radius of fifty feet heard that I was a badly-educated *animal* unfit to be on the same street with ladies and gentlemen. Under the barrage, I beat a hasty retreat around the corner.

The only victory I ever witnessed over the national impulse to get ahead by sheer physical force came to a lone traffic policeman. He too had been caught in a crowd pushing to catch a bus. The policeman was knocked down by the mob and only managed to get to his feet in time to order the driver to leave the scene with his vehicle empty. "Now you can just wait here until you've learned to act like human beings instead of *animales*," he ordered, then strode triumphantly away, his dignity fully restored.

However, I've always thought that one of the greatest charms of the Argentine is his steadfast refusal to submit to the yoke of discipline. He is an individualist, even a maverick. Perhaps, this trait has its roots in a fierce pride which flares in nearly every Argentine; an almost psychopathic craving to put both his best feet forward in the least possible time.

The city of Buenos Aires, as well as each individual Argentine, mirrors the importance of maintaining a good "front." It penetrates all social strata.

An under-paid clerk may be down to his last peso, but he will spend it to treat a friend to a coffee or insist that he pay his friend's fare on a street car or bus. He would rather walk the next day than forego the opportunity of making even the smallest impression of his affluence.

Although his salary be only $50 a month, his pride demands that he keep up appearances of much greater prosperity. One of the most important things in his life is to have a big wedding, with all the trimmings of a church ceremony, including tails for himself and a wedding dress with train for the bride. The costumes may be rented, but who in the audience could be sure of that? In order to finance all this, he may be forced to postpone his marriage for a year or two, but this is of minor consequence compared with the necessity of doing the thing properly and appearing successful before his relatives and friends.

When the children start coming, the man again must demonstrate that he is doing well financially. It wouldn't do to carry the child to the church for baptism; the infant must be taken in a cab, even if the parents live just around the corner from the church and are forced to skimp on a day's food to pay for it.

In the higher social circles, it becomes even more imperative to appear as well off as one's friends and neighbors. It so happens that it is most unfashionable for any members of Argentina's wealthy set—those whose names appear in the Golden Book—to be seen in Buenos Aires during the sweltering summer season. It just isn't done by *las familias "bien."* We were told of one family, in financial difficulties as the vacation season rolled around, who dismissed their servants for the summer and closed up the entire house with the exception of a back room. The family stayed there in seclusion all summer, never venturing out by light of day or when any of their friends might be in the neighborhood. They didn't trust their servants enough to let them in on the secret.

Smart landlords cater to the national penchant for creating a swank façade, and probably no city in the world can boast *porteros* of such elegance and dash as the men who open and close the doors for apartment house dwellers in Buenos Aires. Some of them wear white gloves on duty, and their long coats of maroon, green or grey with matching caps are a dazzling and impressive spectacle. Gold braid was not uncommon to the wardrobes of these doorway custodians until wartime scarcities left only enough for the Army.

We were quite awed when we moved into our first little one-room apartment. The rent was only $47.50 a month, but the spacious entrance had been entirely lined with mirrors, and for the first time in my life I had the heady experience of having a bowing, uniformed attendant push elevator buttons for me and rush to open cab doors.

But my days as a grand *señora* were numbered. I lost my *dignidad*.

This is how it happened. One fine spring day, Leonard and I decided to do our own marketing at the corner *feria*. We sauntered leisurely from stall to stall in an orgy of buying—oranges, celery, meat and cabbage. In the process, we saw and were puzzled by the furtive, hurried air of other customers making their purchases. One gentleman in particular attracted our attention. He was carrying a neat traveling bag, the kind Argentines prefer to take on week-end trips to the country. We noticed him look around, then slip over to a vegetable stall, buy a few centavos worth of food and speedily drop it into his suitcase. This seemed such a curious procedure, that we began to observe other well-dressed persons, also with suitcases that were rapidly being filled with fresh produce. They appeared to be in such haste to get their traveling bags closed that they weren't even bothering to haggle over prices.

Meanwhile, our own paper bags began to bulge with fresh pineapple, stalks of asparagus and those good things that Argentina has in such abundance. Finally, with our pockets nearly empty and our arms full, we hissed for a cab—the only way to get one in Argentina.

It drove us up to our apartment house, and as usual our smiling *portero* paraded out to open the taxi door. But on this occasion the smile fell so completely off his face that I thought he had been stricken with an attack of indigestion. He took a second look at our bundles and then stared the other way, while we struggled to open the apartment house door for ourselves and operated the elevator as best we could.

In all my *yanqui* innocence, I speculated thereafter on the possibility that the porter was allergic to vitamins in the raw. Invariably he blanched at the sight of a cucumber or a carrot and glued his eyes to distant horizons when we sullied his grand lobby with a shopping bag.

Stubbornly I persevered in my flagrant marketing, even when an egg plant slipped out of my arms and bounced at his well-shod feet. But one day fate conspired against me. I passed a shop with an attractive display of week-end luggage, including a smart, imitation leather case for only four pesos. In a few minutes it was mine, and from that day forward the Greenups concealed their carrots from the public gaze, thereby re-establishing diplomatic relations with their porter.

And so we entered skim-milk society by way of our synthetic leather traveling bag. Later we edged a little nearer the top of the Argentine bottle when we hired a maid to carry our shopping bags and rose still closer to the cream level when she in turn began camouflaging her excursions to the butcher with a suitcase.

The cream is rarely tasted by visiting Yankees, who, nevertheless, are tremendously impressed by the aura of super-refinement that envelopes any Argentine who reaches the income tax level. By then, he is repulsed at the thought of carrying a package at all.

J. J. Rugeroni, the Argentine-born publisher of the *Buenos Aires Herald*, used to delight his foreign readers by chronicling the mores of this upper crust.

One day, Mr. Rugeroni recalled with some amusement the horror of a young American, only recently arrived in the country, who burst into the American Club at the lunch hour, still excited over a scene he had just witnessed in a near-by shoe store.

An Argentine near the young man had selected a pair of shoes and handed a one hundred peso note to the clerk. When he received his change, he informed the employee that the shoes must be delivered before two o'clock at his home. The clerk apologized, saying that the delivery wagon had already gone, and therefore the shoes couldn't be sent out until four o'clock. His customer protested that he couldn't wait that long; he was on his way home for lunch, and he wanted the shoes there when he had finished his meal. The clerk then offered to wrap the purchase in as small a parcel as possible so the gentleman could carry it home himself. The customer drew himself up. Did the shop person think that he was attending a servant? "No! By no means! Impossible!" He did not carry parcels and was not going to begin to do so at this time of life. The attendant then said that under the circumstances it would be better if he took his money back—and that was exactly what happened.

In attempting to explain the attitude of the *niño* "*bien*" who wouldn't carry home his own new shoes, Mr. Rugeroni pointed out, "You see, his father never carried a parcel in his life though his grandfather may well have carried a hod."

The publisher then proceeded to tell of one of his own acquaintances, a "cove who had his chauffeur carry his overcoat in the lift up to his offices as he considers it below his dignity to have anything in his hands even in a lift."

One well-known Buenos Aires businessman, who fancied himself something of an authority on how to get ahead in the land of the River Plate, once disclosed to a new arrival in the country some of the minor secrets of creating a favorable impression in society.

In all seriousness, he told him that in Argentina it is more important to have a chauffeur than an automobile. Why? Because the chauffeur can be shown off in the club or office while the car—if indeed the man has one—must obviously remain parked on the street. And men who get their hair cut at the ultra-fashionable Jockey Club have a distinct social edge on the patrons of an ordinary barber shop.

While only a sprinkling are ever privileged to submit to the shears in the luxurious salons of one of the world's most exclusive clubs, the Argentine man, nevertheless, considers himself the best-groomed and best-dressed on the globe. Clothes are highly important to him because better than anything else they can give the impression of success. Consequently each man spends a good part of his time and his money on his tailor-made wardrobe. And he keeps it spic and span, too. I learned one of the tricks of his superb street appearance while working at Reuters, where most of the staff members are Argentines and men.

As each cable writer and translator entered the office he walked over to my desk, not to greet me but to reach for his "work pants" hanging back of my chair. Then he would retreat to the men's room and come back a few minutes later in his old clothes. His street trousers were smoothed on a hanger and his coat draped neatly on top. This daily ritual completed, he was ready for work. Nothing ever changed this routine, not even the revolution or the fall of Mussolini. And when the entire staff was mobilized for D-Day, the translators spent hectic hours supplying flashes for the innumerable extras put out over the city—but not until they had taken off their good pants first.

Most of the suits hanging so carefully behind me were painstakingly tailored, with heavily padded shoulders and wasp waists in typical *porteño* fashion, and their hues were as cautious and somber as the dour, unsmiling expression the Argentine assumes for public appearances when he's cut off from the close ties of his family and friends.

While the Argentine man is justifiably pleased with his own appearance, he takes even greater pride in that of his wife. Newspapers print editorials praising the grooming of the country's women, and both *La Nación* and *La Prensa* carry special Sunday features with photographs showing the latest styles from New York and Paris, which are copied promptly and skilfully by every neighborhood *modista* (dressmaker).

Although the women traditionally follow the dictates of Paris, during the war years old issues of *Vogue* and *Harper's Bazaar* became so sought after that one news stand was asking and getting $2.50 a copy. With the liberation of Paris, however, the feminine half of the nation turned its eyes again toward Europe; and before even General De Gaulle could get back home, news of what the French had designed during the occupation had already been relayed to Buenos Aires. Soon, fashionable Argentine women began appearing in duplicates of the French layer-cake hats which greeted Allied troops when they first entered the great fashion center.

The women of Buenos Aires spend many more hours assembling their wardrobes than their sisters in the United States. The exclusive shops with ready-made dresses are too expensive for most pocketbooks; consequently it is necessary to visit a little *modista* whose talented fingers create a stunning model from any of a variety of superb British, national or American materials which fill shelves throughout the country. Granted, the *señora* may have to go back again and again for fittings in the *modista's* humble dwelling before the dress is finished, but when it is, she provides real justification for the national pride in grooming. American women, she believes, are not as well-dressed as she is, because their clothes are too much alike, being produced in dozen lots. The Argentine woman need have little fear of encountering a dress just like her own at a party, a disaster she has observed more than once in the Hollywood movies. Her hats, shoes and even her handbag can be just as distinctive as her dresses, for she can have them designed especially for her, at only a fraction more than she would pay for the mass-produced articles.

Nor is there a single unbecoming note to mar the picture of elegance she creates when she sallies out for tea. Every hair has been lacquered into perfection by one of the hundreds of beauticians, both male and female, who do a land-office business. Prices in beauty parlors are only a fraction of what they are in the United States. As late as 1945, after fees were upped about 30 per cent by government decree, the shop I visited charged less than $3 for a permanent; and a shampoo, finger wave and manicure came to only a dollar. Even with the price rise, the beauty parlor remained an institution to be visited with regularity and devotion. Servants spend almost as much time as their mistresses in the parlors, and when they serve the table at dinner their coiffures may be as elaborate and shining as the sculptured heads of the guests.

In this glossy atmosphere flourish many aids to grooming. False hair and wig merchants are plentiful and prosperous, their windows displaying a fascinating array of curls, buns, rolls and complete head covering ranging in hues from blonde to rosy red.

Near by, perfume is sold not by the dram alone but in bottles as big as milk containers. And fashionable women spray it on with such abandon that Calle Florida at the tea hour becomes suffocating with the mingled scents of a thousand and one flowers. Significantly, the cosmetic counter was one of the few institutions in the land strong enough to withstand unscathed the revolution and the changes it brought. The metal lipstick stayed the same simulated gold under Perón—even when the new government got so hard up for metal that it denied visiting Uruguayan athletes permission to take home the loving cups they had won in Argentina. And the women continued to apply its fruity hues as liberally as ever, along with such quantities of pancake makeup, powder, rouge and mascara that a friend of mine, recently arrived in the country from Europe, got the mistaken notion that the entire female population of Buenos Aires was made up of actresses.

Yet it is easy to acquire mistaken ideas about the people of Argentina, and one of them would be to assume that they have no other cult than the pursuit of beauty; for them the grooming of the mind is as important as the grooming of the body. Beauty parlors thrive but so do bookstores, and they stay open longer.

One of the things I like best about Buenos Aires is these wonderful bookstores—from little secondhand shops along Calle Corrientes that stay open until midnight every night, to the spectacular establishments in elite shopping districts.

Of the latter, my favorite is the new Peuser's, which is so considerate of its customers that it has installed big easy chairs and arranged the books around them, thus enabling the patron to relax in comfort while he decides what he would like to buy, if anything.

Unless summoned, salesmen politely ignore the readers, even if they stay an hour or two and walk out with empty hands. The store not only carries the latest best sellers in English, a great variety of works in French and the best in Spanish literature, but is also equipped with a large art gallery in the rear. The display of handsome leather-bound *criollo* classics is enough to make any collector's eyes glisten with acquisitiveness. Invariably these visits to Peuser's left me disgruntled with the limited buying power of fourth estate salaries. I still handle reverently the gorgeous handtooled leather volume of *Rasjidos*, a collection of *criollo* songs, which Leonard bought for me there one Christmas. There were many other volumes just as beautiful that we couldn't afford, including a cow-hide, illustrated edition of *Martín Fierro*, which we admired on repeated occasions. These finely printed and bound books are also out of reach of most Argentines, the price for some being about $15 or $20 a volume, but big stores all over the city continue to display these treasures with great pride, and the proportion of deluxe volumes they offer seems to be higher than in New York. However, only such classics of Argentine literature as *Martín Fierro, Fausto, Facundo* and *Don Segundo Sombra* ever repose between fine covers. Most contemporary authors—foreign and national alike—reach the public by way of paper jacket, the average retailing for between fifty and seventy-five cents. Most of them come from printing presses only a few blocks away which have kept so busy during the past few years that Buenos Aires has become the publishing center of the Spanish-speaking world.

This new industrial and cultural plum fell to the Argentines at the end of the Spanish Civil War, when many important Spanish publishing houses fled Europe to locate in the friendlier atmosphere of the River Plate. They brought with them an industrial knowhow, as well as a cosmopolitan taste in literature, which has improved the reading habits of an entire continent, and at the same time enhanced immensely Argentina's prestige as a cultural leader.

Today, Argentina leads all other Latin American countries in the exportation of books, and I've seen books from Buenos Aires occupying choice spots on book shelves from Santiago to the Texas border. Some of the smaller Latin American countries depend almost entirely on Argentina for books, and smart *porteño* publishers have been clever about organizing traveling book exhibitions. Some of the earliest ones were sent to neighboring capitals such as La Paz, Bolivia, but the industry has now branched out to the European continent, and the exhibit held in Lisbon, Portugal in 1945 attracted diplomats and educational leaders alike.

It is even claimed that Spanish readers now prefer books published in Buenos Aires to those coming from printing presses in their own country. Most of Argentina's books are put out by 150 commercial printing establishments, although universities and official and specialized institutions also do a heavy volume of printing.

The exportation of novels and books of non-fiction rose from 7,160,000 in 1941 to 17,000,000 in 1944, the value in that year being placed at 107,000,000 pesos. In 1933, when the national register for intellectual production was first opened, 509 works were entered. In 1943 the annual entries totalled 4,923.

One of the remarkable features of this cultural bonanza has been how little it has profited the Argentine author. He still can't make a living by his books alone, and even such a well-known novelist as the pro-Fascist Hugo Wast held another job while he was doing his most successful writing. Leonard and I never stopped being amazed by the number of authors we found in newspaper and news agency offices working on war communiques and other routine news. The news manager at Reuters was widely hailed by the critics as a promising young novelist and had had several books published. Yet he confessed to me one day that he needed his job in order to live.

Perhaps, a glance at the shelves of any bookstore or home library is the answer to why the Argentine writer isn't rich or even prosperous. His fellow citizens prefer the foreign product.

Most bookstores in Buenos Aires are as international as an atlas, and even the smallest ones cater heavily to translations of American and English books. Although the educated Argentine has spent his life with the best of French, Italian and German literature, the war has brought a shift in his reading habits. Cut off from Europe, he began turning to New York and London, and now it isn't unusual to see a Spanish translation of an American best seller reach the shelves a few weeks after the English-language original has arrived in the country. As in the United States, up-and-coming booksellers now fill their windows with translations of the Hollywood offerings currently showing in the first-run movie houses.

I used to take a certain pride in this, for many of the translations had been made on slack Sunday afternoons at Reuters by the desk men. And if the Argentine reading public is now familiar with such varied phases of American life as the zoot suit, the hill-billy and shortnin' bread, I can take a small share of the credit for it. For it was my explanations of these phenomena that were translated into precise *castellano* by our Spanish colonel. A large proportion of the translation of English books is done by news agency men fluent and rapid in both Spanish and English, and they are paid in the neighborhood of $125 for a completed novel. This runs a little higher with works of non-fiction and extra long novels and somewhat less for detective thrillers.

Argentine publishers have found the interest in John Dos Passos, Sinclair Lewis, Louis Bromfield, Ernest Hemingway and Sherwood Anderson sufficient to publish these authors' works in Spanish, and a well-stocked bookstore in Buenos Aires has on its shelves Dos Passos' *La primera catastrofe, El gran dinero, Manhattan Transfer,* and *Rocinante vuelve al camino,* selling from $1 to $1.75 a copy.

John Hersey's *Una campana para Adano* is available for $1.50, and Erskine Caldwell's *Tierra trágica* for $1.25.

But while the Argentine intellectual may speak admiringly of the works of Faulkner, the man on Calle Corrientes is willing to pay his money to read of Rhett Butler and Scarlett O'Hara. *Gone with the Wind* enjoyed such great popularity in Argentina that even the railway station news stands stocked it in both Spanish and English. *Ana y el rey de Siam* by Margaret Landon is a more recent favorite.

However, the record for light fiction goes to Kathleen Winsor's *Por siempre Ámbar,* which so titillated the Argentines that they didn't even wait for the release of the movie to begin buying copies at twelve pesos or $3 each. A friend who worked in a book store in Buenos Aires described its success thus: "*Forever Amber* sells like hot cakes. It's got so that people blush when they ask for it. You can make it a lot more uncomfortable for them if you stare hard at them and set your mouth in a firm thin line of disapproval. They blush all the harder." (She soon lost her job.) The same house that published the Spanish version of *Amber* also released John Steinbeck's *Los Arrabales de Cannery* but at the more modest price of $1.25 a copy.

The Valley of Decision by Marcia Davenport also has been a best seller in Argentina, but its sales undoubtedly were bolstered by the appearance of the motion picture of the same name.

The popularity of detective fiction is growing, as is that of such authors as Theodore Dreiser, Carl Sandburg and Mark Twain.

Novels are the most popular form of literature, with biography and history second. A poll on reading tastes taken by a Buenos Aires publishing house was of particular interest to *El Pueblo*, the Catholic newspaper, which often concerns itself with what its readers should or should not have on their library shelves. It had this to say of the poll results:

"In roaming the thoroughfares of the city, one may observe street corner idlers gazing at the sky and the earth by turns, for hours at a time. Silent gazers may be seen in cafes, bars and plazas, and we are told that they are the philosophers who presumably account for the 2.5 per cent who read philosophical works.

"Poetry occupies the lowest place on the list. Only 0.40 per cent of the readers want it. This seems almost incredible, because most people number many acquaintances who write verses; consequently it would appear that there are more poets than readers of poetry!"

Few peoples have developed such an attachment for the printed word as the Argentines, and even more than New Yorkers they bury their heads in newspapers and magazines the moment they step into a train or a subway.

The man of the family carefully deliberates over his newspaper, and the one he reads is an excellent clue to his income, general political and social beliefs, and even his nationality. The two internationally famous dailies, *La Prensa* and *La Nación*, are the favorites of the upper and middle classes, with *La Nación* perhaps more editorially acceptable to the Argentine Rural Society and the Jockey Club.

La Prensa is something of a lower case Bible to its over 400,000 readers, and a faithful subscriber seldom questions anything he reads in its typographically neat pages. Almost any argument can be settled ultimately in Argentina merely by announcing that "*La Prensa* said so."

This remarkable paper's front page is devoted to classified advertising, and the revenue is so great from this source alone that *La Prensa* is completely independent of any possible pressure from a big advertiser. Oil paintings hang in the editorial offices, and the young man who gets a job on that newspaper seldom quits its offices until he is ready to receive his journalist's old-age pension. Rumor has it that over a period of years *La Prensa* has found it necessary to discharge three employees, but two of them were said to have been re-instated later in different jobs.

Many other fine newspapers are published in Buenos Aires, and the one with the largest circulation is the tabloid-size *El Mundo* with nearly 500,000 readers each morning. *El Mundo's* lively format and liberal use of pictures disguises a sober tone seldom observed in the North American tabloid. Juicy domestic scandals are as absent from its pages as they are from *La Nación*.

In the afternoon field, the big three are *La Crítica*, *La Razón*, and *Noticias Gráficas*, which boast a combined circulation of over 700,000. All three newspapers play up foreign cable news but print full accounts of crime stories on their inside pages, give extensive coverage to sports events, and publish the American "funnies" translated into Spanish.

All of these major independent newspapers supported the Allied cause during the war and are pro-democratic. Their opposition to certain policies of the military government brought a variety of penalties, ranging from stoning of their offices by Perón's *descamisados* to suspension and even arrests of many of the editors.

La Vanguardia, the organ of the Socialist party, is one of the outstanding newspapers of South America and probably has been the most consistent critic of the Army regime and Perón. It is outspoken and fearless and has a great following among conservatives, radicals and persons of many political complexions. It is also read in neighboring countries.

The newest comers to the ranks of Buenos Aires daily newspapers are the pro-Perón sheets, *La Época* and *La Tribuna*, which devote a considerable portion of their news space eulogizing their political hero or scourging his enemies.

Besides these and still other Spanish-language newspapers, each foreign community in Argentina supports one or more dailies in its native tongue. *The Standard*, printed in English, is the oldest newspaper in Argentina, having been established in 1861, and the *Buenos Aires Herald* was founded only a few years later.

The newsstands in Buenos Aires have for years offered a bewildering assortment of newspapers printed locally in such a Babel of languages that I never did learn to recognize more than a third of them, let alone read them. German and Yiddish publications have been on sale side by side, and the Japanese cleaner could buy a newspaper in his native language as easily as I could in mine.

Over sixty newspapers are published daily in Buenos Aires, and they are a study in contrast when it comes to appearance and viewpoints. However, they share one feature in common. The news stories in them are written to be read from beginning to end. The essential facts aren't given in a first paragraph containing the who, what, where, the when and the how in the traditional North American news style. With the exception of the cable reports supplied by foreign agencies, the news stories in the Spanish-language press are written in a leisurely manner. The reporter may start out by describing the weather at a particular hour in the day, and some paragraphs later reveal that a murder has been committed. The name of the victim may not be supplied until farther down the page. The reader finds no reason to quarrel with this procedure, for he has plenty of time—and enjoys it—to study the day's news.

I always got the impression from reading an Argentine newspaper that it was produced primarily for the masculine reader. Most of the newspapers do carry some fashion news daily and layouts of the latest styles in their Sunday editions, but the women's page has not been developed to the extent it has in the United States. The society editor's accounts are brief and to the point, perhaps because after the editor has listed the long double-barrelled names of the guests, including the married women's maiden names plus those of their husbands, there is little space remaining for elaborate descriptions of parties. A Cholly Knickerbocker writing society gossip for the newspapers is an unknown quantity, for persons important enough to be listed on the society page are treated with formality and respect. In the Spanish-language papers, special women's features are a rarity except for those picked up from North American syndicates. And those get comparatively little space. It's still a man's world as far as the newspapers go, and the number of columns given over to sports completely dwarfs that allotted to strictly feminine interests. News-paperwomen are few and far between, except on the newspapers printed in English. When Leila Drew of the *Herald* scooped every newspaperman in Buenos Aires with her news story of the birth of quintuplets in Argentina, she was almost as newsworthy as the quints themselves. Editors assigned their reporters to interview her. Her picture was printed in newspapers and magazines and fan letters began to trickle into her office. The editorial offices of news-papers in Argentina are strictly masculine affairs, and even on the *Herald* the women reporters are sheltered in a separate room, a hall apart from the opposite sex.

The dominant masculine tone of the newspapers may have something to do with the fact that the magazine field has flourished. Women are seen reading magazines much more frequently than newspapers.

The Argentine reader has an abundant and varied selection of periodicals from which to choose, and there are enough fashion and homemaking magazines to delight the housewife.

One of the most important magazines published on the South American continent is *Sur,* established and edited by Victoria Ocampo, recognized as the foremost feminine intellectual of Argentina. Strictly highbrow in appeal, it publishes selections from the world's outstanding literary figures and essays of topical interest. It most resembles *Harper's* in the North American field.

The Argentine counterpart of *Vogue* is the slick-paper, beauti-fully illustrated *Atlántida*, which publishes full-page advertisements in color of expensive jewelry, mink coats, French furniture and other luxury articles. Much of its space is devoted to the activities of the rich. Each issue contains studio photographs of the country's wealthiest and most socially prominent brides in their elaborate wedding dresses. During the summer, the magazine prints dozens of discreetly informal photographs of prominent families at the beach resort of Mar del Plata or entertaining in their great seaside chalets. In the winter months, the magazine's photographers focus their cameras on the same faces, but in different settings. They may be at cocktail parties, weddings, balls or at the international live-stock show in Buenos Aires. And at least once during the season, the wealthy are shown in ski costume in the Bavarian-like resort center of Bariloche. For fashions, the magazine's editors rely largely on still photographs from Hollywood of movie stars in glamorous evening dress, in bathing costume or in sophisticated town suit.

Other women's magazines such as *El Hogar, Rosalinda, Maribel* and *Chabela* also cater to the public's interest in high Argentine society, and they too publish photographs of lavish parties. Some of these magazines send their staff artists out to sketch the most dazzling gowns of the guests at big social functions, which is a boon to the alert subscriber seeking style on a budget. If she can sew herself, or can bring pressure on her *modista*, she may wear an exact copy of a rich debutante's dress a few days after her favorite magazine has come off the press. Photographs of brides are tradi-tional features of all the popular women's magazines, as are fashions in colors, needlework directions and recipes. A good part of the fiction is reprinted from North American magazines. *Para Ti,* with a circulation of nearly 300,000, is one of the most widely read women's magazines in the republic. It publishes Dorothy Dix along with homemaking suggestions and many pages of brightly-hued fashions.

Two magazines catering to rural readers are *Pampa Argentina* and *La Chacra. Aquí Está!* is a popular bi-weekly, carrying news features on Argentine and foreign subjects, and *Leoplán* is a book magazine designed for men. There are magazines dedicated exclu-sively to sports, to interior decoration, to geography, to the local movie industry, to Argentine radio stars, and to living to a ripe old age, but the periodical with the greatest general circulation is *Selecciones del Reader's Digest,* which has been received with en-thusiasm. Its appearance on the streets is something of an occasion as vendors yell out *"Selecciones! Selecciones!"* in loud, clear voices. The *porteño* hurries to buy his copy with just a shade less eager-ness than when he grabs for a paper with the week's lottery results.

I have never recovered from my surprise at learning that Argentines much prefer their fiction—whether it be novels or a short short in one of the magazines—to have a happy ending. This seems incredibly out of character in a country where the rhythmic sorrow of the tango is heard around the clock from radio stations, *boîtes* and most restaurants and bars. We were awakened in the mornings to these tales of heartbreak, as little *criolla* maids sang of unrequited love while doing their daily chores. By tea time, orchestras in sandwich and cake emporiums all over town had tuned up their instruments to tell, to the tune of the tango, the sad plight of fair ladies deserted by their lovers. By the cocktail hour, husbands had become unfaithful in song, if not in reality. And so on into the night. No evening at a night club or *confitería* could be called a gay one unless the tango singer had killed off a considerable proportion of the pampas' population with bloodshed and tears. Faithless mistresses died of stab wounds in the arms of the men they had betrayed; men killed themselves because the ones they loved loved someone else; and the woman scorned took not only her own life but that of the man who had done her wrong.

Although the tango has been in respectable Argentine society for not more than a generation—having first been introduced into Paris by gay young blades from Buenos Aires, adopted there and then exported back to Argentina—it enjoys enormous popularity and prestige throughout the country today. Carlos Gardel, a tango singer long dead in his grave, is still the idol of millions, his fly-specked picture adorning many a bar room. Postal cards with his photograph continue to enjoy enormous sales.

In 1945, amazing scenes were witnessed in La Plata, the provincial capital, when one cinema house advertised three Gardel picture revivals on one program. When word spread that Gardel could be seen in the local movie house, the inhabitants left their homes as though an earthquake had occurred, and a few hundred lucky ones succeeded in obtaining the available seats. Thousands, however, crowded into the movie entrance hall and overflowed into the adjoining street, struggling and pushing in their vain effort to reach the box office. Traffic became snarled and for awhile it looked as though the activities of the entire city of more than 250,000 would be stalled. Only through the combined efforts of policemen on horseback and firemen with their hose was order restored. While no current favorite has risen to challenge the lofty position occupied by the deceased Gardel, tango singers and orchestras enjoy immense followings, *porteños* going time and again to hear their favorites perform.

But woe be to the foreigner, no matter how skilled a musician he may be, who is presumptuous enough to attempt to play the tango. Our favorite cafe orchestra was directed by a Romanian, and most of his men were European refugees. We became such enthusiastic devotees of the orchestra that we dropped in two or three times a week to hear the maestro play Strauss waltzes, the classics, "Indian Love Call," "The Lady in Red" and tangos. Often we invited Argentine friends, who applauded just as loudly as we did until the maestro was bold enough to strike up a tango. Then our guests invariably began to criticize. He played too fast, or the rhythm wasn't right, or it should have been loud where the Romanian played it soft.

But the disapproval of our guests was nothing compared with the barrage of hisses, whistles and slurring comments which greets any Hollywood attempt to present a tango. Hell has no fury like an Argentine witnessing such desecration, and motion picture theater owners actually fear for their property. On the other hand, musicians from all over the world have been given a warm welcome when they reached the shores of the River Plate.

And they have made Buenos Aires a city of music. I know of no other metropolis in the hemisphere where such a variety of music is played in such a variety of places before such a variety of people. *Porteños* drink coffee and tea to music, and transact business to music. The white collar worker treating his family to seventy-five-cent dinners hears music while he dines, as do the wealthy who patronize the expensive international-type hotels. And music is as much a part of the atmosphere in waterfront dives as it is in the magnificent Teatro Colón, one of the finest opera houses in the world.

The Colón, which occupies an entire city block and was patterned after the opera house in Paris, is a most impressive monument to the cultural aspirations of the Argentines. Before the revolution of 1943, some of the greatest figures in the world of music journeyed to the Argentine each year to appear in the brilliant

winter season. However, the importation of foreign talent to the
giant stage—it accommodates comfortably over 600 performers—
was discouraged during the first phase of the nationalistic military
regime. The foreigners are rapidly reappearing, but young Argentine singers now fill some of the roles which used to be reserved
for talent from abroad.

The attempted "nationalization" of the Colón was a slower
process in regard to the music itself, even though two Argentine
operas, *Aurora* by Hector Panizza, and *Ollantay* by Constantino
Gaito were presented in the 1945 season. The other operas included
such old favorites as Verdi's *Rigoletto*, and *Hansel and Gretel*.

But the glory of the Colón does not rest entirely on the quality
of the performers or what they sing. It is still one of the best places
in the republic for well-dressed ladies and gentlemen to see and be
seen. Regardless of whether the president of the country is rich and
"reactionary" or whether he is a self-proclaimed man of the people,
he still finds it necessary to be in his box at the Colón, along with
his first lady or his daughters, on certain state occasions. It would
be a national scandal if he failed to appear there in all of his official
finery on Independence Day. Politicians, social leaders and other
mere citizens who wish to shine in his reflected glory, scramble for
tickets far in advance of that date.

Perhaps from the standpoint of actual music, the Argentine
enjoys just as much the concerts of the splendid Philharmonic
Association of Buenos Aires, which sometimes are staged at the
Luna Park boxing arena when the wrestlers and prize fighters have
a night off.

Another popular musical event is the open air opera and ballet
held during the summer months, which any person may attend for
less than a quarter. The performance is staged in an open air theater
and attracts an audience of some ten thousand spectators each night,
composed of people from all walks of life in the capital—diplomats,
tradesmen, office workers, rich and poor. Those who want to sit
down in front for the operas can get special reserve seats in advance,
ranging in price from twenty-five to fifty cents.

The legitimate theater also enjoys a popularity unknown to
other South American countries, and only New York and London
have more stage shows running simultaneously during the season.

In 1945, twenty-five legitimate theaters in Buenos Aires offered the public such diverse fare as Benavente, Ibsen, Molière, Barrie, Shaw, Richard Wright and John Van Druten.

Like the other phases of cultural life in Argentina, the theater is international even though most of the performers are native-born Argentines. It is in the theater that the influence of Spain is especially strong, for many of the biggest hits come from Spanish pens. One of the most interesting theaters is the sixteen-year-old Teatro del Pueblo which offers drama to the public at movie admission prices. Its 1945 season included not only three Spanish classics, but Shaw, Sophocles and Beaumarchais' *The Barber of Seville.*

Many of the legitimate theaters are interspersed between movie houses for several blocks amid the bright lights of Calle Corrientes, the Broadway of Argentina. But each night when the entertainment houses start disgorging their patrons, it is from the movie palaces that the great tides sweep forth, filling streets with larger crowds at midnight than at noon. The center of Buenos Aires alone has 193 movie houses, not counting the 237 in the province of Buenos Aires and the outskirts of the city. And there are 1,495 motion picture theaters with a seating capacity of 695,010 in the country.

Most of the seats are filled from 1 P.M. until midnight each night, while the avid addicts of Hollywood sit not through the double-feature, but triple and even quadruple ones. Only a handful of the most exclusive houses in the capital can get by with showing merely a single full-length picture, the Argentine newsreel, foreign news, a travelogue and a cartoon. Most of the theaters we attended—the ones charging less than a quarter on week days and thirty cents on Sunday—gave us our money's worth. On many a winter evening, we shivered our way through three entire pictures, plus a couple of newsreels and a comedy. Even the most flea-bitten establishments, where as many as four features are shown for fifteen cents, present patrons with printed programs listing each picture to be shown and the names of the cast. And it was in one of these that Leonard was most in need of a *criolla* Emily Post. It was our first week in the country and our first visit to an Argentine movie. The usher guided us to our seats by flashlight and courteously handed us a program. Leonard responded with a *"gracias,"* one of the few

Spanish words he knew. But still the usher stayed by our side, his flashlight shining in our faces. His electric torch spotlighted us for the audience, and we squirmed at this unprecedented attention. It was difficult to concentrate on the screen with our escort maintaining his vigil at the flashlight. After an uncomfortable interval, Leonard's hand reached for his pocket for twenty centavos to offer the usher as a bribe for obscurity. From that day forward, he always reached for his twenty centavos before starting down any theater aisle.

It isn't unusual to enter a movie house at 7 o'clock at night and be there until it closes at 12. These movie marathons are broken up by ten-minute intervals between pictures when the lights are turned on and vendors circulate through the audience selling ice cream, candy and other nourishment. Then the program resumes, the customer sufficiently strengthened for another hour and a half.

I didn't encounter a single person in Argentina who didn't like movies, and many of them bought tickets in advance for Saturday and Sunday night shows then went once or twice during the week besides. One Saturday night, Leonard and I walked more than a mile and visited at least twenty theaters before we were able to get a seat.

Besides the regular motion picture theaters, there are several devoted entirely to newsreels. In the early days of the war, Berlin fought Hollywood, and lost, on the motion picture front of Buenos Aires. The *porteño* public had already become too fascinated with Rita Hayworth's figure and Fred Astaire's dancing to pay good money to see storm troopers salute Hitler. Consequently, there were always plenty of empty seats in the German film houses, and the addition of Japanese and Italian propaganda offerings were little better bait for the customers.

The triumph of Hollywood found "neutral" Argentines cheering loudly each time an Ally mowed down a German, preferably a Gestapo agent. And hisses penetrated through each house when it became obvious that the Argentine government had blacked out the Spanish sub-titles in which the Axis was portrayed in an unfavorable light. I'll never forget how the customers stamped the floor and whistled their disapproval when Tarzan's activities against the Nazis were censored. As our jungle hero wandered through the trees shouting, "Nazi, Nazi," in English, the non-belligerent sub-title in Spanish had him calling, "*Enemigo* (enemy), *enemigo*."

The motion picture theater became such a forum for democracy that soon houses all over the country were ordered to flash notices on the screen warning customers against applauding for any power at war.

But not through political ideas alone has the Hollywood influence attained its present importance. It has infiltrated the entire social fabric. In no other place have I heard movies discussed so often and in such detail. Young people have learned English just to understand and enjoy the *cine* better. The interest in English as a "second language" is said to be increasing at the expense of French. *Señoritas* copy their clothes and hair styles from the reigning Hollywood favorite. When Veronica Lake first appeared with unhampered locks obscuring one eye, dozens of dark-haired beauties reached for the peroxide bottle and came out in society a few days later with blonde tresses neatly draped over the same eye.

When Argentines talk of visiting the States some day, it is not the White House they are the most eager to see, but Hollywood. A wealthy *estanciero*, who was planning his first trip to the United States, once asked Leonard in all earnestness, if it would be possible for him to get a date with Ginger Rogers.

Quite fittingly, one of the most popular *norteamericanos* in Argentina is a film star. He is *El Pato Donald* (Donald Duck), whose every quack of frustration brings chuckles of appreciation and sympathy.

The admiration of American movie stars has made competition stiff for the local motion picture product.

Argentina's own film industry was born some fifteen years ago. For many years, the River Plate films were so technically inferior to Hollywood that the overwhelming majority of theater-goers shunned the home-produced efforts for the more glittering spectacles from abroad. About the only time they saw an Argentine picture was when it was teamed on a double-feature with one from Hollywood.

However, the war clouds in Europe brought several experienced technicians from Paris and other capitals. Pierre Chanal, the famous

French director, became an outstanding figure in the Argentine film industry. Besides the new blood from Europe, there was another valuable addition in the person of Oren (Bob) Roberts, an American trained in the California studios, who introduced the Hollywood technique into Argentine movies. His work as photographic director for Pampa films has earned him numerous tributes. By 1942, the industry had so mushroomed that fifty-seven films from Argentine studios reached the screen. Then lack of supplies from abroad forced the Argentine industry to limit its activities. Fewer pictures were produced, but they were better ones. The local producers dipped into the pages of Argentine history for some splendid historical films such as *Su mejor alumno* (His Best Pupil) which dramatically brought to the screen the times of Sarmiento and that turbulent phase in the nation's development. The story of the liberating armies of northern Argentina, from the pen of one of the country's foremost writers, Leopoldo Lugones, was told in another success, *La guerra gaucha* (The Gaucho War).

Although Argentine film companies presented some drawing room comedies, such as *Nace un amor* and *El muerto falta a la cita*, their most popular works have been those capturing the flavor and spirit of the country. Among those were *Prisioneros de la tierra* and *Tres hombres del río*.

Their films *Santa Rosa de Lima* and *Villa Rica del Espíritu Santo*, stressing the Spanish-Catholic heritage of South America, found ready markets in other Latin capitals, as did their interpretations of literary classics by Balzac, Daudet, Zweig and Ibsen.

In the main, Argentine producers have been too clever to try to imitate Hollywood with lavish musicals, and they lack the facilities to attempt expensive technicolor epics such as *Gone with the Wind*. However, they have been able to take advantage of the absence of films depicting a way of life that the Latin truly understands. The average Argentine movie-goer may enjoy the antics of Andy Hardy and other Hollywood characters, but they are as remote from his own experiences as if they had taken place on another planet. No Argentine matron is able to identify herself with a slack-clad heroine working on a factory assembly line, nor can she even picture herself in the rôle of a career girl living in an apartment of her own. She has often seen *yanqui* film heroines get drunk in public bars and divorce their husbands, but such behavior still remains as shocking to her as it is foreign.

Consequently, the Argentine producer, by his ability to select story material in keeping with his audiences' tastes and experiences, is able to a certain extent to counter the technical and financial advantages of Hollywood.

Hollywood's answer to the growing competition from Latin American film companies has been the picture with the dubbed-in Spanish sound track. But this has not met with unqualified enthusiasm in Buenos Aires, where the movie fans are almost as familiar with the real voice of Charles Boyer as they are with that of their president.

Accustomed to their hero's tender murmurings in richly-accented English, they found the Castilian flowing so freely from his lips in *Gaslight,* one of the first dubbed-in pictures, somewhat disconcerting.

Some discerning fans have protested that the dubbed-in pictures offended them from an artistic standpoint. "For us, it is like going to an opera where the singing is done by people hidden in the wings, while a few good looking people stand on the stage making gestures," one Argentine observed. "We like to hear the voices that go with the faces, even if we don't understand all they say."

In the interior of the country, however, where fewer members of the audience understand English and where the people are not quite so agile at reading sub-titles, the movies with Spanish sound tracks have been a real boon. The residents of these provincial towns have shown preference for movies in Spanish, and from them the Argentine producer has always been assured revenue on his pictures.

The big market, of course, is Buenos Aires, and film companies from all over the world send their films to the movie-crazed Argentine capital. English pictures have been generally well-received, and *The Seventh Veil,* starring James Mason, was a great hit.

French films are also popular because many Argentines understand the language and are almost as familiar with the life led by the French and depicted in their movies as they are with that in their own country. The Mexican and Spanish pictures have the advantage of being in Spanish and following familiar patterns of South American life and interests.

Anastacia, who was typically Argentine in her love for the movies, had seen so many Hollywood productions that when she came to work for us she already knew something about hamburgers and apple pie. She prided herself on being able to adjust to strange *yanqui* ways, even when it came to putting ice cubes in glasses of plain water and mayonnaise on top of fruit salad.

But there was one thing she never quite understood or forgave, and that was our taste in Argentine art.

Like most Americans in Buenos Aires, we developed an early enthusiasm for the remarkable *gaucho* drawings of Molina Campos. Leonard gave me a collection of his prints on our first Christmas in the Argentine, and we had them framed as a first wedding anniversary present to ourselves.

By that time, however, Anastacia had taken command of the household. She decided what we should eat, tried to tell us how to furnish the apartment, and never hesitated to let us know which of our friends met with her approval and which of them did not. So it was no surprise when Anastacia again felt called upon to express an opinion, this time on the subject of art.

When I called in Anastacia to help me hang our new Molina Campos prints in the front room, she was noticeably unenthusiastic. She sniffed and commented that she had the same pictures on her *Alpargatas* calendar at home, but she kept it in the kitchen and made it all too clear that that was where she thought our prized prints belonged too. One after another was scorned as *"Qué fea!"* (How ugly!)

Like Anastacia, the Argentines who visited us invariably commented on our choice of art. Some of them confessed that they too appreciated Señor Campos' delightful interpretations of life on the pampas but wouldn't dream of having them on their own walls. What would their friends think? After all, he was a "calendar artist." So they decorated their homes with somber religious paintings, or reproductions of them.

But most of the Americans we knew collected Molina Campos' prints with gusto and often got to be such students of his calendars that they could speak with some authority on little changes in the artist's style and subject matter from year to year. Some collected only his horses and others only his *boliche* (bar) scenes. Campos' prestige went up considerably with his fellow countrymen when he was commissioned by Walt Disney to do the horses in the pampas sequences of *Saludos Amigos*. In 1941, Buenos Aires *librerías* still had a wide selection of his prints for thirty cents each, but by 1946 after *Saludos Amigos* had appeared in nearly every neighborhood theater in the land, some of his prints had risen to as high as $5 and $6 apiece.

Each year, the *Alpargatas* company, the makers of rope-soled canvas shoes, releases a dozen of Campos' prints on their calendars, and the person who gets a calendar is fortunate. Some foresighted *porteños* have saved their calendars and later turned them into a handsome profit for themselves—enough to buy several pairs of *alpargatas*. A few *librerías* began to collect them years ago and now rip off a page at a time for twenty or twenty-five pesos, depending on how popular the particular print has become.

Molina Campos is one of the most financially successful artists in the country too and lives in a spacious north side Buenos Aires apartment, busily at work on future calendars which come out much too infrequently for his fans.

His closest rival in the calendar field is Carybé, who produced a brilliant series of Argentine scenes for the Esso calendar, which were promptly gobbled up by amateur collectors. These two artists have so captivated Americans in Argentina that few of them can resist the temptation of covering their walls with these works or at least filling their suitcases with the prints as mementos of Argentina when they finally leave the country.

When we moved into a boardinghouse in the heart of the city, I soon discovered many privately-owned art galleries in the neighborhood, and I enjoyed following the *porteño* custom of visiting a show room or two before dinner.

It was always a pleasure to discover pictures of pampas scenes and colorful *criollo* types, although there weren't nearly enough to satisfy me. The French influence is pronounced. Most of the better known artists of the country have either studied in Europe or were born there and migrated to Buenos Aires. Perhaps the best known one today is Quinquela Martín, a foundling of the tough Boca waterfront district, who rose from youth as a coal-heaver to international recognition. He is best when painting his own waterfront area and the men at work there. His own success has brought good fortune to the whole quarter, for he is responsible for a modern school in the heart of the poor district. He has decorated the school with his own murals so that children can learn to appreciate art and beauty early in life. The children of waterfront workers who show any talent are given free instruction in painting and sculpture. His own studio is a penthouse on the roof of the school, from where he can look out over the waterfront that brought him riches.

Pío Collivadino, Cesáreo Bernaldo de Quirós and Emilio Centurión are three of the most famous artists of the country, but my own favorite is Miguel Viladrich, a Spanish artist, whose *Tipos argentinos* are strikingly beautiful.

Curiously, it has been the foreign artist, like Viladrich, who has pioneered in discovering Argentina. Emeric Essex Vidal, who came to Buenos Aires at the time of the British invasion, was charmed by the country's architecture, types, costumes and life, which he sketched enthusiastically. His works were published in London in 1820, and today they furnish one of the best records available of life on the River Plate in the last century. The prints are highly esteemed and have even found their way into quite a number of Argentine homes. A French naval officer, Adolfo d'Hastrel, who entered the River Plate for battle at the time of Rosas, was another who succumbed to the lure of the pampas and painted many colorful *gaucho* scenes, as did the talented Raimundo Monvoisin whose *Soldado de rosas* and *Gaucho federal* are famous.

Perhaps the most tragic story of Argentine painting is that of Carlos Morel, whose wonderful scenes of *gaucho* life captivate anyone visiting the Bellas Artes museum. He was one of the first native Argentines to paint his fellow countrymen. But his career as an artist was a short one. Although he lived to be eighty-one years old, he ceased painting at thirty-two—a victim of the tyranny of Rosas. He had been sentenced to death, and when the reprieve came just a short time before his hour to die, his mind had become so deranged that he could never paint again.

One of the most brilliant of Argentine painters was Prilidiano

Pueyrredón, whose landscapes, portraits and *gauchos* are considered some of the best ever painted in the country.

The lusty characters painted by these artists of a century ago bear little resemblance to the refined, pale countenances seen on the canvases of today's society painters. And a comparison of the early works with the fashionable modern portraits is one way to discover what has happened to the Argentine people in the last one hundred years.

The Indian strain so obvious in the features of the men immortalized by Pueyrredón, Ballerini and Boneo, has long since vanished from the countenances of the first families of the country and from most of the residents of Buenos Aires. The complexions have been bleached by huge migrations from Italy and Spain, from France, Britain and Germany, until today approximately 78 per cent of the entire population is of European extraction with about 19 per cent being foreign-born. This is especially true of the federal capital, where the *porteño* looks more like a European than he does a *criollo*.

This new Argentine of the expensive portrait keeps his eyes toward Europe as resolutely as any British civil servant sent to an outpost of the empire; his back is still turned on the heritage left him by those remote *gaucho* ancestors who sat around their campfires devouring great chunks of half-cooked meat. He prefers, instead, to be one of the select company sipping cocktails at Harrod's each Saturday noon.

Yet, contrary to what might be supposed, the cultured Argentine is not effete. He is a man of surprising resourcefulness and energy and something of a shock to the North American preconception that all Latins are lackadaisical builders. He loves to watch football games, so he has erected modern stadiums to house them. He likes horse races, and he installs them in settings of extraordinary beauty. And he likes to live in a glittering place, so he has fashioned Buenos Aires into a jewel of a city, sparkling with emerald-like parks and traced with flowers of ruby-red elegance. He needed subways to enhance the usefulness of his city; yet, refusing to accept utility at its own drab face value, he painted huge murals on tile in the walls of his stations, so that a ride on the subway came to be a journey through the nation's history in technicolor. Still not satisfied with the appearance of the city, he demolishes whole blocks of comparatively new apartment edifices in the heart of the city and clears the stone away to make room for the widest avenue in the world. He seems to be always in the midst of a building boom, even during the materials shortages of the late war. His passion for new construction seems beyond restraint.

The Argentine is ambitious to a fault. He follows his career with energy and cunning, in spite of the handicaps imposed by the traditional dominance of an enormously wealthy class that has little real interest in seeing the standard of living raised. He is cold and sometimes rude to those he doesn't know personally but courteous and generous to his friends. He has a soft heart for the right cause, as witnessed by the fact that after the San Juan earthquake disaster he contributed nearly a dollar for every man, woman and child in Argentina for the reconstruction of the fallen city. True, the city has not been re-built, but that was because of incompetence and graft in high places, rather than any lack of generosity on the part of the people. He is unsparing of his time in helping his friends.

Leonard and I might have had to wait weeks to be married, but for the unflagging interest and assistance of an Argentine student friend who guided Leonard through the maze of pre-marital red tape. Argentines are also helpful and courteous in piloting friendly *norteamericanos* through the initial mysteries of the Spanish language; they are astonishingly hospitable to those who respect them and make an attempt to understand their ways.

The Argentine has an enormous store of good qualities to offset his human frailties. I am aware that I have paid less attention to his good points, yet it is natural that his idiosyncracies should prove of more interest than his everyday virtues, particularly when his pecularities are such an enchanting mixture of the subtle and the dramatic.

One of his most spectacular traits, from my point of view, is his anxious ambition to die in style and repose ever after in elegance.

While his grandfather was content to live, die and be buried under the stars, the Argentine of these 1940's must give considerable thought and effort to his last resting place if he expects to anchor his own name and secure the right social position for his survivors.

The ultimate goal of the high-reaching Argentine is to get his remains into a lead-covered shell, placed inside an elaborately carved wood coffin and deposited in one of the swank vaults of the Recoleta Cemetery. After he dies, that is the only way he can stay put with the right people.

A friend and I spent one summer morning wandering through this burial place of presidents, cabinet members, poets, publishers and aristocratic old families. The names on the vaults read like pages from an Argentine history book. In the friendly sunlight lay the quiet, narrow streets, lined and overshadowed by the marble palaces of the dead. I could look through big windows at tiers of caskets inside some mausoleums, and candles flickered in most of the vaults of these great families, casting their glow over bouquets of fresh flowers and brass polished to the perfection of mirrors. Marble angels with outspread wings sheltered some of these family resting places, others were topped ornately with excellent statuary; a splendid barbaric concept of death embellished with the civilized arts, a luxurious city peopled with ghosts. I recalled that Recoleta had been the scene of the country's most hair-raising ghost stories, and decided it was not a place I would choose for a stroll in the moonlight.

Recoleta Cemetery (population unknown) is so crowded that the only way a newly rich industrial family can hope to attain a place there, is to buy space already occupied by an old but impoverished family. And this is difficult. Even though such a sale brings about $1,000 per square yard, women sacrifice their jewels, and men their homes, before bowing to this most crushing of humiliations.

That morning, I saw a mausoleum being emptied of its residents to make room for more prosperous tenants. It was a depressing spectacle, enlivened only by the certainty that any Argentine so outrageously treated would manage to restore his *dignidad* by becoming a very belligerent ghost.

"I LIKE THE UNITED STATES, BUT...."

IN MOST WAYS, BUENOS AIRES IS STARTLINGLY NEW AND MODERN, but in one respect the city is gratifyingly far behind the times. That is the *pensión*, or boarding house, which has not yet given way to the automat or the self-service cafeteria. There are scores of *pensiones* still flourishing in the heart of the city. And it was our good fortune to live for a few months in one that was almost legendary for its cuisine. That was the *pensión* of the Madam Luisa Seigneureau, whose fame had spread so far that she was able to lure cooks from the homes of millionaires to do post-graduate study in her establishment.

Madam Luisa was so French that she had never bothered to master the Spanish language, but in the international language of food she was the most talented and literate person I have ever known. To Madam Luisa, the preparation and serving of food was an art, and she personally saw to the seasoning of each dish in the five-course lunches and six-course dinners she offered. We had heard wonderful stories of her cooking before we went to live there and were somewhat amazed to find that the truth was even better in the eating.

That is why we were so surprised one of those first nights when one of the charming lady boarders skipped her filet mignon and dessert to go "count the horses." Explanations certainly seemed in order, especially since Madam Luisa had already spoken to us with pride of having such a distinguished guest—a widely traveled gentle-woman holding a responsible position in an embassy. Surely, Ruth and I must have misunderstood the lady. It could not have been counting the horses she had mentioned as she left the table, it must have been a rubber of bridge. But she returned to the *pensión* in less than an hour, much too quickly for an evening at cards.

The next night, she hardly touched the chicken. And this time we were absolutely sure she said she was going to count the horses. By now our curiosity was thoroughly aroused and we debated following her to find out what she was really up to. But Madam Luisa's cooking kept us in our places.

In the end, we were counting horses too. However, we never found it necessary to leave the table early in order to do so. There were two places we counted the horses, one was outside the entrance to the American Embassy, the other was half a block away at the corner of Calle Florida and Diagonal Norte. The number of horses at the corner told us the internal state of the nation; if there were ten or more horses there, we could expect trouble of some sort. And the horses at the entrance to the embassy furnished a reliable barometer of Argentine–United States relations, usually a far better clue than the newspapers or the radio. If only two of the police mounts were standing there, we were sure that everything was rosy. Four was also a safe number, and six or eight gave no cause for alarm. But if the number crept up beyond a dozen, it was time to think of putting your passport in order. Many a time, a larger number was on hand, indicating great tension between the United States and Argentina.

Long before that, even before Pearl Harbor, we had come to recognize the storm signals in the Buenos Aires–Washington relations. Some of these were almost daily phenomena. Many of them came from our Argentine friends and most of them started with, "I like the United States, but . . ." The emphasis was invariably on the "but" and not on the "like." This was the way our polite friends prefaced their grudges against the "colossus of the north."

In those days, Argentines always seemed to be foaming at the mouth because "you Americans think you are too good to eat our beef." That was ridiculous, because the statement always seemed to come about the time I was easily cutting my two-inch steak with a fork. I sometimes tried to explain to them that while there was undoubtedly much lobbying in Washington to keep the cheap and excellent Argentine beef from competing with the North American product, it was a fact that American cattle growers were genuinely concerned about the danger of importing hoof-and-mouth disease. This argument never set well with my Argentine friends, and I am afraid I never succeeded in convincing them that hoof-and-mouth disease is much more serious if it breaks out in the United States than it is in Argentina. In the mild climate of the pampas, the cattle are able to feed in the open the year round and a steer can have hoof-and-mouth disease without deteriorating greatly in health or market value, whereas in the United States hoof-and-mouth was very often fatal, and the stock raisers had destroyed millions of dollars worth of cattle to eradicate epidemics.

After Pearl Harbor, Argentine resentment over the United States sanitary embargo on Argentine beef dwindled to almost nothing. We had committed—and kept right on committing—far greater sins for them to talk about.

One of the things Argentine officials did not like was the pressure brought upon Argentina to sever relations with the Axis countries after the sneak attack on Pearl Harbor. It was true that at the Foreign Ministers' Conference in Havana in July, 1940, Argentina had subscribed to the following: "Any attempt by a non-American state against the integrity or inviolability of the territory, against the sovereignty or independence of an American state, shall be considered as an act of aggression against all the states signing this declaration."

But Argentine diplomats quickly pointed out that this declaration had never been ratified by the Argentine Congress, and there were many other Argentines—some official and some not—who insisted that Hawaii was not a part of the American continent, hence Argentina and the other Latin American nations should not consider they had been attacked. They added that if the United States had not had an imperialistic policy, it would have no need for defending distant islands in the Pacific.

The Conference of Foreign Ministers in Rio de Janeiro, six weeks after Pearl Harbor, tended to appease isolationist Argentines. The man in the street seemed to take some pride in what he considered Argentina's victory over the United States at the conference. The United States had wanted a unanimous "resolution" for an immediate rupture of relations with the Axis. But owing to resistance by Argentina and to a lesser extent Chile, she got only a "recommendation" for the American nations to break with the Axis at their convenience.

It was two years before Argentina broke relations with Germany and Japan, and in that time President Castillo was ousted by the Army. Relations between Washington and Buenos Aires quickly went from bad to worse.

One dull Sunday afternoon, I discussed the situation with a translator in the United Press office. In friendly fashion, we talked over the objectives of the United States and the objections of Argentina. And then Señor G—— calmly knocked my arguments aside with a figure of speech.

"Argentina is like a beautiful woman," he explained earnestly. "She has had many lovers and she welcomes them. She likes to be wined and dined and wooed. She likes flattery and fine phrases. But, you must never forget that she can be seduced, but she can't be raped."

And Señor G—— suggested that the United States change its tactics toward Argentina.

This candid prescription for intimate international relations closely followed Secretary of State Cordell Hull's scathing note to Admiral Segundo Storni informing the new Foreign Minister that the Argentine military government would get none of the Lend-Lease equipment it had asked from the United States.

Newspapers printed the full texts of the Storni request and the Hull refusal. It was a sunny, spring day in September, and hundreds of *porteños* sat on park benches poring over every word of the two documents. One park bench occupant after another began to strike up conversation with his neighbor, and soon hands were flying in gestures of excitement and surprise, and voices grew louder and louder.

I heard exclamations such as *"Qué bruto!"* (How crude!) referring to Mr. Hull more than once that day. On one street car, an elderly man sat quietly reading his paper a few seats ahead of me; suddenly he burst out with, "Down with Cordell Hull!" and then went on with his reading.

A year later I heard men still deploring the *insulto*, although I'm sure some of them would have had difficulty recalling what Mr. Hull had said to offend them in the first place.

Several thoughtful Argentines told me they agreed perfectly with Mr. Hull's position. However, they had been shocked at his plain speaking. He had attacked Admiral Storni with a pickaxe when a rapier would have been just as effective and certainly a more fitting weapon for one diplomat to use against another. They reminded me that a straight line is not necessarily the shortest distance between two points, especially in Argentina. I suspected that they were also embarrassed that Admiral Storni had used the direct approach and had stumbled so naively into the path of Mr. Hull's tirade. But they were also annoyed with Cordell Hull for having taken advantage of Storni's innocence.

Thereafter, whenever I discussed Cordell Hull with the Argentines, we were talking about two different men. To me he was always a good, gray political saint; to some of them he was a scold, a brute and an ogre.

Whenever the pro-Axis press printed a statement by Mr. Hull, it was accompanied by a cartoon of him with his mouth open, still scolding. Soon after, theater-goers in Buenos Aires were startled to see an animated cartoon showing Mr. Hull side by side on the screen with Donald Duck, both quacking furiously. Some Argentines roared with delight, but many were annoyed that their government could have been so crude; they realized that the cartoon could never have appeared without official sanction.

Fed by the pro-Axis newspapers and government-sponsored digs, the ill-feeling became intense by the middle of 1944. One of my English friends told me that when she asked for sugar in a suburban grocery store, the owner had asked whether she was English or American. "I'm English," she said. "Why do you ask?"

"Well," the man confessed, "if you had been *norteamericana* there wouldn't have been any sugar."

It would be unfair, however, to give the impression that all of the coals were heaped on the silvery head of Mr. Hull. The pet peeve of some of our democratic Argentine friends was the former Under-Secretary of State, Sumner Welles. For many months, his column appeared on the front page of *La Nación*, and they contended that his criticism of State Department policy on Argentina played into the hands of the military regime. The Welles articles were frequently reprinted on the front pages of the Nazi-controlled newspapers. One of these, *El Pampero* (which later became *El Federal*) was edited by Enrique Oses, a leading nationalist who made every attempt to convince the Argentine people that the State Department did not reflect the true sentiments of the United States.

Some Argentine democrats argued that the division in U. S. opinion regarding Argentina, as evidenced by Sumner Welles' almost weekly sniping at the State Department, not only weakened the United States' position in regard to Argentina, but also dampened their own hopes of ridding themselves of the dictatorship. So Ruth and I were puzzled one day when an Argentine friend, a law student at the University of La Plata, made this rather unusual remark to us:

"The students of La Plata are going to take up a collection to send two cases of champagne to Summer Welles."

"But why?" we asked. "We thought you didn't agree with Sumner Welles."

The student demanded, "Well, not even Señor Welles can drink and talk at the same time, can he?"

In all fairness, it must be said that Sumner Welles never praised the pro-Nazi military dictatorships that succeeded President Castillo, he merely defended their right to exist in the Western Hemisphere at a time when many of the American countries were at war with Germany. One Argentine indignantly denied Welles' charge that the State Department was intervening in the internal affairs of Argentina by non-recognition and was thereby alienating the Argentine people.

By the same line of reasoning, he contended, recognition could be regarded as intervention. If the United States re-established diplomatic relations with Argentina, other nations in the hemisphere would also do so, and therefore the Farrell-Perón government would be strengthened enormously both at home and abroad at the expense of the democratic forces within the country.

In defense of Sumner Welles, it had to be admitted that he was less concerned with the passionate ins-and-outs of the Argentine situation than he was with the over-all condition of the inter-American system. He feared that the U.S.-Argentine dispute would, if long continued, tear apart the entire structure he had helped so carefully to elaborate during his tenure in the State Department. And Mr. Welles' extreme affection for the entire inter-American system led him, temporarily at least, into three fallacies, all of which can readily be excused by his intense desire for the survival of the model international system in the new world. The first error derived from his apparent loss of direct touch with the internal situation of Argentina, and the failure to understand fully that what went on inside that country had direct bearing on the inter-American system itself. It was after Mr. Welles resigned from the State Department that the suppression of individual liberties inside Argentina reached its worst point; it was then also that Argentine connivance made possible the successful operation of a vast ring of espionage throughout the hemisphere, causing direct loss of Allied lives and treasure that was only partly curtailed by the maintenance of an expensive and laborious system of Allied counter-espionage inside Argentina.

Even more dangerous was the damage that could be—and was—done to the inter-American cause by the disruptive activities of the pro-Nazi government in Argentina, which spoke solemnly of desiring inter-American "solidarity" while it attempted to subvert or wean away its neighboring governments from the democratic cause. Mr. Welles was so concerned about the appearances of hemispheric amity that he overlooked one of the facts of life in the new world; Argentina had seldom if ever given its wholehearted support to the inter-American system, as evidenced by her ratification of only an insignificant fraction of the acts, agreements and resolutions reached at inter-American gatherings. Hence Mr. Welles was hardly justified in thinking the elaborate system might fall because of Argentina's absence from the fold.

In the same manner, I believe Mr. Welles also vastly underestimated the strength of the system he had helped to build. If the structure was so flimsy that it might collapse under the withdrawal of an uncertain member or two, how could it possibly survive the impact of a world war, and of what real use could it ever be in furthering the interests of Mexico, or Ecuador, or any of the other member nations?

Of course, there were Argentines who thoroughly enjoyed and who found gratification in every fresh storm of opinion provoked abroad concerning Argentina. It fed the national feeling of importance to see banner headlines and long stories in their newspapers reporting what London and Washington were saying about Argentina.

I recall a friend at one point saying, with mingled pride and amusement, "Look at us now. The whole world is talking about Argentina!"

I have long suspected that the Argentines consider the Americans a nation of the guileless. They were too polite ever to say this in so many words, but more than once they beat dangerously close to the bush.

One such time was in November, 1944, when a dispatch from Washington quoted Dr. Samuel Guy Inman, the eminent authority on Latin America, as saying that "85 per cent of the Argentines are pro-United States and democratic." More than one translator called my attention to the story. They agreed that at least 85 per cent of their fellow countrymen were democratic but chuckled over the idea that that automatically made them pro-United States. There is a difference, you know. They pointed out that the United States had no monopoly on democracy, that France had thought of it first. I was reminded of the Magna Carta and the Rights of Man and even had some of the U.S. Declaration of Independence and the Constitution quoted to me.

It was also suggested that the people of the United States erred (and along with them our news agencies and correspondents) in over-simplifying Argentine-United States relations by classifying each crisis as a clear-cut choice between fascism and democracy, in trying to pigeon-hole the Argentine officials and people as either the blackest of totalitarians who hated North Americans or snow-white democrats and idealists who dearly loved the United States and all it stood for.

To speak of the Argentine people as a homogeneous group of nearly fourteen million souls, all wanting the same thing, all burning in indignation over the same issue, all rising up to howl when their sovereignty had been infringed, was obviously ridiculous.

During the heyday of the Perón-Farrell regime, it was true that hardly a day passed without some newspaper or nationalist spokesman charging that the United States was meddling in Argentine affairs. But we also knew a group of Argentine conservatives who took us to task at every opportunity because the United States was not doing enough to fight the military government. We were accused of merely talking tough when we should have been acting. And we were warned that it would be disastrous if the United States recognized the Argentine regime, that the democratic forces would never forgive Washington.

One militant underground leader, also a member of the Conservative party, deplored the fact that the United States had not taken positive measures to get Perón and Farrell out of Casa Rosada. He had figured out how to do it. "Just ship us two thousand machine-guns—we'll pay for them—and we can do the rest for ourselves. That's all we need. Just get those machine-guns to us!" he pleaded.

That same week a liberal Argentine freely criticized the inconsistency of United States policy. Although he was anti-Perón, he thought it ridiculous for the United States to act so piously regarding Argentina and the military men in power while it continued to do business with Franco. "Everybody knows that Franco is worse than Perón," he said. "Why aren't you doing something about him?"

I hadn't been in Argentina many months before I was made to understand that there is only one thing the United States does right, and that is the construction and operation of the assembly line. Otherwise we are to the Argentines a nation of irresponsible and largely incompetent and uncultured souls, stumbling clumsily if somewhat luckily through domestic troubles and international complications. In short, the United States is Argentina's No. 1 whipping boy. Argentines in nearly every walk of life have some complaint about the United States—some well justified and others so ridiculous that it hardly seemed worth the effort of setting the critics straight.

Some of the leftist newspapermen we knew used to upbraid us about Wall Street, as if Ruth and I personally held seats on the New York Stock Exchange. They found Wall Street lurking behind every news item, extending its sinister tentacles all over South America to make life unbearable for those who would not bend to the "colossus of the north." Some of these Argentines would scan a Washington dispatch concerning some new phase of Argentine-U.S. policy, then lift their eyebrows and observe, "Wall

Street." When Harry Truman replaced Henry Wallace as Franklin D. Roosevelt's running mate, I was informed that Wall Street was to blame, but I was made to feel as if it were my own responsibility. Most of the Argentines we knew, came around to register a personal dissent on the dropping of Wallace, who was a hero to many of them. The candy man at the corner indignantly demanded that we explain why Wallace had been let out, while a school supervisor said in shocked surprise that Argentina had lost her best Good Neighbor.

I was also held personally to account for other misdeeds of the American people, such as the case of discrimination against the Mexicans in Texas. Sumner Welles had reported in one of his columns that Mexicans were not allowed in some theaters. This was called to my attention by an indignant white-collar worker who perhaps had never met a Mexican and had previously shown little interest in their affairs.

Another horrible subject that I was never allowed to forget was the lynching of Negroes in the southern states at home. A news story of a lynching might not run more than two paragraphs, but the alert translators never failed to seek me out each time to deplore the tragedy. They firmly believed that over a hundred Negroes were lynched in the United States each year, and I was not able to shake this conviction by showing the statistics in the World Almanac.

One day I had had about enough of this, and I asked one translator just why it was that Argentines disliked Americans so much. After a few polite denials, he finally told me: "Because North Americans look down on Argentines. Why, they think that we are just like the rest of the South Americans—that we are all Negroes here!"

As a matter of fact, that is only a partial and inaccurate answer as I learned through experience and observation. Part of the damage to our national reputation has been done by Americans themselves living in Argentina and a large share by the nationals of other countries living in Buenos Aires: the British, the Spanish, the Germans, Italians and French. The remainder of the damage is owing to extreme Argentine nationalists, the Catholic church and, paradoxically, its opponent the Communist party, which has energetically drummed up anti-U.S. sentiment in Argentina since Moscow changed the "party line" for the hemisphere.

The little causes of friction between Americans and Argentines in Buenos Aires are many. One of them is the great discrepancy in salaries. American men often are sent down from the States at high salaries to work in American firms in Buenos Aires. The Argentine resents the fact that for performing virtually the same functions he gets only from a half to a tenth as much pay as the Yankee. It doesn't help matters any that the American can afford to live on a much higher scale than the Argentine of similar capabilities.

The average American in Argentina lives much better than he ever did at home. His wife not only does not wash her own pots and pans but more often than not also requires her maid to answer the telephone and the doorbell. The little woman who thought nothing of washing the baby's diapers back in Chicago finds in her new environment many strange and wonderful things. Before long she discovers that it is an absolute "must" to have a maid in crisp uniform to serve her table. And if she is ambitious at all, a couple is finally hired—a woman to do the cooking and a man to open the door, pick up the newspapers and clean the ash trays. After she has been in the country awhile, she would no more think of touching a mop than her husband would a lawnmower.

Some Americans explain their impressive "front" as a business necessity, yet the sad truth is that many of them in Buenos Aires waste it on each other rather than on the Argentines. The tendency is to congregate into groups like any small community in the United States. The men gather at the American men's club and their wives at the American women's club or the Methodist church. They entertain each other at dinner and meet for cocktails. When the "girls" gather for tea, there is seldom an Argentine among them—and you may hear the accents of the Bronx, Des Moines or Dallas, Texas, but hardly ever of Córdoba, Mendoza or Catamarca.

Naturally, the ambitious Argentine looks with envious eyes at the gilded life of the *yanqui*. He watches the Americans in his company come to work in private automobiles or taxis. They wear expensive suits, often smoke good cigars or American-manufactured cigarettes and live in fine, big apartments. The Argentine employee is often forced to live with relatives in a small apartment; he comes to work in a crowded bus, smokes cheap cigarettes or none at all, and buys his suits on a precarious installment plan.

The Argentine thinks of his American fellow worker and asks, "What can he do that I can't do? Why should I get only a fifth of what he does?" One Argentine accountant was bitterly resentful when an American was employed in a similar capacity at 1,200 pesos a month. His own salary was 350 pesos.

There have been cases where Argentines have waited for years to get a promotion to a good job, only to be disappointed by having the company send down an American to take the post.

The Argentines who would like to know the people of the United States better simply can't afford to keep up with the American Joneses.

Ruth reported one luncheon meeting of university women in Buenos Aires at which the speaker asked all of those who had ever been invited to an Argentine home to raise their hands. Only a sprinkling of hands was lifted. The speaker then urged them to attempt to get acquainted with Argentine women.

One young woman interrupted, Ruth said, with the question, "But I'd like to know the best Argentine families, just how do I do it?"

A Spanish friend, married to an American, snickered at this. "Now isn't that just like you Americans?" she complained. "You want to know the 'best' people but you don't care anything about the plain people, the ones like yourselves."

It was more difficult, she pointed out, for an American business man and his wife to enter Argentine high society than it was for the camel to pass through the proverbial eye of the needle. The wealthy Argentine, who was as much at home in Europe as he was in South America, tended to find Americans provincial. He winced inwardly at their Spanish and it was difficult for him to understand why they could speak only one or two languages, while he was fluent in several.

Argentine wives, who still lead relatively secluded lives, were somewhat scandalized by the freedom of American women and the way they drank and smoked in public. The fact that an attractive divorcée has her name in the social register back in New York would not admit her to select circles in Buenos Aires. One beautiful and wealthy American woman was a case in point. Married to an Argentine diplomat after being divorced, she was one of the most socially acceptable women in Washington. Yet when she accompanied her husband back to his home, she found many Argentine doors closed to her, for in the eyes of the strict Catholic families she was not recognized as the diplomat's wife. She found herself with so much leisure that she took up writing as a pastime.

Argentines are shocked at the high divorce rate in the United States, and the nationalist press never misses an opportunity to deplore the impermanence of matrimony among the Yankees.

Informality in American customs and manners also serves to alienate the Argentines. One American man I knew reluctantly turned down a much better job in the United States because his Argentine wife was unwilling to risk possible injury to her dignity. "How could I be happy in a country where the President holds press conferences in his shirt sleeves?" she asked.

The shirt sleeve is diplomatic dynamite as far as Latin Americans are concerned. The Axis-financed press in Argentina used to pounce with glee on what it called, "diplomacy in shirt sleeves," referring to the United States' brand, of course. Even the unsavory *Clarinada* poked fun at Cordell Hull as the exponent of this type of statesmanship. A young American friend was threatened with a fine when police caught him strolling in shirt sleeves along Buenos Aires' landscaped riverfront promenade on a hot day in 1942.

But Perón now has his masses of "shirtless ones." And in 1947 Perón and other government officials—all in their shirt sleeves— spoke to a huge gathering of laborers in the ornate Teatro Colón. However, Perón and the others arrived at the theater with their coats on. The act of removing the coat is merely a political gesture not practiced in business or social circles.

Argentines are so gifted at languages that they are amazed by the average American's difficulty in picking up their tongue. Yet I've noticed they don't criticize this failure in the English as much as they do in the Americans. The English are not a bit better at learning Spanish than the Americans, and they may even be worse. I've known Englishmen who have lived in the country for thirty years without learning Spanish. Some have developed a sort of bastard tongue in which they resort to an English word whenever they don't know the Spanish equivalent. Yet the English manage to escape most of the censure to which the Americans are subjected. The difference may be that the Argentines respect the English.

The English don't try so hard to be liked. But they have earned so much respect that when an Argentine wants to insist that he is telling the truth, he calls it *palabra inglesa* (word of an Englishman). And when a person wants to make sure that his Argentine friend will be on time for some function, he specifies that it will begin at the *"hora inglesa."* And the biggest compliment one Argentine man can pay another is to call him a "gentleman."

To learn why Americans are not popular with the Argentines it is also necessary to dip into the history and economy of the country.

In the first place, there is that hard core of nationalists who hate not only the "colossus of the north," but other foreign lands as well. Their hatred has been fed on the fact that up until the recent war their country had been relegated to a colonial place in the world economy.

Even the most internationally-minded and pro-democratic Argentine sometimes rankles under the foreign control of so many of his activities. For example, until President Perón began a drive to nationalize all public utilities, the *porteño* rode in from the suburbs in trains owned by the British. At both Retiro and Constitución stations were streetcars bought by British capital waiting to take him to his office. When he picked up a telephone, it was American owned. When he sat down to dinner at night, his *bife* most likely had been processed by an American or British packing company. It had been broiled by electricity or gas, supplied by one of several foreign owned power companies.

Perón has changed this by purchase of the British railway systems and the American controlled telephone company. But tens of thousands of Argentine workers still receive their pay checks from Dutch, British, French, Spanish, American or Italian companies. And many of the newspapers they read continue to give more space to the cables supplied by American and British news agencies than they do to what is happening inside the country.

Long before the Second World War, small, anti-plutocratic and pro-Fascist groups, all hating the foreigner and his money, sprang up throughout Argentina. In the beginning most of the venom was directed against England because the City—British big business— had always regarded the Argentine as the "Sixth Dominion," and British investments were roughly double the American.

In time, however, the Anglophobia developed distinct symptoms of Yankeephobia. After Pearl Harbor, when the United States sought a united front in the Western Hemisphere against the Axis, most of the hatred of the nationalist, pro-Fascist elements turned on her. After the revolutionary government came to power—bringing with it men who openly proclaimed they wanted to make the nation self-sufficient—the United States inherited much of the resentment that had been directed against British capital, plus a substantial share of ill-will in her own right. For it was Washington which challenged the authority of the colonels and generals in Casa Rosada—the men best equipped to rid the country of the dominance of the foreigner.

British business interests were understandably happy to have the heat taken off them, and they certainly did nothing to put out the Argentine nationalist flame as it moved onto the Americans. There is some evidence they helped to fuel the fire. The men most powerful in London's business circles had never looked with any great favor on Argentina's falling completely within the orbit of Pan-Americanism where she would be subject to strong economic influence from the United States. Argentina, they reasoned, more rightly belonged within the British sphere of influence, regardless of that Act of God which located her geographically though not spiritually on the American continent. These men were alarmed to see American businessmen seeking to expand their own interests in Buenos Aires during the war when some circles in Britain began to look on the Argentine situation as not a conflict between fascism and democracy but a battle between the pound sterling and the American dollar for one of Britain's dwindling world markets.

It was grim and funny in the years after the June, 1943 revolution to watch the allies of the battlefield—Britain and the United States—snarl over the commercial spoils of Argentina. American business representatives in Buenos Aires prayed that their State

Department would not get too tough with the Argentine dictatorship, while their British rivals welcomed Hull's harsh words and simultaneously beseeched White Hall not to follow his example.

This was meat and drink for the Axis press, which front-paged any evidences of disagreement between Britain and the United States regarding Argentina. One article from *The Economist* of London must have delighted the editors. Speaking of U.S. attempts to get Britain to bring pressure on Argentina, the writer declared that Britain was "no longer rich enough to afford fits of uncalculated ill temper. Britain has shown herself prepared to make any sacrifice whatever for the sake of victory but not necessarily for the sake of extending Washington's influence to Cape Horn."

The South American Journal, a British financial publication with a limited circulation, poured out thousands of soothing words to Argentines ruffled by blunt criticisms from Washington. In time, the siren song of this publication almost drowned out disapproval of the Argentine regime voiced by the great dailies of London and the Foreign Office itself.

Some of my English friends deplored more than once the seeming reluctance of London to go all of the way with Washington in a "get-tough" policy with Argentina. But they pointed out it was not an easy matter for Britain; her food supplies were short already, and it would be impossible for the British to live without Argentine beef.

One important class of Argentines—the *estancieros*—have long resented the United States because in normal times the landowning families of Argentina are competitors of the American farmer for the sale of wool, meat, hides, wheat and corn in the world market. Naturally, their ties are with Europe, especially England, which has helped them prosper by building railways to bring their stock to packing plants and by providing refrigerated ships to transport their beef to appreciative London dinner tables.

Then there are those Argentines—many of them in high places in government and finance and industry—imbued with the mission to have Buenos Aires dominate, at least economically, Uruguay, Paraguay, Chile and Bolivia. The United States is the main obstacle to their converting these smaller powers into satellites of Argentina, and they would much prefer to see the Pan-American Union over-

shadowed by a similar organization of Latin American states, with
the United States excluded. Buenos Aires thus would become the
super-capital of the Hispanic-American world, with Portuguese-
speaking Brazil probably invited to join.

Hispanidad has been a handy and much-used tool, although the
1946 model seen in Argentina bears little resemblance to the product exported by Franco. Immediately after his victory in the
Spanish Civil War, Franco set out to revive the spiritual and political dominance of Spain over the Latin American republics.

In some conservative Argentine circles, this idea was well received. However, before long an unmistakable *criollo* stamp had
been put on the Iberian import. Argentine politicians showed a
fondness for expressing lyrical admiration for the glories of old
Spain and its culture, especially when dealing with any of the other
Latin American nations. And it was a popular device when Argentina was attempting to counteract the influence of the United States
in South American affairs. The cozy tie of the common Spanish
motherland, culture and tongue was dusted off for the benefit of a
wavering Chile, Peru or Uruguay.

However, any idea of Buenos Aires serving as a moon to the
Madrid political sun was quite preposterous to the average Argentine. Naturally, there would have to be two suns—one shining in
Argentina and the other in Spain—and obviously the moons, the
other South American countries, would revolve around Buenos
Aires. Another Argentine conception was based on the traditional
Spanish family life. In this case, Spain was the venerable old man,
not as spry as he used to be, and Argentina was the oldest and most
prosperous son, who exercised the filial prerogative of bossing
around his younger brothers. He would also listen respectfully to
the old man's words of wisdom but would disregard the advice
except where it suited his own interest. And, having already
amassed a considerably larger fortune than his father, he would
affectionately lend money to the old man to keep the family's home
estate in good repair.

With or without justification, the Argentines considered themselves superior to the Spaniards. The people thought of themselves
as Argentines, not Spaniards, and they have a word, *gallegos*, which
they use in referring condescendingly to individuals of the mother

race. Their tone of voice in using the word is about the same as
Americans employ when they say "those limeys."

Hispanidad, most dictionaries have it, means only "that which
refers to the Spanish language," but it came to have another and
much less innocent meaning after Franco came to power. It became
a valuable accessory to the penetration of the Falange in the Western
Hemisphere. During the war the Falange worked hand in hand with
the Hitler propaganda machine to depict the United States as a
giant bully holding a great club over the South American countries.
Uncle Sam was also shown as a greedy old man who supported
"Godless Russian Bolshevism," at the same time serving as a tool
for Free Masonry and Jewry.

The Franco-Spanish propaganda was not as spectacular or crude
as the Germans. But it had entree in more high places. Under the
cloak of culture, it was welcomed in the wealthier homes, the
schools and the churches. And it had splendid apostles in the
hundreds of Spanish priests who entered Argentina after the civil
war in Spain.

Unfortunately, one of the most consistent and influential critics
the United States has in Argentina is the hierarchy of the Catholic
church, with Monsignor De Andrea being a notable exception.
But dissension arose in the ranks of the Catholics in 1944 when the
eloquent French liberal, Father Ducattillon, visited Argentina and
attracted an enormous following of pro-democratic members of the
church. The old-line Catholics became alarmed for a time when
the Ducattillon supporters stayed away en masse from the Eucharistic Congress of that year, and the rift was acknowledged by *El
Pueblo,* the official Catholic newspaper, in an article by Manuel
Gálvez. The writer referred in sympathetic terms to the pro-Axis
Catholics in Argentina, who he said mainly desired to see the defeat
of the Communists and the attainment of "order and social justice."
Manuel Gálvez was less charitable toward the pro-democratic
faction. He charged that "whole families absented themselves from
Buenos Aires in order not to take part in what they called the 'Nazi
Congress'. . . . This flight from the city revealed an antagonism
towards the government which I cannot understand, for it would
make one believe that these Catholics wished the country to be
subordinated to the United States. . . ."

Ruth and I numbered among our friends many devout Catholics. We were surprised that not a person among them had attended the Eucharistic Congress, while we—both non-Catholics—had. This huge gathering of Catholics from all over Argentina and many of the neighboring republics was a spectacle I'll never forget. Women kneeled in the streets to pray, heedless of the crowds milling about them. One middle-aged woman in black was on her knees praying only a few feet away from a sidewalk cafe where men sat at little tables, talking and laughing as they drank cold beer and ate peanuts.

The existence of a large pro-democratic element within the Catholic church in Argentina, however, had little apparent effect on church policies. In early 1945, many Argentine Catholics as well as foreigners, were shocked by a Pastoral Letter from the Cardinal Primate, Archbishops and Bishops in the country, denouncing all Protestant organizations and prohibiting Catholic support of such institutions as the Salvation Army, the Young Women's Christian Association and the Young Men's Christian Association.

The Protestant missionary has, of course, long been a cactus plant in the Catholic garden in Argentina. But in the last few years he has become the favorite scapegoat for many North Americans seeking to put the blame somewhere for the unsatisfactory relations between the United States and Argentina.

Frankly, I can't recall ever meeting an Argentine who was losing any sleep over the presence of American missionaries on the soil of the *patria*. An exception, however, might be the sleuth-like reporter of *El Pueblo* who discovered that 182 boxes of Bibles—"heretic" Bibles—had been brought to Argentine shores by vessels of the state merchant fleet. "The evil implied by such importation," he warned, "is made worse by the fact that the state fleet should have carried these books which are designed to undermine one of the pillars of the state—the Catholic religion."

I met one Argentine who resented the fact that some American missionaries thought they were coming to the country to "civilize" the Argentines. He asked me how people in the United States would feel if suddenly a group of Argentines, with only the sketchiest knowledge of English, were suddenly to arrive in New

York harbor with the announcement they were going to "civilize" the savage inhabitants of Long Island.

The newest and most enthusiastic recruit to the anti-United States ranks in Argentina (as elsewhere in Latin America) is the Communist party. Until Moscow and Buenos Aires established relations in the middle of 1946, the Argentine Communists had fought Perón tooth and nail—first underground and then openly and legally in the presidential elections. But a few months after his election the Communists had made their peace with Perón and had transferred their onslaught to another foe—this time the ancient bogey of "Yankee Imperialism." Numerically the party was still weak, in 1946 an optimistic member estimating a total following of fifty thousand (the actual membership figure is probably between twenty and thirty thousand). However, the Communists turned to attack the United States with venom and vigor, employing many of the same tactics used by the Nazis during the late war. In fact, the attack was so similar that many a bewildered Argentine wondered if Moscow had not modelled its propaganda on some back copies of the Goebbels-inspired sheets or at least hired a few of the most gifted staff members of those publications.

Undoubtedly, the Communists and all the other native and foreign groups in Argentina lobbying for and against the United States have had something to do with U.S.-Argentine relations. Flaws—either real or imagined—in the official North American attitude or actions toward Argentina are glaringly exposed by these interested groups. Uncle Sam is always under the microscope, for everything he does is magnified and dissected by his myriad critics and his good friends.

But what of the future of Argentine-U.S. relations?

Today, the issue governing official relations is more clear cut than it has been at any time since the late thirties.

The question is, simply, SHALL WE ARM ARGENTINA, OR SHALL WE NOT? Or, in view of the elections and the consolidation of Perón's position: SHALL WE ARM PERON, OR SHALL WE NOT?

Perón has asked to be armed. He has requested first-class military equipment—tanks, artillery, rapid-fire guns and heavy bombers. He has money and is willing to pay for them. He asks the United

States to send top-notch military missions to Argentina to instruct his troops and his aviators in the use of the most modern armaments.

There are two main schools of thought in the United States bearing on this basic issue of arming Perón.

One argument runs: "Certainly, we should arm Perón. He will help fight the spread of communism in South America. Perón will be a good ally if it should become necessary to go to war with Russia. Perón is a strong man, but he's smart and, after all, the Argentine people did elect him. If he doesn't get guns from us, there are plenty of others he can buy them from. Let's give them to him now, and have him for a friend. We need solidarity in Latin America for the hemisphere defense."

The other school says: "Perón hasn't fulfilled the commitments he has already made. Until he does, can we be sure how he will use any arms he might get from us? If we can't trust him to keep his promises without modern arms, how can we possibly trust him with them? And besides, the only thing Perón wants from us is armaments; if we give them to him, there goes our trump card. Let's wait to see if we can trust Perón."

It becomes apparent that although the issue is simple, its solution is not. The factors still to be considered are the attitude of the Argentine people towards arming Perón and the opinion of the people of the United States and the other nineteen American republics, both now and at some conjectural date in the future.

If we supply arms to Perón, does the United States assume a moral responsibility for the manner in which those arms are used? We must think carefully—now—of the eventualities.

What will Brazil think if the United States drastically increases the strength of Perón by supplying him with new weapons? How will Chile, Uruguay, and Paraguay feel, having a stronger neighbor? Consider the unlikely event that Argentina should go to war with Chile, using arms we had sold or leased to Perón. Would the other republics recall charitably that we had strengthened Perón expressly for the *defense* of the hemisphere? Would they hold the United States blameless? And what about the people of the United States; would we feel that we were responsible for an act of armed aggression, and would we be willing to spend our blood and treasure to stop something that we had unwittingly started? Would we at any chosen moment be strong enough to do it?

Suppose a revolution were to break out against Perón and that the weapons we had supplied him were used to kill rebelling Argentine civilians; could we shrug off the inevitable accusations of the Argentine people?

Is it necessary to purchase the everlasting good will of Perón by supplying him with the arms he requests? Could the United States really buy Perón?

The answer is "no" in both cases. Perón can be counted on to act in his own self-interest in any given situation, and Argentina likewise—regardless of what man is in power—will act in her national self-interest. As far as communism is concerned, Perón will fight it naturally and relentlessly—even while maintaining a façade of friendship and normal diplomatic relations with the Soviet Union—because the formidable position of the Catholic church in Argentina would not permit him to do otherwise. And Perón will not honor any "deal" he has made with anyone, if it later proves unsuited to his own interests. Perón is a "smart man," as the men who want to supply him with arms will testify. Perón is pro-Perón and pro-Argentina, and he is sure he knows what is good for both.

Neither can the friendship of the Argentine people be bought and sold. Four years in Argentina was time enough to convince me that whatever the United States does—give arms or withhold them —many Argentines will like it and many won't. Today, I can't think of a single thing the United States could do that would be liked by every Argentine.

Come what may, the Argentines will keep right on doing what comes naturally, and we undoubtedly will remain in the role of scapegoat No. 1. The Argentines are happier to have it so. What we can do is to make sure that our policy toward Argentina contains the ingredients of common sense and remembrance of our own principles—and aspirins, of course.

INDEX